The Necessity for Love

The History of Interpersonal Relations

By the same author

Ed. AUTHORITY IN A CHANGING SOCIETY
THE NEW CHURCH IN THE NEW AGE
MUSICAL INSTRUMENTS AND THE ORCHESTRA

CLIFFORD RHODES

The Necessity for Love

The History of Interpersonal Relations

CONSTABLE LONDON

First published in Great Britain 1972
by Constable and Company Ltd,
10 Orange Street London WC2H 7EG
Copyright © 1972 by Clifford Rhodes

ISBN 0 09 455900 7

Set in Monotype Perpetua
Printed in Great Britain by
Western Printing Services Ltd, Bristol

Acknowledgements

I should like to thank J. M. Dent and Sons Ltd., for permission to quote from Socratic Discourses, tr. J. Wright, Everyman's Library, 1910, and from Five Dialogues of Plato, Everyman's Library, 1942. Also, the Loeb Classical Library for permission to quote from Plato, tr. W. R. Lamb, 1927, and Xenophon, tr. E. C. Marchant, 1959, Harvard University Press: Heinemann Ltd. All Biblical quotations are taken from the New English Bible, second edition, c. 1970, by permission of the Oxford and Cambridge University Presses.

Contents

Preface

In writing this account of what the leading minds of our Western tradition have thought about interpersonal relations, I have found two major difficulties apart from the obvious one of mastering the material. One of them is semantic. Most of the authors whose thought I present were innovators of the highest order; writers for whose insights the language of their period provided only inadequate means of expression. Not only did they have to invent a terminology of their own, using words in a special sense, different from that of ordinary speech, but also their search for precision sometimes led them into tortuous arguments of daunting obscurity. To avoid the confusion and the frustration that can arise from this I have interpreted and paraphrased freely in modern literary language while trying to retain the flavour of the original.

When constructing my bibliography, I noticed at an early stage that other writers on the subject have eschewed the historical approach and I began to wonder whether they were the reluctant angels. Historians of moral philosophy, by contrast, can confine themselves to a succession of fairly clear-cut answers to perennial questions: what is the good life; what is the ground of moral obligation; on what principles are we to conduct ourselves as members of human society. Here our scope is much wider. We have to pass almost in the same breath from the master-slave relation to the conduct of a casual love affair and to the most exalted mysticism. We range over the whole gamut from the sublime to the near-pornographic. The central word is 'love'; but it is a word that has been given a multitude of shades of meaning, while the questions asked about it have changed from century to century. This suggests that the experience itself may have changed its nature. Certainly the practices associated with it have changed. The interpersonal relations of Greeks of the age of Pericles were different from those of Londoners or New Yorkers in the technological period.

But this is not all. My object is not so much to produce an academic history of philosophy as to contribute what I can to the understanding of interpersonal relations. To have confined myself to the philosophers would have been misleading and the book would have been worth little from the standpoint of gaining insight into our contemporary situation. Poets, psychologists, theologians, the Bible itself and, even, descriptions that have come down to us of great experiences such as that of Heloise and her Abelard, have all influenced the development of our thought and practice. Some of the authors I interpret are more than one of these at the same time. But to cover historically all who have made a contribution would be the work of a life-time and the result, total confusion.

My solution is to organise this wealth of material under traditions, or themes, and to select from each only the most significant figures. When this has appeared to make for a more logical sequence and greater intelligibility I have not hesitated to break away from strict chronological order. It is much more sensible, for instance, to consider Plotinus as the culmination of the Greek tradition than as the chronological successor of Ovid. To treat St Augustine as the predecessor of Boethius would be quite absurd. Augustine was a father of the Christian Church: Boethius was the last of the Roman patricians. Finally, in the interest of realism, I have related the thought of my chosen authors to their lives and times and the practices prevalent among their contemporaries.

Because I seemed to be bombarding the reader with a hail of apparently unrelated ideas, at the end of the fourth chapter I have included a special section, a kind of parenthesis, in which I have tried to draw together what has gone before and to provide guidelines to what follows. I hope this will make for intelligibility. In the last chapter I have tried to reassemble the salient thoughts and, in the light of them, to discuss our own troubled situation.

I should like warmly to thank Mr Claud W. H. Sutton who,

many years ago, had the onerous task of teaching me philosophy at Oxford, for reading the MS and giving it the same critical attention that he did to those earlier essays. Warm thanks are due, also, to Dr Marcus Gregory, with whom I have worked on other enterprises in the past, for reading the MS from the standpoint of depth psychology. Professor Basil Mitchell, of Oxford, has won my deep gratitude by writing me a critique that was of invaluable assistance in making the final revision. None of these are responsible for any of the views expressed; but all of them have made suggestions that I have been glad to have. Also, I want to thank Mr Benjamin Glazebrook, of Constable's, for encouraging me to write the book in the first place and for his patience and forbearance in waiting for it two or three times as long as I had led him to expect.

CLIFFORD RHODES,
Somerton,
Oxfordshire,
October 1971

Chapter One

Classical Background

THE HEROIC AGE

Since it is the first period in the history of the West about which we possess written information, the Heroic Age is the natural starting point for this book. We cannot rely upon Homer either for accurate observation, such as would satisfy a modern sociologist, or for systematic theorising; but we can learn from his great epic what a man of distinction and refinement, who wrote some time between 1250 and 850 B.C., admired or deprecated in human conduct.

Homer's characters give an impression of extraordinary spontaneity and freedom. Such inhibitions as they felt were minimal. They lived in a world peopled almost as much by gods and spirits as by men and women. Ten were major gods and the rest minor. But, surely, Hesiod, who wrote during the eighth century B.C., is over-indulging his poetic licence when he says that there are 30,000 spirits:

> To spirits thrice ten thousand by God's will 'tis assigned
> Through all the fruitful earth to watch o'er humankind.
> Deathless, hidden in darkness, wandering everywhere,
> They watch all judgments given, all evil that men dare.
> *Works and Days*, 252–5, tr. Lucas

They mingled freely with the human inhabitants of the earth and there was usually one at hand in a crisis, whether welcome or not, and they could be useful: a pregnant girl could always find an accommodating deity to take the blame. They were astonishingly human in their emotions and reactions.

Government was by the king in the council of notables but it had to carry the people with it. Central authority was weak: the family was the important social unit. Several families would join together to form a clan. This was the bronze age and the menfolk were mostly warriors or shepherds, whose long absences from home left their women with a good measure of authority and responsibility in family affairs. The outstanding example was that of Penelope who, during the twenty years that Odysseus was away on the Trojan expedition, was in charge of affairs at home in Ithaca and conducted herself with perfect wisdom and loyalty.

The story of Odysseus and Nausicaa exemplifies the unaffectedness of relations between the sexes. Cast ashore on the coast of Phaeacia, naked and unkempt, Odysseus is disturbed by Nausicaa, daughter of King Alcinous, at play by the river's mouth with her young women. The two at once strike up a friendship and Nausicaa leads Odysseus home to the palace, where he spends his time sociably with Alcinous until he is ready to go his way. There is no sign of suspicion or of fear or false modesty.

Marriage was, in many instances, more by capture than by rapture. Women taken captive in war became the slaves of their captors, whatever their social rank. After the fall of Troy the males of the city were massacred and the women distributed among the Greek army. Hecuba, King Priam's queen, fell by lot to Odysseus, while Agamemnon took home with him the mad prophetess, Cassandra. Helen, the loveliest woman in the world and paramour of Paris, who was the cause of all the trouble, returned home with her rightful husband, Menelaus. Universally hated though she was, Menelaus refrained from killing her as he had been authorised to do if he wished. Women enslaved in conquest were often treated with tenderness and respect, as in the case of Briseis who won the love of Achilles.

More usually, marriage was arranged by the parents of the young people and was accompanied by the payment of a bride price. Between the two the relation was that of mutuality and respect. Men and women mingled freely at their work and in their recreation and a woman could have friendships outside marriage without arousing her husband's jealousy. Marital fidelity in women was a highly honoured virtue.

It has been said that romantic love is a relatively modern invention; but this is hard to credit. The traditions and rituals with which it is surrounded, and the convention that bases marriage upon it, are indeed relatively new; but the phenomenon itself is one that we encounter again and again in Homer and in every period of history since. The passage in which Hector and Andromache take leave of each other on the walls of Troy, their little son with them, before battle begins, would be a classic of love in any period.

> And by his side Andromache, that wept the while,
> Clasping her hand in her husband's, 'Dear one, thy dauntless heart',
> She said, 'will surely slay thee – ah, pitiless thou art
> Both to thy little son and my unhappiness.
> For soon I shall be thy widow – I know the Greeks will press,
> Massed as one man, to kill thee. And once I sit bereft
> Of thee, the grave were better – there is no comfort left
> In the whole world for me, the day that thou shalt die –
> Nothing but grief. . . .

Hector did not return. The next Andromache saw of him was his body being dragged over the ground behind the chariot of Achilles. Thereafter, for twelve days Achilles dragged the body round the tomb of his friend, Patroclus, whom Hector had killed in battle. With the weapons of the time battle meant close personal combat and, in instances such as this, engendered a deep, personal hatred. There was little either of chivalry or of humanity in the treatment of such an enemy. But the situation could also produce the opposite effect. When Diomed encountered his friend and kinsman, Glaucus, in the mêlée the two fraternised and exchanged armour.

Not all family life was sweet. When Agamemnon was on his way to Troy the Greek fleet of a thousand ships lay storm-bound at Aulis. The seer, Calchas, advised that only by sacrificing his daughter, Iphigenia, to the goddess Artemis would Agamemnon be able to regain the open sea. On a lying pretext, Iphigenia was accordingly brought from home and offered as a blood sacrifice.

In hatred for her husband, the outraged mother, Clytemnestra, avenged her daughter by taking as her lover his enemy, Agistheus. When, twenty years later, Agamemnon returned home Clytemnestra was awaiting him with the murderess's dagger.

In primitive societies, where law and its administration are still no more than embryonic, revenge is the only form of justice available and in the Heroic Age it had the sanction of religion. In killing her husband, Clytemnestra was doing no more than fulfilling her duty to her murdered daughter. But her action was sinful in spite of that for, to that period, no crimes were more dastardly than those within the family. The agent of revenge had to be the son of the murdered Agamemnon, Orestes, driven now to the murder of his own mother. Fearful afterwards of the nemesis following his dreadful deed, Orestes wandered over the earth in the search for freedom and escape. Aeschylus, whose great theme was that both gods and men learn through suffering, showed in his play, the *Eumenides* (458 B.C.), how this dialectic of horrors was ended when Orestes threw himself upon the mercy of the goddess Athena, who used the opportunity to teach forgiveness as the only way of breaking the tragic cycle of vengeance. Against the spirit of the feud she insisted that the obligations of justice must ultimately give way before the obligations of mercy.

But forgiveness is too personal and too difficult a solution to be practised by any except an ethical élite. The principles of justice and mercy must be incarnated in an institution. The only answer to the blood feud capable of universal application is a system of enforceable and impersonal law. To meet this need Athena ordained the establishment of the Council of the Areopagus as a court to deal with cases of killing.

Towards the end of the *Odyssey* is a touching passage on the friendship between humans and their domestic animals. It should not be surprising to find this because the records suggest that, in Egypt, this relation between dogs and men had existed thousands of years before Homer. When Odysseus returned home, as he approached his palace he saw lying on a dunghill the flea-ridden and neglected hound he had been training as a puppy when he left for Troy twenty years before:

There outstretched lay Argus and the ticks swarmed in his
  hide;
And yet, when he saw Odysseus, standing by his side,
He wagged his tail, and backwards he let fall either ear,
Too weak to creep to his master. But the King wiped off a
  tear. . . .

THE GREAT PERIOD OF GREECE

Among the Greeks of Aeolis the freedom and spontaneity that
characterised the Homeric period lasted for long after it had
begun to disappear from Greece itself. This was a more cosmo-
politan society. There was a high culture from which women
were not excluded. Here, on the Island of Lesbos, about the year
610 B.C., was born the poetess Sappho, who married and had a
daughter, Kleis, to whom she was devoted. The legend that her
infatuation with a young man caused her to fling herself to death
from a headland is nowadays thought to be fictitious. Her poems
leave no doubt that her most intense passion was for women. For
this she offers neither reason nor justification but accepts the fact
simply and without self-consciousness. An example is her poem to
The Beloved, which is as unmistakable as it is graceful. Evidently it
is addressed to a married woman:

> Him I hold as happy as God in Heaven,
> Who can sit and gaze on your face before him,
> Who can sit and hear from your lips that sweetest
>   Music they utter –
>
> Hear your lovely laughter, that sets a-tremble
> All my heart with flutterings wild as terror.
> For, when I behold you an instant, straightway
>   All my words fail me;
>
> Helpless halts my tongue; a devouring fever
> Runs in flame through every vein within me;
> Darkness veils my vision; my ears are deafened,
>   Beating like hammers;

Cold the sweat runs down me; a sudden trembling
Sets my lips a-quiver; my face grows paler
Than the grass in summer; I see before me
    Death stand, and madness.

(Tr. F. L. Lucas)

Sappho is unaffected by guilt-feeling and there is no sign of public disapproval of her wayward passion. When these are absent, so also will be the ill consequences that usually flow from them. Yet there is the same unfulfilled longing, the same unsatisfied desire, as in heterosexual love.

Sparta was one of the first organised communities in Europe about which we have objective and historical accounts. Since the Spartans themselves did not produce literary men or academics we have to rely upon outside historians, notably Herodotus and Xenophon. The period of Spartan greatness lasted from the seventh to the third centuries B.C. Because the political constitution and the social system had the backing of religious sanctions they changed little during those centuries. The Spartan way of life is understandable only on the assumption that it was designed with a view mainly to the production of an efficient army.

There were three social classes: a serf class, the Helots, who were tied to the land and supervised by a strict secret police; a middle class of farmers and traders, the Periocoi; and the Spartans themselves, a military caste numbering in their heyday about 10,000, who owned the land and provided the government. The nobles had their own family domains while the rest were allotted land by the State. Nobody was impoverished and, since the labouring work was done by the Helots and commerce was conducted by the Periocoi, the Spartans themselves were virtually a small, leisured aristocracy. But, whereas the usual tendency for social groups of the kind is to give themselves to the pursuit of pleasure, the Spartans dedicated themselves to militarism. Conscious of the possibility of a Helot revolt, they dared not relax their discipline. The Spartan way of life was much admired throughout Greece and provided the basis for Plato's ideal state; but because it was that of a tiny community living under peculiar social conditions it cannot be realistically treated as a model. It is one of history's aberrations.

Militarism's first demand is for a healthy population. Shortly after birth every child was examined by a committee of elders and, if weakly or suffering from any disability, was left to die by exposure on the slopes of Mount Taygetus, just outside the city. At the age of seven, boys were removed from their parents and spent the next period of their lives living communally according to a military pattern. The nearest comparison is the English public school system. The girls, too, had to be brought up to be fit mothers of soldiers. Their training was largely gymnastic and boys and girls normally did their exercises together, unimpeded by clothing. Their dress at other times was the lightest of tunics, open down the side and making little attempt at concealment.

Bachelorhood was frowned upon as unproductive. Men could marry at the age of twenty, the ceremony consisting of a mock abduction of the bride by the groom. The bride then had her own house, of which she was absolute mistress, while her husband returned to communal living with his own age-group of young men for the next ten years. During that time the husband could not visit his wife except clandestinely, a prohibition that must at least have combated over-familiarity. At the age of thirty the man became a fully fledged citizen and was allowed to live with his wife. He remained a soldier until he was sixty and at that age could hold public office.

Husbands allowed their wives to cohabit with other men and accepted as their own the children of these extra-marital unions. Since a husband's own children by other men's wives were being similarly brought up by the other men he had no just cause for complaint. Women inherited property equally with men and some women of wealth maintained two households with a husband in each. While the main purpose of this strange system was to produce efficient soldiers there is no evidence that it worked less well or less happily than any other. Certainly the Spartans tolerated it for four centuries and their neighbours were envious. At the same time we must surely take with a pinch of salt Charles Seltman's claim, in his *Women in Antiquity*, that there was no jealousy, no bastardy, no divorce, no homosexuality and no adultery, as we understand the term. Bury (*History of Greece*) suggests that a half-caste class of Mothones probably sprang from the illicit unions between Spartan men and Helot women. If true, this would qualify Seltman's eulogy.

Not far from Sparta, but in strong contrast, was Athens, greatest of the several remarkable city states of Hellas, city of thinkers and poets, architects, sculptors and playwrights; all these and fine soldiers and sailors, too. Culturally, Athens had everything, including depth. Her citizens were far from being the mere novelty tasters that the slighting reference to them in the Acts of the Apostles suggests: 'Now the Athenians in general and the foreigners there had no time for anything but talking or hearing about the latest new thing.' (*Acts* 17, 21.) One of their outstanding characteristics was, in fact, a passionate intellectual curiosity.

St Paul's famous speech on the Areopagus started with a theological solecism: 'As I was going around looking at the objects of your worship, I noticed among other things an altar bearing the inscription, "To an unknown God". What you worship but do not know – this is what I now proclaim.' (*Acts* 17, 23.) But the Athenians had thousands of unknown gods, minor deities, whose ritual observances they cleared off in one comprehensive feast day. None of them was remotely comparable with the creator God of the Christian Scriptures. St Paul was comparing like with unlike. The outlook of Greek mythology was totally different from that of the Hebrews.

In their social relations the Athenians were less enviable. While the women were not by any means housebound and while divorce, on both sides, was easy, marriage was in practice far from being an equal partnership. Women received minimal education and were little more than housekeepers. As such, they were mistresses in their own domain but were inadequate as companions to their husbands. Yet, the *Supplices* of Aeschylus, first produced some time between 499 and 472 B.C., has as its theme the warfare between the sexes and concludes that, while sexual experience when forced upon women against their will, is vile, sexuality is redeemed by love. That there was tenderness between husbands and wives is shown by the number of tomb-stones erected in honour of young wives. But Athenian society was predominantly a male society and women did not mix easily in it.

There was a class of prostitutes and call-girls. Brothels were licensed. Some of the most eminent and remarkable of Athenian women were the *hetairi*, a superior type of courtesan. These were often highly intelligent women who repudiated the housewife's rôle. They were at least as well educated as most men and lived a life of cultured leisure and freedom. Some of them became women of means. It was with these that men of wealth found the feminine companionship they needed. A few of the *hetairi* even found a niche in history. The most famous of all was Aspasia, mistress of Pericles, greatest of Athenian orators and statesmen. For her sake Pericles ultimately divorced his wife. She was his constant companion and influenced his thinking. She is said to have composed some of his finest speeches.

One consequence of this unsatisfactory situation was the practice of paederasty. Much has been made of this; but in the absence of scientific social observation its extent and depth are matters for speculation. Philosophers spoke favourably of close relations between older men and youths and they were un-doubtedly frequent: but they did not necessarily involve physical intimacy. The same philosophers spoke contemptuously of men who exploited such relations for sensual purposes. The relation they approved more resembled that between a good schoolmaster and a promising pupil. The youth gained a wise counsellor and the older man benefited from the vitality and cheerfulness of his young friend. It is true that when the philosophers wrote of love, as often as not they were referring to the feelings of friendship that exist between men; and it is also true that Socrates and Plato attributed almost mystical significance to such friendship, regard-ing it as one of the highways to salvation. But it should by no means be assumed, as it sometimes is, that paederasty was either conventional or even generally tolerated in Athens during its great period, because this would be a distortion.

ROME

As would be expected in the home of the world's greatest law-givers, family relations in Rome were subject to strict and detailed legislation. In the days of the Republic, women had no rights whatever. While twelve was the age of legal capability, women could exercise such rights as they had only under the supervision of a guardian, who would be either her father or her husband. The father's power over his daughter was absolute. He could kill her if he thought fit. The test case was that of Virginius, an army officer, upon whose daughter the powerful patrician, Appius Claudius, cast a lecherous eye. To save his daughter from degradation, Virginius stabbed her to death. This was within his rights and the public applauded his action.

Except under the severest tyranny, the law is no stronger than public opinion. With the coming of the Empire and its wide extension, the new cosmopolitanism of the people greatly mitigated the harshness of the law. In practice, the utmost freedom prevailed. There were three forms of marriage. The first was the *conferatio*, which was contracted at a religious ceremony in the presence of a patrician. This initiated both husband and wife into the priesthood of Jupiter and divorce was forbidden. In time this prohibition was felt to be irksome and the rule had to be relaxed. The second form of marriage was the *co-emptio*, which consisted of a fictitious sale of the girl by her father to the groom. The third, and ultimately the most popular, was the *usus*. If a man and woman cohabited for twelve months, having been separated for no more than three nights during that period, they were considered to be legally married.

Divorce was easy and, in the later Empire, was frequent, often for trivial reasons. Officially, a wife's adultery was punishable either by death or by the loss of half her dowry and one-third of her other possessions, and banishment. A husband's adultery was punishable by the loss of one-half of his possessions and banishment. The double standard of morality did not apply in this case. But there was a way of evading these provisions. Law is seldom successful in its attempts to control private morals. If a woman wanted sexual freedom she need only register as a prostitute and then she was no longer subject to restriction. Many women of good family did this. Married women became legally independent after the birth of their third child and single women were always independent. Abortion was forbidden and severely punished; but this did not stop women making the attempt, often with disastrous results. In A.D. 322 the Emperor Constantine enacted that children whose parents were unable to support them should be clothed and fed at the expense of the State. Fifty years later, Valentinian made that most gruesome of all methods of family planning, infanticide, a capital offence.

Even during the early days of the Republic, women were held in great respect. The law did not accurately reflect the attitude of the Roman people. The *materfamilias*, in particular, was a great personage. Often there was genuine tenderness between husband and wife. Ill-treatment of a wife was actionable in the courts. Girls and boys were educated in exactly the same way at the public expense. As they grew up, women could earn their living in the trades and professions.

Rome was based on slavery. During the republican period slaves were treated with the utmost harshness and cruelty. In the courts, for example, their evidence was admissible only if extracted under torture. If the head of a household died by violence all his slaves were tortured just in case one of them might chance to have relevant information. Slaves were absolutely at the disposal of their owners, among whom a merciless attitude was prevalent. Later, under Greek influence, that spirit died away. Ill-treatment of slaves incurred social disapproval. Under the humane Emperor Antoninus (A.D. 138–61) owners were forbidden to kill their slaves and, if their cruelty to them became intolerable, they could be ordered to sell them. Under later emperors the practice of inquisitorial torture was abolished and the use of slaves as prostitutes was forbidden.

Such was the background of the philosophers of antiquity. The differences in the conditions and the nature of personal relations between different regions and between different periods were marked. To go from Sparta to Athens or Rome was to move into different worlds. Yet people found happiness and fulfilment in all of them. The differences between their mores appeared to have little influence either on their military effectiveness or their commercial prosperity. Athens, Sparta and Rome were all powerful in their day. The notion that the decline of Rome was due to the immorality of her citizens has, of course, been long ago discredited.

Chapter Two

The Greek Philosophers

SOCRATES, XENOPHON, PLATO

Preferring the subtleties and nuances of conversation to the inflexibility of the pen, Socrates (469–399 B.C.) left no writings and founded no institutions. We know of him mainly through records of his discussions made by his devoted admirer, Xenophon, and his pupil and successor, Plato. Neither of these was objective. Both selected from his talk what appealed most to their own minds and sifted it through their own understanding. Both used their records as vehicles for their own prejudices and ideas. It is an indication of his intellectual power and personal strength that Socrates, the man, emerges from this handling as clearly as he does.

Xenophon (*c.*430–*c.*355 B.C.) has had unkindly treatment from historians of philosophy. Bertrand Russell describes him as 'not very liberally endowed with brains' and adds, 'I would rather be reported by my bitterest enemy in philosophy than by a friend innocent of philosophy'. Actually, Xenophon was a soldier of distinction and outstanding as a chronicler of military and political affairs. He was a keen sportsman and farmer and, at the same time, a man of considerable independence of character. But, as we should expect of a man with these interests, his abilities were practical and it is the practical aspects of Socrates' teaching that he reports. Certainly, he never accompanies his hero to the heights of mysticism as Plato does.

Plato (*c.*427–*c.*347 B.C.) was quite a different sort of person. Of noble parentage, he was aristocratic in outlook and urbane in manner. He wrote derogatorily of the arts and especially of poetry. He taught the idea that since the things of the temporal world were copies of the eternal realities, art was no more than a copy of a copy. But he himself was a poet. It has been suggested that his deprecation of poetry was the consequence of the conflict within himself between philosopher and poet in which the poet had to be severely repressed. All his philosophical writing has an aesthetic quality. Whenever he reaches a point beyond which reason will not take him he falls back on the direct intuition and the luxuriant imagery which are the quintessence of poetry. While he learned much from Socrates he so developed what he had learned that the teaching of the master is swamped in the thought of the pupil. It is impossible to distinguish with any precision the one from the other.

Through the eyes of these widely different observers we see Socrates as a man of the better artisan class who enjoyed mixing with people of all types, was modest in his demeanour and frugal in his habits. Although not a man of means, he counted himself rich because his needs were so small. Yet he claimed to have more satisfaction from life than those who lived extravagantly. A crust of bread was ambrosial because he never ate until he was hungry: a cup of water was delicious because he never drank until he was thirsty. Perhaps this accounts for the shrewishness attributed to his wife, Xanthippe.

At the centre of Socrates' thought was the conviction that, since people never knowingly do evil, to be aware of the eternal verities was to live by them. Virtue was equated with knowledge of the good. Socrates adopted as his own the motto of the Delphic Oracle, 'Know thyself'. In taking this line he grievously underestimated the human capacity for self-deception. If it suits them, people are infinitely capable of persuading themselves that the worse is the better cause. But emphasis on the intellect at the expense of the will was characteristic of Greek thinking. In the end, the enemies that his unsparing tongue inevitably made for him justified their revenge with a blatant rationalisation. He was charged with, 'not believing in the gods, whom the city held sacred; but, as designing to introduce other and new deities; and, likewise, of his having corrupted the youth'. Sentenced to death by a draught of hemlock, he talked calmly with his friends to the last, philosophising on the theme of the soul's immortality, and finally met his end with dignity.

Rather than attempting to disentangle the thoughts of Socrates, Xenophon and Plato, it will be as well for present purposes to treat them as a trinity and to start with the highly practical advice Socrates, as reported by Xenophon, offers on the daily conduct of personal relations. Rebuking his son, Lamprocles, for disrespect to his mother, he talks in much the same terms as any father in any age. First, he elicits from Lamprocles the admission that ingratitude for favours received is an example of pure injustice which rightly earns the disapproval of society. Socrates points out that there can be no greater obligation than that of children to their parents for it is to them they owe life itself and all the enjoyments it affords. Lamprocles is not to imagine that parents have children merely for the pleasure of begetting them. Men could easily satisfy their instinctual urges in brothels without troubling to marry. A man chooses for his wife the woman he thinks will bear the best children and who will best raise a family. The mother endures the pains and perils of pregnancy and of parturition solely for the sake of the child. She nourishes it from her own body, rears it, cares for it, teaches it and thinks for it without ever knowing what return there will be for her.

We sense a row beginning to develop. Lamprocles replies:

'Nay, but even if she has done all this and far more than this, no one could put up with her vile temper.'

'Which, think you,' asks Socrates, 'is the harder to bear, a wild beast's brutality or a mother's?'

'I should say a mother's when she's like mine.'

'Well now, how many people get bitten or kicked by wild beasts; has she ever done you an injury of that sort?'

'Oh no, but she says things one wouldn't listen to for anything in the world.'

'Well, how much trouble do you think you have given her by your peevish words and froward acts day and night since you were a little child; and how much pain when you were ill?'

'But I have never said or done anything to cause her shame.'

In these reported dialogues nobody is ever allowed to have the better of Socrates; least of all his own son. Lamprocles is told that he should treat his mother's ill-temper as a tragic actor treats the abuse and menaces flung at him across the stage, knowing full well that there is no real malice behind them. If he shows respect to outsiders from whom he may some day need assistance, how much more should he respect his mother, who cares for him with infinite pains all the time? Society disapproves so strongly of people who are disrespectful to their parents that, unless he mends his ways, he might find himself ostracised or even, when the time comes, excluded from public office because of it. If he is ungrateful to his parents nobody will think him capable of any right feeling in any circumstances whatever.

On another occasion, Socrates rebukes a young man, Chaerecrates, for quarrelling with his elder brother, Chaerophon. Evidently the cause of the dispute is the division of property between them. Socrates begins by protesting that, surely, his brother is more important than mere chattels. Everybody agrees that no individual loses by reason of the fact that some members of the community are richer than others. It is better to belong to a community while secure in the possession of a sufficiency than to be wealthy but isolated. Can they not see that the same principle applies to brothers? They have friends outside the family because they feel they have need of them; but they behave as if there could be friendship between fellow citizens but not between brothers! Yet common parentage should be a tie of affection.

Chaerecrates is not to be mollified. He would have agreed with Socrates if Chaerophon's behaviour were brotherly; but it is the opposite, and this makes friendship impossible. What particularly annoys him is that, while his brother can be charming to other people, he himself has nothing but contumely from him. Socrates answers that he should behave towards him as he would to a growling sheepdog, taming him by kindness. If he wants kindness from other people he knows he has to show kindness to them. If Chaerophon fails to respond he knows he has at least demonstrated his own brotherliness and has put Chaerophon in the wrong. In the meanwhile, their behaviour resembles that of a pair of hands or a pair of feet that refuse to co-operate with each other. The partnership of brothers can and should be stronger than that even of a person's hands or feet.

Although friends are the most precious of all possessions, Socrates is astonished at men's carelessness in acquiring them and at their negligence in keeping them. Friendship has to be worked for and is worth the effort. Yet there are people who will go to endless trouble for a servant who is ill but do nothing for a friend in similar circumstances. Like other possessions, friends differ in value; but the moral of this is not that a man should weigh his friends in terms of their value to him but, rather, should ask himself how valuable he is to them. The more valuable he makes himself to them the less likely will they be to betray his friendship.

When choosing friends it is wise to avoid men who are dominated by selfish vices and to seek out those who have already shown their capacity for friendship with others. But, it is objected, since rogues cannot be expected to form durable friendships with each other, and since even good men are apt to fall out with each other, upon whom is it possible to rely? Socrates concedes the point and goes on to describe his ideal 'gentleman', whose friendship is worth having above that of all others. He is moderate in his ambitions and his desires, unselfish to the point of sharing what he has even in times of distress, a stranger to covetousness and jealousy, conciliatory in his attitude and public spirited: in short, a man of goodwill who wants to gain the corresponding goodwill of others. Such a man will welcome friends as partners, fellow-workers and allies. When such a man is found it is worth straining every nerve to acquire and cultivate his friendship. Socrates tells his interlocutor that the first step is to be a gentleman himself, so that his own friendship will be worth having. He will be glad to commend him to any gentleman he wishes and to make the introduction; but he will have to do so without dissembling. The best matchmakers have found that it does not pay to 'oversell' the person for whom they are trying to arrange a marriage. The same applies to friendship. True friendship can arise only when people are honest with each other.

Warning against sensual passion, Socrates says: 'Avoid it resolutely: it is not easy to control yourself once you meddle with that sort of thing . . . you lose your liberty in a trice and become a slave.' There is dangerous poison in a kiss. Indeed, the young and fair can inject poison from a distance without any contact at all. 'Nay, I advise you Xenophon,' he says, 'as soon as you see a pretty face to take to your heels and fly: and you, Critobulus, I advise to spend a year abroad. It will certainly take you at least as long as that to recover from the bite.' Those whose passions are not under complete control should limit themselves to such indulgence as the soul would reject unless the need of the body were pressing but such as will do no harm when the need is there.

> 'As for his own conduct in the matter,' writes Xenophon, 'it was evident that he had trained himself to avoid the fairest and most attractive more easily than others avoid the ugly and repulsive. Concerning eating and drinking, then, and carnal indulgence such were his views, and he thought that a due portion of pleasure would be no more lacking to him than to those who give themselves up much to these, and that much less trouble would fall to his lot.'

Since this is Socrates' attitude it seems odd to find him offering excellent advice to a courtesan (hetaira) on how to look after her clients. The woman is Theodote, famous for her looks and much sought after by artists as a model. When Socrates and his friends visited her they found her living in a lavishly furnished house, looked after by several pretty maids who were obviously well cared for. She herself was sumptuously dressed and her mother at her side was also wearing fine clothes and jewellery.

Theodote tells Socrates that she lives on the generosity of her friends and on knowing how to retain their friendship. He advises her to appoint an agent who will seek out rich men and bring them to her. She should use more careful skill and art in keeping them. She should ask of them such favours as they will be glad to grant immediately and should repay them with the same spontaneity. She should not press her favours upon her suitors but wait until they ask for them. When they are satisfied she should wait a while before offering herself to them again and play 'hard to get'. Suitors tend to recoil with a certain nausea from a woman who is too overpowering. Theodote is so pleased with this advice, which can hardly have been original even in the fifth century B.C., that she immediately wants Socrates himself, who is neither rich nor handsome, as one of her friends; but he courteously excuses himself and makes his escape.

In the *Oeconomicus* we have Xenophon's ideas on estate management tempered, no doubt, by the reflections of Socrates. What is said here of the relation between husbands and wives is of interest for the light it sheds on Athenian home life. Socrates remarks that, while some men increase their estates by winning the co-operation of their wives, others ruin them by their failure in this respect. If a husband does not instruct his wife adequately he has only himself to blame for his misfortunes. Socrates asks:

'Is there anyone to whom you commit more affairs of importance than to your wife?'
'There is not.'
'Is there anyone with whom you talk less?'
'There are few or none, I confess.'
'And you married her when she was a mere child and had seen and heard almost nothing?'
'Certainly.'
'Then it would be far more surprising if she understood what she should say and do than if she made mistakes.'

Socrates goes on to say that the wife who is a good partner in the household contributes just as much as her husband because, while the husband brings in the income, the wife is responsible for spending it.

Later, Socrates enters into discussion of this subject with Ischomachus because he has the reputation of a 'gentleman', defined as a man who is both handsome and of good character. The subject is introduced by Ischomachus who tells Socrates that he is able to pass his time out of doors because his wife is quite capable of looking after the household by herself. When they married she was not yet fifteen and had until then been tied to her mother's apron strings. Her character training had been excellent but she had learned nothing except the most elementary household affairs.

Such was the upbringing and education of Athenian girls. An intelligent young woman who valued her freedom and a rich social and cultural life, and who wanted to develop herself, had little option but to become a hetaira. It was hardly surprising that the menfolk found little satisfaction in the companionship of women who had nothing to offer. This was a blemish on Athenian civilisation.

Ischomachus was exceptional and his example salutary. First, he and the girl had offered sacrifices and prayers. As soon as the girl was ready to discuss such matters he explained to her that marriage meant far more than bedding together. Both of them were to put into the home all they had to give:

'And we are not to reckon up which of us has actually contributed the greater amount, but we should know of a surety that the one who proves the better partner makes the more valuable contribution. . . . For it seems to me, dear, that the gods with great discernment have coupled together male and female, as they are called, chiefly in order that they may form a perfect partnership in mutual service.'

In their wisdom the gods have made men and women complementary to each other: the men by character and physique more suited to the outdoor tasks; the women, by reason of their greater affection for children and their sensitiveness, to the indoor tasks and the guardianship of property. The intellectual gifts, 'memory and attention', are impartially distributed. So, too, are the qualities of character such as self-control. Husband and wife need each other because each is competent where the other is deficient: they are equal but different.

Having agreed on these first principles, the two then agreed on a fair division of labour. The husband is to spend his time out of doors, superintending the estates, while the wife is to be responsible for everything pertaining to the household. She is to teach the servants their tasks and allocate their work, to care for the health of the staff, to maintain and distribute the stores and take full charge of all the household expenditure. In every way the wife is to maintain the dignity and fulfil the responsibilities of a mistress of the household.

Perhaps a little unfairly, Ischomachus lectures his young wife on make-up. When she came to him one day much painted and powdered he asked her what she would think if he came to her similarly disguised. Repelled by the thought, she agrees that she would much prefer him as a hale and strong man, whereupon he points out that he does not want to make love to an armful of cosmetics either. He would much rather have her as she really is, without artificiality. Living a healthy and active life, and maintaining her dignity as mistress of the household, would do far more for her appearance than any amount of beauty preparations.

In the *Banquet*, Xenophon describes a social occasion at which Socrates was present, when the conversation turned to light-hearted banter about love. Socrates tells the company that he cannot remember a time when he was not in love. He rallies his friends about their own love affairs without showing the least disapproval because they appear to have chosen men or women indiscriminately as the objects of their affections. His concern is whether the attraction is for the body or the soul. He is contemptuous of men who indulge homosexual passion carnally. He cannot, he says, make up his mind whether there is only one Venus or two: the first a celestial Venus who is worshipped in purity and sanctity of life and inspires the mind with love of the other soul, with friendship and with a desire for noble actions; the second, the vulgar Venus who inspires mankind only with love for the body.

Physical love vanishes as the beauty that evoked it decays. Sometimes it is accompanied even by dislike or hatred for the personality of the beloved. It palls with indulgence. But the soul is different, for with greater maturity her loveliness, also, increases. With the passage of time, spiritual love becomes more and more ardent, knowing no satiety. Since such love begins with admiration for the noble qualities of the beloved, rather than with the desire for selfish pleasure, it always elicits a response. How is it possible to respond otherwise than in a friendly way to deeply felt respect and esteem?

In view of what is often said about Greek paederasty it is interesting that Socrates should be able to assume the concurrence of his hearers in his condemnation of sensual indulgence. Why should someone who cares only for the external appearance of a person, for the pleasure it gives him, expect any return? He gives nothing and enjoys what he wants. Here is no true mingling of thought and feeling, no self-giving. On the contrary, while the one gains pleasure the other is likely to feel only shame. Because of social disapproval their affair has to be clandestine and furtive. To the argument that disapproval should be confined to those who use violence, and withheld from those who rely on persuasion, Socrates replies that the use of persuasion to gain the satisfaction of desire is even more to be deprecated. It results not only in the exploitation of the body but also in the thorough corruption of the whole person. As for those who purchase compliance, they can expect no more affection than the shopper can expect from the tradesman. Except as an ingredient in a much greater passion, physical attraction is on all grounds totally unsatisfactory as a basis for love.

To turn from Xenophon's reporting to Plato's is to leave behind earthy commonsense and lilt into the realm of the intellectual and spiritual. But when Plato wrote the *Lysis* he was still very much the pupil of Socrates. He had not yet spread his wings and the *Lysis* is a tedious work spun out with intellectual conundrums and word play. The question with which it begins is an important one: what kind of people become friends and why? In pursuit of the answer, Plato runs through every possible permutation of the good and the evil. Are good men friendly with other good men, good men friendly with evil men, evil men friendly with other evil men, good men with an evil streak friendly with wholly good men – and so on. The conclusion of an over-long discussion is that no universal formula can be found and there appears to be no reason why anybody should be friendly with anybody else! Friendship is indefinable.

This lame conclusion is due to the tendency to argue in black and white ethical terms whereas the question with which the debate starts is a psychological one. People become friends for all kinds of different reasons: sometimes because of a community of interest and feeling, sometimes because each finds his complement in the other, or because each sees himself in the other so that his own identity is confirmed and enhanced. It is not unknown for two people to be bound together in a community of vice which neither is capable of breaking. Their dependence upon each other is complete and they are inseparable.

The *Phaedrus* is more characteristic. Plato's method of starting with the earthy and soaring to celestial heights where reason is left behind is here perfectly exemplified. Socrates and Phaedrus are depicted ambling at their leisure through the countryside near Athens, looking for some delectably cool and shady place where they can while away the time. When they are settled, Phaedrus reads aloud a speech by a well-known writer, Lysias, on the subject of love.

He was against it. The speech, which has thrown poor Phaedrus into ecstasies, turns out to be stilted and uninspired stuff. Lysias deprecates warmth or passion in human relations and extols the more calculated kind of friendship. Love, he claims, leads men to neglect their private affairs and brings bitterness and disappointment in its train. It causes men to act and talk foolishly and in such a way as to earn social disapproval. Love is lacking in judgment and discrimination and in a sense of proportion. The lovers themselves are possessive and tend to isolate themselves from society. Passionless relations, on the other hand, leave men masters of themselves and able to dispose of their favours with a view to their own future advantage.

Wishing to pull his companion's leg, Socrates listens patiently to this platitudinous tirade and pretends to be delighted with it. But he then turns his derision onto it and announces that he could do better himself. Still pretending, he proceeds to build a case similar to that of Lysias. Passionate love, he says, is inordinate desire for a person and this could be only degrading to its object. Longing to have the beloved for his own pleasure, the lover would try to keep him ignorant, cowardly and weak, grudging him friends and encouraging him in soft living and womanish ways, making him such a person as will 'not fail in time of battle and all

serious emergencies to inspire his enemies with confidence and
his friends and lovers with alarm'. He would want him always
inferior to himself so that he could dominate him. Yet, since the
lover will always be an old man and the beloved a youth, the
relation between them can only be such as to fill the beloved with
shame and self-disgust. As for the lover himself, when finally he
has wearied of the relation, he will find he has accumulated debts
for the payment of which the formerly beloved will pursue him
relentlessly and subject him to blackmail. Socrates then asks
Phaedrus whether this kind of treatment of the subject is not both
shocking and worthless.

Up to this point the purpose of the argument has been to reveal
by reduction to absurdity the futility of contemporary discussions
of love, which worked on the lowest level and so ended by confusing the most discreditable concupiscence and uncontrolled
lust with the ennobling passion that love can be. The writers of the
time failed to distinguish between undisguised lechery and high
aspiration. Socrates begins his own exposition.

Suppose that passionate love is, indeed, a madness: what of it?
The prophetess at Delphi and the priestesses of Dodona were mad.
At least love is a divine madness, the inspiration of heaven and
more glorious than sober sense. Without madness there is neither
poetry nor art. It is important to understand that the soul is
immortal: it is uncreated and deathless. But what is the soul?
Warming to his theme, Socrates deserts reasoned argument and
enters into myth. The soul, he says, resembles a pair of winged
steeds and a charioteer. Unlike those of the gods, these steeds are
of different breeds; one of them in every way splendid, the other
undisciplined and unmanageable. When the wings of the soul are
fully feathered it roams with its two steeds in the upper air. The
immortals rise with the gods to that 'region beyond the sky of
which no earthly bard has ever yet sung, or ever will sing in
worthy strains', a region where the eternal realities are seen in
their purity – colourless, formless and intangible, visible only to
the intelligence: absolute justice, temperance and science. This
is the supreme ecstasy.

Those who are not divinities have to struggle desperately to make the ascent, being held back all the way by the vicious steed. In the confusion and stampede that results, many souls lose their wings altogether and fall to the earth where they inhabit a body appropriate to their performance in the heavenly sphere. The soul that has done well is given the body of a contemplative philosopher – somebody like Plato himself, for instance! – when it has a chance of regaining its feathers in a relatively short time. Souls that have done less well have to content themselves with the bodies of such people as politicians, economists or teachers of gymnastics. The ninth, and lowest, type of body in this classification is that of the absolute monarch. At death the souls are judged and given another life in accordance with the judgment. No soul that has not had at least a minimal vision of the truth can take to itself a human body: souls such as these become animals.

Standing aside from human affairs as he does, rapt in contemplation of the eternal realities, it is hardly surprising if ordinary folk conclude that the philosopher is mad.

This is an abridgment of the myth: Plato revels in a wealth of symbolism and imagery. But the myth contains the germ of the mature philosophy that Plato was to develop later. The eternal realities of which he speaks are prototypes of which the greatest marvels of this world are no better than copies. The world of time and space is a pale reflection of eternity. This is exactly the opposite of the modern world view. According to Plato the man whom the modern world thinks of as the realist is not dealing with realities at all but is playing with shadows.

When the soul takes to itself a human body it still carries within it faint recollections of what it has experienced in the celestial sphere. According as a man retains his integrity, or is sullied by the evils of this life, so these recollections are more or less clear and vivid. When the eyes of the virtuous man are caught by earthly beauty, the eternal beauty returns to his mind in all its delight and grandeur. He is at once carried to the heights. Since sight is the sharpest of the senses, it is visual beauty that most readily stimulates recollection. Were wisdom available to sight, the vision of the ultimate wisdom would be of such intensity as to be too terrible for humanity to sustain. It is more particularly in

human loveliness that we see the divine reflection: but, whereas
the perverse man in the grip of evil is stirred by it to unworthy
desires, the man of virtue is raised to the heavens.

> The man, it is true, whose initiation is of ancient date, or who has
> lost his purity here, is slow in being carried hence to the essential
> beauty of the upper world, when he sees that which bears his name in
> this. Accordingly, he feels no reverence as he gazes on the beautiful
> object, but, abandoning himself to lust, attempts like a brute beast to
> gratify his appetite, and in his wanton approaches knows no fear nor
> shame at this unnatural pursuit of pleasure. But whenever one who is
> fresh from those mysteries, who saw much of that heavenly vision,
> beholds in any god-like face or form a successful copy of original
> beauty, he first of all feels a shuddering chill, and there creep over
> him some of those terrors that assailed him in that dire struggle;
> then, as he continues to gaze, he is inspired with reverential awe, and
> did he not fear the repute of exceeding madness, he would offer
> sacrifice to his beloved as to the image of a god.

As the soul gazes on the beloved person it is warmed and
relieved of its pain so that the feathers of its wings start up again
from their roots. When separated, the process is reversed and the
pain of life multiplied. These variations cause a state of bewilder-
ment and perplexity that destroys happiness and peace of mind
until the vision is renewed.

> And therefore, if it can help, it never quits the side of its beloved,
> nor holds any of more account than him, but forgets father and
> mother, and brothers and friends, and though its substance be wasting
> by neglect, it regards that as nothing, and of all observances and
> decorums, on which it prided itself once, it now thinks with scorn,
> and is ready to be a slave and lie down as closely as may be to the
> object of its yearnings; for, besides its reverence for the possessor of
> beauty, it has found in him the sole physician for its bitterest pains.

This passionate affection is the god, Eros. The love is not a wound
inflicted by the arrow of Eros but is itself the god.

Plato now reverts to the metaphor of the charioteer with his
two ill-matched horses. The well-behaved, noble animal is the

reasoning faculty: the self-willed, ungovernable one represents the instinctual drives. As they approach the beloved the charioteer is hard put to it to maintain control. Reason is in conflict with desire. But, with the blessed vision as inspiration, the well-behaved horse is strengthened to restrain the ferocity of his unruly mate and, as a result, a chaste and honourable relation with the beloved is established. Even if, in a moment of weakness, the unruly horse does gain the upper hand it is never able to run spare; for the charioteer always has the other on the reins to pull against it. Since the vision is all-in-all to the lover he gives without stint to the beloved whatever will assist him in achieving still greater nobility. Affection so expressed cannot fail to evoke an appropriate response. Lover and beloved will rise to the heights in each other's company, although the vision itself is essentially a solitary experience.

This exposition concluded, Socrates is made to lecture Phaedrus on the perils of slick rhetoric and to explain the technical reasons of presentation that made this exposition so much more acceptable than that of Lysias. The dialogue ends with a prayer:

> Beloved Pan, and all ye other gods who here abide, grant me to be beautiful in the inner man, and all I have of outer things to be at peace with those within. May I count the wise man only rich. And may my store of gold be such as none but the good can bear.

Probably the best known of all the Socratic dialogues is the *Symposium*. Like the *Phaedrus*, it belongs to the period of Plato's maturity, when his thought was well developed. It is an account of a party at which Socrates and several friends are present. Evidently, most of them are recovering from a hangover because they begin by agreeing that they do not want two heavy drinking sessions, one immediately after another. They will drink for refreshment only. One of the company, Eryximachus, suggests that instead of drinking they should entertain themselves with conversation. He proposes as the subject, 'love', about which each is to give his opinion in turn. Phaedrus begins.

Love, he says, is the greatest among the gods and the worship of him is the oldest of all, since he was unbegotten. No mention of his parentage is to be found in either prose or verse. Love inspires men to noble actions, kindles their valour in war and is a powerful motive for self-sacrifice.

Pausanias starts by rebuking Phaedrus for indulging in mere eulogy. There are two kinds of love, he says, the first identified with the heavenly Aphrodite, the uncreated daughter of the heavens themselves, and the second, the earthly Aphrodite, the daughter of Zeus and Dione. The latter wants nothing but sensual pleasure, which it will take wherever it is to be had. The former is innocent of any lewdness and entirely masculine in character. It is therefore directed most appropriately to the male, preferring the more vigorous and intellectual bent. Although the law of Athens permits sexual relations between men and youths, public opinion disapproves and any father will try to save his son from that predicament. Were it known of a boy that he had been so used he would be the butt of his companions. But the influence of the heavenly love is virtuous and there can be no objection to that. This is what the law wishes to encourage.

Next comes Eryximachus, a medical man and the bore of the party, who asserts that medicine is under the sole direction of love since its object is to impose harmony on the discords of the body.

Aristophanes, the comic playwright, begs the company not to laugh at the serious theory he is about to propound. This was the origin and the power of love. Originally there were three sexes; male, female and hermaphrodite. All of them were globular in shape and had double what everybody has now: two faces, four arms, four legs, and so on. They faced in opposite directions at the same time, and were very strong and mobile. When they ran, they simply stuck out all their eight limbs and did cartwheels, which enabled them to bowl along at great speed. So conceited did they become that they tried to scale the heavens and oust the gods. To this attempt, Zeus replied by slicing them in half. This suited the gods well because, while human strength was halved they themselves would enjoy twice the number of sacrifices. Zeus screwed round the heads of these new half-men and drew their skins together and tied them up at what became the navel.

This bisection completed, each half longed to be a whole again and could do nothing but run about looking for another half to which it could cling. So absorbed were they with this that they were likely to die of starvation, until Zeus took pity on them and rearranged their genitals so that they could satisfy their longing with sexual intercourse, which relieved them of their obsession and freed them for other activities. Those that had been half a male became homosexual, the half females became Lesbians and the half hermaphrodies became heterosexual. That is why lovers of all kinds desire nothing more than to be together all their lives. They are nostalgic for their primaeval wholeness.

Agathon having delivered a panegyric, Socrates takes up the tale. Love, he says, is always love for something or somebody. What we love we long for, so love is always a longing and indicates the lack of something. While it is true that if what we love comes into our possession we cease to long for it we still long to continue in possession – as in the case of strength or riches. It is a mistake, therefore, to say that love is either beautiful or good in itself because these qualities are what we love or long for precisely because we lack them.

Having established this point, Socrates proceeds to recapitulate what he has learned from a wise woman of Mantinea, Diotima, who taught him all he knew about love. Since love does not in itself possess moral or aesthetic qualities, but longs for them, it cannot be a god, as they thought. Since obviously it is not a man, either, it must be between the two, a great and powerful spirit, a messenger of the gods, carrying our own prayers heavenward and returning with the answers.

This was the manner of the birth of love. On the day of Aphrodite's birth the gods were celebrating the event. Resource, the son of Craft, having drunk freely, wandered into the garden of Zeus to sleep it off. There he was found by Need who, thinking that to have a child by Resource would relieve her poverty, lay down beside him and conceived. Love was the child of the union and became the follower and servant of Aphrodite because he was born on her birthday. He loved the beautiful because Aphrodite herself was beautiful.

Then again, as the son of Resource and Need, it has been his fate to be always needy; nor is he delicate and lovely as most of us believe, but harsh and arid, barefoot and homeless, sleeping on the naked earth, in doorways, or in the very streets, beneath the stars of heaven, and always partaking of his mother's poverty. But, secondly, he brings his father's resourcefulness to his designs upon the beautiful and the good; for he is gallant, impetuous and energetic, a mighty hunter, and a master of device and artifice; at once desirous and full of wisdom, a lifelong seeker after truth, an adept in sorcery, enchantment and seduction. He is neither mortal nor immortal; for in the space of a day he will be now, when all goes well with him, alive and blooming, and now dying, to be born again by virtue of his father's nature, while what he gains will always ebb away as fast. So love is never altogether in or out of need; and stands, moreover, midway between ignorance and wisdom.

Popular error about the nature of love is due to the confusion of the lover with the beloved; for the beloved must, indeed, be beautiful and wise and good. Since love is the longing for what is lovely, love is a seeker after truth because wisdom is beautiful. Truth and beauty are good and, as with possession of the good comes happiness, all people are alike in being lovers for they all want happiness and the good is the only road to it. Yet there is one activity above all others that characterises love. To love is 'to beget upon the beautiful both in body and soul'. It appears, then, that love is not so much a love of the beautiful for its own sake as for the conception and generation that the beautiful effects. This comes of man's longing for immortality, which is the only means whereby he can make the good his own forever. One incentive, and one only, rivals that of procreation, namely fame. Glory alone provides an immortality greater than that of children and children's children.

Those whose procreation is of the spirit rather than of the flesh conceive and bear the things of the spirit: wisdom and all her sister virtues. The most important kind of wisdom is that governing the ordering of society. So if a young man already in possession of the virtues meets a companion who is not only physically attractive but also shares his love of wisdom they will together develop each other and from their spiritual intercourse great works of the spirit will be brought forth. And who would not prefer the greatness of a Homer or a Hesiod, a Lycurgus or a Solon, to the propagation of children, if that were the alternative? Is there anybody whose mortal children have brought him such fame?

Here the mystic takes charge and soars away. Loving one human person, the lover realises that if it is to loveliness of form that he is devoted he must extend his love to include many others besides. He must learn to love every lovely body and realise the insignificance of his passion for the one. From there he must pass to the realisation that the beauties of the body are of little importance by comparison with the beauties of the soul. He will learn to cherish spiritual loveliness even in a person whose outward appearance is ugly. Then he will turn to the beauty of laws and institutions and to the sciences and all kinds of knowledge. At the last, his contemplation will bring him to the ultimate beauty. Diotima continues:

> Whoever has been initiated so far in the mysteries of love and has viewed all these aspects of the beautiful in due succession, is at last drawing near the final revelation. And now, Socrates, there bursts upon him that wondrous vision which is the very soul of beauty he has toiled for so long. It is an everlasting loveliness that neither comes nor goes, which neither flowers nor fades; for such beauty is the same on every hand, the same to every worshipper as it is to every other.

As Socrates concludes his account of Diotima's ideas the sound of revellers is heard outside. One of them, the brilliant playboy, politician and general, Alcibiades, is admitted to the party and, after the usual banter, delivers himself of a eulogy of Socrates. The gist of it is that he thinks Socrates to be the greatest of leg-pullers and to be smiling up his sleeve at everybody most of the time. Yet, on examination, his talk is always full of substance and his arguments irrefutable. He himself used to be sure that Socrates was in love with him. Confident in his own attractiveness, he did his best to seduce him but none of his blandishments moved

Socrates in the least. He went to the length even of inveigling Socrates to spend the night with him and, in the middle of the night, crept under his covering and held him in his arms but, 'believe it or not, gentlemen, when I got up next morning, I had no more *slept* with Socrates in the meaning of the act, than if he'd been my father or an elder brother'. Alcibiades then describes the imperturbable behaviour of Socrates as a soldier in battle and his capacity for enduring hardship. He tells how once he saw Socrates standing perfectly still on the same spot for twenty-four hours, rapt in contemplation.

As Alcibiades ends, the revellers burst in and take charge of the proceedings, which at once degenerates into a noisy and drunken party. After a time the guests, both invited and uninvited, go home; but Agathon, Aristophanes and Socrates continue to talk. As day breaks, Agathon and Aristophanes nod off. Socrates carefully tucks them up and, after calling at the Lyceum for a bath, spends the rest of the day as usual and then goes home to bed.

In the quotation from the *Phaedrus*, Plato emphasises that when once the lover has seen the beloved he wants always to remain with him and he forsakes all other companionship. With separation from the beloved he loses sight of the heavenly vision and the pain of life returns. In Diotima's discourse the beloved is only the first rung of a ladder reaching to the celestial sphere. Some critics suggest that the ladder is kicked away as soon as the soul apprehends the heavenly vision. Surely this is an exaggeration. The lover will still find fulfilment in the company of so faithful a copy of the original beauty. As a poor simile we may take the young soldier on campaign who is reminded of the delights of home by a photograph of his girl friend. He does not throw the picture away when he has once been reminded, but keeps it in his wallet and gazes upon it whenever he has the opportunity.

But the contradiction between the *Phaedrus* and the *Symposium* is deceptive. In reality, Diotima's discourse is a valid development of the *Phaedrus* theme. Despite the splendour of their conception, neither of the two satisfies as an analysis of interpersonal love. Certainly they describe genuine human experiences, and those some of the most valuable. The grandeur of the mountains and the glory of the blossom does, indeed, uplift the spirit and stimulate reflection on the ultimate values. In the presence of human greatness we feel elevated ourselves and find new meaning in life. Falling in love is a psychedelic experience. There are echoes of this in the nature mysticism of Wordsworth and in the Jesus mysticism of the Christian, who deepens his knowledge of God by contemplation of the Christ.

But, when all this has been said, neither in the *Phaedrus* nor in the *Symposium* is Plato talking of love for a human person: he is describing love for the qualities of a person, his beauty or his virtue, which is quite a different matter. It is love for the patience, generosity, wisdom, intelligence and appearance of the person and not for what he is in himself. What Plato overlooks in the *Phaedrus* but makes clear in Diotima's discourse is that if the lover discovers similar qualities in other people he is logically obliged to include those others in the scope of his affections. But does anybody feel passionately for virtues? Surely, only as we love a Constable picture or a Beethoven symphony; not as we love a human person. What we feel for the virtuous resembles more a strong admiration. Any philosophy of love must find room for grief. Plato makes only a half-hearted attempt to do so and even this is abandoned in the *Symposium*. If we love a person for his qualities we would certainly regret his loss but we should not experience inconsolable grief. Surely grief is not an ignoble emotion, to be ignored. If we loved someone only for his qualities we would put flowers on his grave and immediately go in search of someone else with similar qualities.

Plato misses the uniqueness of each human person and therefore the irreplaceability of the beloved. We feel grief because we know that what we have lost can never be replaced. Nobody else will do. A bereaved husband may, after an interval, fall in love with some other woman but the relation would be new and different. The second wife would be deeply offended if she felt she was only a substitute for the previous one. A human person is not merely the addition: generosity + patience + wisdom + intelligence + physical attractiveness. Any whole is always more than the sum of its parts. We like a person who has virtues that he shares with others; we might not love a person who was deficient in the virtues: but what we love is the particularity, that which distinguishes him from everybody else. It is always from the encounter of individuals in their particularity that love arises. We may well imagine that, in his private life, Plato experienced love in its depths; but his philosophy misses the inwardness of the experience.

Against what social background does Plato envisage his ideal of interpersonal relations? His Utopian dreams are set out in the *Republic*, a work that is the fruit of his reflection on the political situation of his time. He had been brought up during the tumult and disillusion of the long-drawn Peloponnesian War which had ended in the crushing defeat of Athens by Sparta. Thereafter, Athens fell into the hands of a harsh and tyrannical oligarchy, The Thirty. Under their rule Plato was deeply shocked by the judicial murder of Socrates. His own political experience was small. Asked to co-operate with The Thirty he disassociated himself from them after a time. He also spent a brief period in Syracuse as an adviser to the ruler, but had no success in this capacity and returned. Yet he was a shrewd observer of events, as any admirer and pupil of Socrates was likely to be.

In the *Republic* he discusses the meaning of justice but, finding it impossible to define the term adequately, he concludes that it could be recognised only in the perfect State in which everything was fitly proportioned and harmoniously organised. He describes this ideal State. While it is evident that he had learned much from the Spartan system, his republic turns out to be a State such as never had existed, never has since and never could. This he acknowledges. He is not, he says, projecting a programme of constitutional and social reform but establishing principles upon which satisfactory community life should be based.

Plato, the aristocrat, thinks in terms of an élite. The community was to be divided into two main classes: the first, that of the producers and men of commerce and the professions; the second, a semi-military caste on the Spartan model. The members of the second class would be carefully selected, would live strenuously and frugally, dwelling in tents. Those most distinguished by wisdom and experience would form a group of Guardians, who would be the philosopher rulers. Only philosophers were suited for rule for they alone had insight into reality and could discriminate between the true and the false, the genuine and the counterfeit. They would hold all goods in common.

Personal relations, too, were to be communal, with little privacy for anybody. The superior class would live in community. Women would live in strict equality with men, receiving the same education and working and training with them and going to war with them. In everything except physical strength, Plato believed in the equality of the sexes. But men and women would be forbidden to form liaisons with each other. Only those whom the magistrates introduced to each other were to be allowed to procreate and the selection was to be made on genetic principles with a view to the production of strong, intelligent and virtuous children. Procreation was to be permitted only between the ages, for men, of thirty to fifty-five years; of women, of twenty to forty years. As a reward for distinguished service men would be allowed more frequent associations with women. Men and women over those ages could form unions as they pleased, provided they did their best to avoid child bearing.

Immediately after birth, babies were to be taken from their mothers and were to be brought up communally. Every possible measure was to be taken to ensure that parents could never recognise their own children; but for the satisfaction of parental affection parents could regard as their own all the children who could have been born within the period of weeks when they might have given birth to them. Similarly, these children would regard as their own all who might have been their parents.

It is difficult to see how, in this soulless and inhuman regime anybody could qualify for rule by becoming a philosopher. Nor could the sensitive personal relations Plato describes in other writings exist. But Plato is surely right in contending that justice does not consist in the application of a formula but only in the operation of the social system as a whole. Satisfactory personal relations can exist only under the same conditions. Recent European experience has shown how an evilly contrived system can be destructive of all humane values. Justice is conditional upon the just society.

Most distinguished of Plato's pupils, Aristotle (384–322 B.C.) became, in his turn, tutor to the greatest conqueror of ancient times, Alexander of Macedon. Although for nearly a thousand years his reputation was overshadowed by that of his master, in the ninth century A.D. Moslem philosophers began to appreciate his importance. Through them, and through the Jews, his work became known in Christendom and profoundly influenced Scholasticism. Many of his ideas have become part of the normal furniture of our minds.

Although he admired Plato and learned much from him, Aristotle differed profoundly from him both in temperament and outlook. There was little in him of the mystic. For him this world was the real world and reality was to be experienced in the things known by the senses. He was a close and accurate observer of nature. Following Gilbert and Sullivan, it has been said that every baby is born either a little Platonist or a little Aristotelian. But it is Aristotle's misfortune that, in the lecture notes form in which they have come down to us, his writings have none of the literary style and charm that characterise those of Plato and make them so delightful to read. He is severely analytical and his writing is compact and concise to a fault. Translators complain feelingly of the difficulties with which he presents them. Yet, by skilful editing, J. A. K. Thomson did manage to make his version of the *Ethics* readable and I rely upon him here. It is here that Aristotle writes of friendship (*Nichomachean Ethics*, Books 8 and 9).

Like Plato, Aristotle thinks mainly in terms of friendship between men, but he does admit that a woman can be taken as a friend. Unlike Plato he deals with the question almost entirely on the secular plane. He does not think in terms of the absolute imperatives of conscience. For instance, he would have had no sympathy with such commands as that we should treat every man as an end in himself and never as a means. Nor would he have had much sympathy with the statement in the Scottish catechism that the true end of man is 'to glorify God and enjoy him for ever'. For him the purpose of life was what ordinary decent people regard as their true end, which he said was *eudaimonia*. Professor W. D. Ross points out that, etymologically, this word indicates the state of being 'watched over by a good genius' but that colloquially it meant 'good fortune'. To Aristotle it has a richer meaning. It is more than prosperity, although that would be an ingredient and a pre-condition of it; more than pleasure, although pleasure would normally be an accompaniment. It is broader than virtue; more active than happiness; more positive than welfare or well-being. It means, in fact, all that a good and wise man wishes for his friends.

Much of the *Nichomachean Ethics* is devoted to the means whereby this can be achieved. What emerges is a character strongly resembling that of the man known to the English as a 'natural gentleman'. The virtues Aristotle recommends may be those that are often referred to as the 'bourgeois virtues' but a society that was without them would fare ill, whatever the bohemians may say. Aristotle's ethic is far from being mere hedonism, nor is it in a narrow sense egotistical. From all this it will appear that it is unlikely to be the ethic of the hero, the saint or the prophet but it might well be that of the statesman, the soldier or, still more, the solid and reliable citizen.

Aristotle justifies the attention he gives to friendship on the ground that 'love has somewhat of the character of a virtue, or at any rate involves virtue'. Friendship is indispensable alike to the rich and powerful and to the poor and unfortunate, for who knows when he will need the help and co-operation of a friend? Even among birds and beasts we find friendship. When travelling we feel a certain kinship with strangers, simply because they are our fellow men. Legislators concern themselves more with this feeling than with justice; for what they want is concord among all citizens and this is similar to friendship. Finally, friendship is an ennobling influence.

But what is it? We start by asking what it is that brings friendship into existence. What are its objects? It is generally thought that the object of friendship must be either good, or pleasant or useful. These three may boil down to only two, since the usefulness of friendship may be to bring pleasure. Then is it the good in itself that men love or only what is good *for them*? The fact is that, although it is only the absolute good that is lovable for its own sake, the individual tends to love what seems as if it will be good for him as an individual. Necessary conditions of friendship are that the goodwill one feels for the other should not only be reciprocated but should be known to be reciprocated. An example of what Aristotle means is when, perhaps, a well-known statesman feels enthusiasm for a famous sportsman who happens to be one of his supporters. Unless this mutual respect is known to both of them and the distance between them overcome they cannot be friends.

Corresponding to the three objects of friendship are three different types of friendship. First, there is the kind when the two men do not respect each other so much for their personal qualities as for what they expect to gain by the association, as with men associated in business. Second, there are friendships based on the pleasure each enjoys in the association, finding each other amusing or interesting companions. Such friendships as these two are ephemeral. As soon as the advantage for the pleasure diminishes, so does the friendship. This is most evident in the young who are susceptible to the passion of love which, for the most part is 'a longing for delight working upon the emotions'. Young people will pass from one love affair to another in the course of a single day. Aristotle is evidently thinking of young people brought together by 'chemical' attraction, enjoying wallowing in their own emotions.

Now we come to the core and here, if Aristotle does not quite anticipate modern discussion of the subject, he comes close to it. For he says that true friendship can exist only between two persons who are not only themselves good but also wish the good of each other *for the other's sake*, because of what he essentially is in himself. For instance, I might enjoy a round of golf with a neighbour on a Saturday morning. What I care about is his golfing ability. If he took up rock climbing instead I would lose interest in him. I would look for another golfing partner. But if I cared for a man as an individual and a person our friendship would survive such chances. At the same time, this kind of friendship includes the other two because it brings both pleasure and advantage. Indeed, it might well be that the pleasure and the advantage are the means of introduction to the real person. True friendship takes time to mature. 'Wishing to be friends is quick work, but friendship is a slow ripening fruit.'

Friendship is nourished by shared activities and so, during a prolonged separation, it may die away. But it is a permanent disposition and does not easily wither. To love one's friends is basically to love one's own good since by virtue of becoming the friend of someone else, the good of the other person becomes his own good.

Each of the elements of friendship appears in a man's own self-regard and friendship originates in the sympathetic feelings we have for ourselves. A man is free of inner conflict; he wishes whatever is good for himself; he wants his own survival, which to most men is the greatest of all goods; he enjoys dwelling on his better memories and hopes, and he knows what he likes and dislikes. This is characteristic of friendship, too. In other words, a friend is a second self and affection for him comes to resemble self-love. Friendship differs from goodwill in its intensity and depth; but the qualities that inspire goodwill may also be those that spark off friendship, just as physical attraction often sets off a love affair. Goodwill is inactive or potential friendship. Concord, on the other hand, which arises when two or more people are working together on the achievement of a common aim bears a strong similarity to friendship.

Aristotle now discusses the popular, but sentimentalist notion, that there is something discreditable about self-love, that the good man must always and only act on lofty principles and think nothing of his own interest. This is unrealistic. We shall understand the point better if we remember that the truth seeker is not any the less noble because he hopes to become a better man by

knowing the truth; nor the struggling artist in his garret less to be
admired because he finds personal fulfilment in his painting. The
soldier crawling into No-Man's-Land to rescue a comrade must
needs think of his own safety, and take advantage of every vestige
of cover, if his attempt is to succeed. Tennyson's 'self-knowledge, self-reverence, self-control' aptly expresses Aristotle's
attitude.

We have to distinguish between an ethically sound self-love and
the coarse selfishness of the man who, thoughtless of the interest
of others, grabs at more than his fair share of the good things of
life. There is all the difference in the world between, say, the
young doctor who trains mind and body, and is concerned for his
fitness and efficiency, so that he can go to some area of distress
and bring healing to sick and hungry children, and the *bon viveur*,
overfed and greasy on ill-gotten wealth, or the playboy, living
trivially as a parasite on his family. The man who develops his
personality, striving for things of moral beauty and excellence
because he values them, is in a different league from the man who
spends his life pampering himself. Were everyone to cultivate
true self-love there would be no doubt as to the health of the body
politic. All citizens would be virtuous. Self-love does not exclude
self-sacrifice. On the contrary:

> Many of his actions are performed to serve his friends or his country,
> even if this should involve dying for them. For he is ready to sacrifice
> wealth, honours, all the prizes of life in his eagerness to play a noble
> part. He would prefer one crowded hour of glorious life to a pro-
> tracted period of quiet existence and mild enjoyment spent as an
> ordinary man would spend it – one great and dazzling achievement to
> many small successes. And surely this may be said of those who lay
> down their lives for others; they choose for themselves a crown of
> glory.

Nor does self-love exclude disinterestedness. Aristotle insists that
friendship must be disinterested. It must not depend upon the
ulterior motive or the *arrière pensée*. A man with self-love will be
prepared to sacrifice money and honours and take second place to
his friend when this is the nobler course.

Another confusion is that the man of perfect blessedness will be a recluse or a solitary. Again, the contrary is true. Man is a social animal : nobody would want any or all of the goods that this world affords at the cost of lonely friendlessness. Besides, happiness itself involves activity and the happy man needs friends to share his activities and pursue his aims. When two men take to each other they always want to work together in some way.

Aristotle seems to have had a prejudice against old age, since he repeatedly remarks that old people, being cross-grained and morose, do not make friends easily, whereas young people do. It is possible to *like* a large number of people at the same time, for liking has the character of an emotion. Friendship, by contrast, is a settled disposition, arrived at as a consequence of deliberate choice made on the basis of intimacy and knowledge. It is evident therefore that it is no more possible to have a large number of friends than it is to be in love with many women at the same time.

Friendships of the types so far discussed are based on equality. There are others in which the partners are unequal : those between father and son, older and younger, husband and wife, ruler and ruled. Balance is introduced by the quality and the degree of affection on both sides. Yet, when there is a great gap between two people, such as that of social position, friendships do not occur. In the light of this the notion that friends wish the greatest good for each other needs modification : neither can want the other to rise out of his sphere.

Whereas men like to be honoured because the praise addressed to them confirms their good opinion of themselves, they appreciate affection for its own sake; therefore friendship is more desirable than honour. Friendship is in giving, rather than in receiving, affection. An example of this giving is that of the mother, who still feels affection for her child even if it is brought up by foster parents and has no means of reciprocating. The best and most lasting friendships are those in which affection is mutually bestowed. This puts unequals on a footing of equality, if each bestows affection in accordance with the deserts of the other, particularly when they are similar in goodness. Their goodness is a principle of stability, whereas the vicious have no consistency in themselves and so are fickle.

In every human association some form of friendship is presupposed, as between shipmates on a voyage. Since all such associations are included in the larger body politic this provides us with a basis for the analysis of political constitutions. Of these there are three types, each having a degenerate form as its counterpart: monarchy (tyranny); aristocracy (oligarchy); timocracy, a constitution based upon property qualifications (democracy) · The relation of a father to his sons resembles aristocracy; that of brothers resembles timocracy, while households without a head, or in which authority is weak, resemble democracy.

Here Aristotle interjects a comment on slavery, remarking that there can be no friendship between a master and his slave as such. This relation resembles that between a tyrant and his subjects who are mere tools for his use. There can be no friendship or justice between the human person and inanimate objects or even between the human person and horses or cows. A slave is an animated tool and a tool is an inanimate slave. There is therefore little room for justice between master and slave or between tyrant and subjects. But there are exceptions. Aristotle says that there can be a relation that is good for both between the master and the 'natural-slave', defined as one who has only just enough reason to understand simple orders. Yet most men are not 'natural-slaves'. Evidently nature has not made enough mentally deficients to go round!

Continuing his discussion of the family system, Aristotle bases the parent-child relation on the fact that the parent loves the child as part of himself, while the child loves the parent as the author of his being. But the love of the child is the lesser of the two for the giver of life feels the connection more intimately than the receiver. The giver, also, has known the recipient from the moment of birth.

Brothers love each other by reason of the identity of their parentage. This is a case of 'identity in separation'. They have also enjoyed similar upbringing and are usually of similar age. Their relation strongly resembles that between comrades. Love between husband and wife is natural, for theirs is the most primitive and fundamental of all human relations. In their functions and duties they are complementary to each other and their children are a bond between them. To ask how they should behave towards one another is the same as to ask what behaviour between them justice requires.

Such are Aristotle's thoughts on friendship and it is difficult to argue against any of them. But, at the end, as in all his ethical thinking, it is also difficult to avoid feeling that the element of calculation and prudence is too obtrusive, as if the warmth and spontaneity of experience has been dissipated in the process of dry analysis. In all great human experience there is something that defies analysis and Aristotle misses this. That he would have approved of the men and women of reckless heroism and self-abnegating compassion we may be sure, but whether he would have inspired them is open to question. Those who have dared, adventured and sacrificed for humanity have usually had in their nature a streak of fanaticism that to Aristotle would have been suspect. They were not people of prudent moderation but people who discarded caution and gained their identity by total immersion in a profound love. The Aristotelian ideal is a sound Establishment man.

PLUTARCH

One of the most delightful of essayists, Plutarch (A.D. c.46–c.120) spent most of his life in his beloved Chaeronia, in Boeotia, where he was active in local affairs. He is remembered mainly for his *Parallel Lives*, a series of comparisons between distinguished Greeks and similarly distinguished Romans, from which Shakespeare took some of his plots. Less well known are his *Moralia*, essays on ethical, literary and historical themes. Among them are discussions of personal relations.

Friendship and love imply their opposites; but enmity and hatred are the less popular subjects with authors. Plutarch deals with them from the standpoint of the person who is the object of enmity and hatred, who may have acquired enemies merely because he shares in the hostility directed against his friends. In his essay, 'How to Profit by One's Enemies', he suggests how the situation can be exploited to advantage. Avoiding pious exhortations on how to turn enemies into friends, he confines himself to showing how enmity can be treated like any other evils of life and made to yield benefits.

First, from our enemies we can learn to know ourselves better and, as a consequence, we can eradicate our own weaknesses. Whereas our friends are reluctant to criticise us, our enemies sieze avidly on anything discreditable and make the most of it. If we are wise enough to recognise it as such this is a good turn they are doing us. We are compelled to live circumspectly for fear of providing the enemy with pretexts. By his competition with us he offers us a further incentive to integrity, which is in itself the finest defence against his hostile darts.

That we shall resist the temptation to revile our enemies is unlikely; but we shall cause them far more distress by proving ourselves to be men of kindliness, honour and self-control. If we revile them we must at least ensure that our enemies cannot turn upon us our own allegations, for there is nothing more disgraceful than slander that recoils upon its author. Before vilifying others we must make sure that we are irreproachable ourselves.

When calumniated we should think carefully what there may be in our behaviour to lend colour to the calumny. Often the best reply is silence; for through silence we maintain dignity and, in no circumstances, can silence be quoted against us.

Socrates bore patiently with his waspish wife, Xanthippe, because he felt that by doing so he would train himself to bear with similar good temper the scurrilities of others. But how much better to gain this training through patience with enemies. It is as well to answer contumely and injury with compassion even for the enemy himself when he is in distress. This will win the respect of the onlookers, who are bound to be impressed. They will be still more impressed if, when the enemy has acted worthily, we praise him for it. When, afterwards, we lay complaints they will be all the more readily believed because we have demonstrated our magnanimity and impartiality. In the process we shall have gone some way towards ridding ourselves of unworthy jealousy and envy. Perhaps we should thank our enemies for drawing off jealousy and envy that might otherwise have been directed towards our friends.

After this exercise in ethical expediency we turn with interest to what Plutarch has to say 'On having Many Friends'. This he tends to deprecate on the ground that affection of any depth cannot extend beyond a limited circle. If a man claims to have many friends it is probably because he has none at all of any value. A person desiring many friends is like a promiscuous woman who loses all her lovers because she cannot help skipping from one to another.

'Friendship,' writes Plutarch, 'is a creature that seeks a companion.' It is not satisfied merely with being in company, like cattle in a herd. Companionship of any depth has to be worked for with goodwill, graciousness and virtue. Portioned out among a large number of people it is weak and enfeebled. How unhappy are rich men and rulers, surrounded by the servile and the flatterers, who vanish at the first sign of misfortune!

Those who seek our friendship must be tested to see what their proffered friendship means, for it is as uncomfortable to have the association of an unprincipled friend as it is painful to get rid of him. Chance acquaintances are therefore to be suspect. Close association, regular companionship and deep knowledge are of the stuff of friendship. If we judge would-be friends superficially, by what they can offer us, we have contrariwise to think what they are likely to demand of us.

There is nothing to boast of in having no enemies; for this probably means we have no friends either. Apart from incurring the hostility of the enemies of our friends, our friendly intimacies are sure to arouse jealousy in some of those who are not admitted to them.

'Friendship comes into being through likeness'. Friends must have everything in common, sharing the same views, opinions and feelings as if there were two bodies with only one soul.

On the most intimate of all relations, in his 'Advice to Bride and Groom' Plutarch writes to a young couple of his acquaintance who have recently married, offering marriage guidance counselling that is marred by his over-emphasis on the male point of view. The wife clearly exists merely for the sake of the husband.

Plutarch reminds his young friends that, among their household gods, the ancients gave Hermes a place at the side of Aphrodite and also assigned places to Persuasion and the Graces, in token that married people should 'succeed in their mutual desires by persuasion and not by fighting and quarrelling'. Solon had advised that, before going to bed, the bride (why not the groom as well?) should take a bite of quince so that the pleasure of the lips should be apparent from the start. In Plutarch's own country the bride was customarily crowned with asparagus because this plant gives the best flavoured fruit from the roughest thorns. This symbolises the satisfactions that await the husband if he is willing to put up with his new wife's first displays of ill-temper. On the other hand, young wives who let themselves resent their first marital experiences may find that they have accepted the stings of the bee only to turn away from the honey.

Rows are especially to be avoided in the early stages of marriage because the relation at that time is not strong enough to withstand the strain and may be permanently spoiled. When it has had time to settle down it becomes unbreakable.

Also, the newly-married couple should beware of trusting too much the passions that arise from physical attractiveness. Unless backed by character and temperament these are apt to be unreliable. Similarly, women who employ aphrodisiacs so as to dominate their husbands through pleasure are laying up trouble for themselves. They will find their husbands turning into dull-witted, degenerate fools. The husband, on his part, who has been lucky enough to win a wife of wealth or position should not try to dominate her by humiliating her. He should treat her with the respect that is due.

Plutarch's marriage guidance counselling diverges from that of Socrates and Xenophon when he insists that the woman should be the passive, and the man the leading, partner. A woman, he says, ought to be most in evidence when in the company of her husband so that she can do him credit. But she is to sink her own identity in his. When he is away she ought to hide herself. She should not, as Herodotus had advised, put away her modesty with her underclothing. On the contrary, she should put on modesty instead of her clothes and then, 'both husband and wife bring into their mutual relations the greatest modesty as a token of greatest love'. Just as in music the bass sounds the melody (!) so both husband and wife should act in agreement but it should be the husband's leadership and preferences that prevail.

Should the wife be rich, all the more should she reflect in her own moods those of her husband; whether in seriousness or play-fulness, in gravity or in gaiety, and she should express herself through him. In doing so she will enrich herself and make a stronger impression. If her husband leaves her out of his more licentious enjoyments she should not allow jealousy to take possession of her but should bear in mind that this shows his respect for her. No decoration so adorns a woman as dignity, good-humour and modesty.

On the other side, if the husband does not want to drive her elsewhere, he also will have consideration for his wife's moods and feelings. The analogy to marriage is that of two ropes that gain their strength from being entwined together. As they share each other physically so they should share in everything, even in their worship of their favourite gods, which should be those the husband prefers. However, if a husband finds that his wife cannot be everything to him at once he should reflect that it is unreason-able to expect the same woman to be both wife and paramour. If he chooses her in the first place for her looks he is a fool. Inner sweetness of nature and temperament are far more important.

It is the little, daily irritations that do most harm to marriages. Especially ought husband and wife not to carry on their bickerings in public, any more than they make love in public. Even correct behaviour can be offensive if accompanied by asperity. Rancour and ill-humour have no place in married life. While it is true that the husband should be the leading partner, he should not treat his wife as a chattel but should exercise his influence by entering into her feelings sympathetically just as the soul controls the body. Mutuality is the secret. Couples whose only bond is either that of sex or that of money are not truly united at all; they are still separate persons. They should mix as liquids mix, throughout their whole personalities.

Plutarch does not overlook the mother-in-law problem but his first instinct again is to deal with it from the male point of view. Since mother love is what it is, a wife should seek to gain her husband's affections without alienating him from his mother. Her inclination should be towards his mother and she should do all in her power to win her confidence. She should look to his parents rather than to her own, for confidence begets confidence and love begets love.

If quarrels do break out, then the woman is well-advised to keep quiet until her husband's anger has blown itself out and to speak him fair when he has fallen silent. It is a mistake, on such occasions, to take the huff and sleep apart, for sex is the finest conciliator. They should particularly try to avoid bedroom quarrels for these are the least easily curable. If a woman has reason for jealousy she should not rush straight to the divorce court or allow her grievance to dominate her. This is exactly what her rival wants. It is far better to close her eyes to the affair and let it pass. But both partners do better to reserve themselves for each other. They should not sow seed which, if it should bear fruit, would make them feel ashamed. If a man knows that affairs with other women distress his wife he should not for the sake of 'so trivial a pleasure' cause her pain, any more than he would wear a perfume that upsets her.

Finally, Plutarch advocates intellectual pursuits as the finest uniting influence. The partners should study together the deep things of life. This will affect the whole character and attitude. How could a woman immersed in the study of geometry wish, for instance, to be a dancer, and how could a woman under the charm of Plato or Xenophon fall into superstition? She may not be able to acquire the ornaments of the wealthy but the adornments of the mind, that gave distinction to the great women of history, are available for all, without price.

PLOTINUS

'Good and kindly, singularly gentle and engaging . . . so in fact we found him. Sleeplessly alert, pure of soul, ever striving toward the divine which he loved with all his being, he laboured strenuously to free himself and rise above the bitter waves of this blood-drenched life.' So wrote his friend and pupil, Porphyry, of Plotinus (A.D. 204–70), the last and one of the greatest philosophers of antiquity.

The period through which he lived was an unhappy one. The great age of the Antonine emperors had ended twenty-four years before his birth and the Roman world had been troubled by outbreaks of plague, earthquakes, religious persecutions and frontier wars. The Army became conscious of its power and engineered a succession of palace revolutions. There was frequent turmoil and disorder. The estates of many of the old aristocratic families were confiscated to reward generals who had assisted new emperors to murder their predecessors but who had little else to recommend them besides a talent for brutality. There were economic crises and the civil administration fell into disarray: taxation was burdensome and corruption entrenched.

Porphyry could without hyperbole write of the 'bitter waves of this blood-drenched life'. There was much to discourage men with the qualities of a Plotinus. The traumatic effects on sensitive people of such widespread practices as infanticide and of the brutal entertainments of the arena must have been considerable. To have to endure the spectacle of violence and deliberately inflicted suffering is to recoil. We do not know how much the stories of the debauchery and licence of the time have been exaggerated in the telling but the general climate can hardly have been uplifting.

It is dangerous to generalise about the mood of a period but there are many indications that a feeling of world-weariness and pessimism was widely prevalent. The influence of world-denying oriental religions did nothing to stimulate a more cheerful spirit.

Such was the spiritual environment in which Plotinus lived. Porphyry opens his biography with the remark: 'Plotinus, the philosopher, our contemporary, seemed ashamed of being in the body. So deeply rooted was this feeling that he could never be induced to tell of his ancestry, his parentage or his birthplace.' Despite this reluctance it is known that he was born in Egypt and, at the age of twenty-seven, began his philosophical studies in Alexandria, whose learned men were deeply immersed in the Greek tradition. Plotinus himself was under the influence of Plato more than of any other philosopher and that is why it is appropriate to include him in this chapter. At the age of thirty-nine he joined a military expedition to Persia, led by the Emperor Gordian III, with the intention of using it as an opportunity for studying Eastern thought. But the expedition collapsed when the emperor was assassinated by his own troops. Plotinus made his way to Rome where he settled until shortly before his death. There he conducted a philosophical group, a kind of permanent seminar, and won the friendship of the Emperor Gallienus.

He appears to have been a man of delightful personality. Seldom has a philosopher so precisely exemplified in his way of life the doctrines he taught. It was said of him that he would assist anyone who came to him in need. So well was he thought of both for integrity and for business ability that a number of wealthy men and women made him the trustee of their fortunes and the guardian of their children. He took orphans into his household and supervised their upbringing so that his home was always alive with the gaiety of young people. Like some other philosophers of distinction, he did not start writing until late in life; when he was forty-nine years old. His friends were deeply devoted to him and a number of distinguished women were included in his circle. At one time he entertained the idea of founding in the Campagna a community on the lines of Plato's *Republic*, to be named Plato-nopolis. Gallienus himself was interested in the experiment but later withdrew his support and the scheme fell through.

His personal habits were less pleasing. He abstained from the baths and contented himself with a massage every evening. When his masseurs died of plague he dispensed even with that. At the end of his life he contracted a disease so repulsive as to drive his

friends from him. On his death bed he sent for his friend
Eustochius. To him Plotinus said: 'I have been a long time waiting
for you; I am striving to give back the Divine in myself to the
Divine in the All.' Having so said, he died.

During his life, Plotinus on several occasions experienced the
mystic union. Amid the ugliness and disillusion of his times he won
serenity by personal self-discipline and rigorous concentration on
his intellectual enterprise. Bertrand Russell wrote of him: 'Among
the men who have been unhappy in the mundane sense, but
resolutely determined to find a higher happiness in the world of
theory, Plotinus holds a very high place. . . . Like Spinoza, he has
a certain kind of moral purity and loftiness which is very impressive. He is always sincere, never shrill or censorious, invariably
concerned to tell the reader, as simply as he can, what he believes
to be important. Whatever one may think of him as a theoretical
philosopher, it is impossible not to love him as a man.' His well-
proportioned system has an aesthetic appeal and Bertrand Russell
comments that there are worse reasons than that for admiring a
philosophy. The influence of Plotinus reached far into the future.
His most recent disciple was the late Dr W. R. Inge, Dean of St
Paul's, whose authoritative work on Plotinus was published in
1929.

While Plotinus has much to say about love, he does not so
much analyse the relation as show its place and its rôle in the
entire scheme of things. It is basic to his conception of the
universe. He lifts the relation far above the mundane level and
shows it to be the starting point of personal salvation. His master
work, *The Enneads*, sets out a conception of the divine Trinity;
but this is not to be identified with the Holy Trinity of the
Christian creeds, from which it differs significantly. Although
Plotinus himself refers to this Trinity as God the term could be
misleading because its relation with the universe is not that of
active creator. In the Greek manner, Plotinus personalises it and
turns it into myth; but it is not personal in the living and active
sense.

First in the Trinity is the transcendent ONE; known variously
as the First, the Good, the Absolute and the Unconditioned. The

ONE is dependent on nothing else but is infinite and eternal. It is changeless and within it there is no process. It engages in no activity because activity would involve process and change. It has neither wants nor needs but is completely self-contained. It cannot properly be described even as the First Cause. It is inaccessible to human knowledge and no qualities can be predicated of it. We can multiply negatives about it indefinitely but say nothing positive of it.

Yet, without this ONE nothing could exist. From it, by emanation or irradiation, comes the Intellectual-Principle, the second of the Trinity. In no sense does this emanation result from an act of the will. Plotinus himself uses the analogy of the light of the sun, but to be strictly accurate the sun would not have to give off any energy or be in any way diminished as the light poured from it. Also, there is nothing spatial about the ONE and the Intellectual-Principle. The rays of this sun neither travel a distance nor take time to arrive.

The Intellectual-Principle has two objects: the ONE and itself. It is the highest reality knowable and is the perfection of beauty. Within itself it contains all the ideas – or forms or concepts – of classes of things and even of particular things. These are the divine thoughts that take bodily form in the sensible world. All the phases of existence, down to matter itself, which is in fact only a half-reality, are eternally present in the divine mind or Intellectual-Principle. With remoteness the radiance glows more faintly and in the material world which is the lowest phase of existence this deprivation has evil as its consequence.

Third in the Trinity is the All-Soul, the emanation of the Intellectual-Principle. This has two aspects: the Celestial Soul which is, as it were, turned toward the Intellectual-Principle in perpetual contemplation; and the Lower or Generative Soul, whose function is to fashion the material world as a copy or representation of the Ideas or Forms in the Intellectual-Principle. This Generative Soul is the source of energy and movement – the cause. It is also particularised in the souls of individual human persons. The Generative Soul may be thought to have an affinity with the Christian Logos.

The All-Soul in the human person also has three aspects. First there is the Intellectual-Principle of the Soul, which is forever separate from the body and absorbed in contemplation of the divine. A person is most true to himself when completely identified with that. Second is the Reasoning Soul which is the thinking mind and the seat of the will. Third comes the Unreasoning-Soul which is the instinctual nature of a man.

This world is 'a clear image, beautifully formed, of the Intellectual Divinities'. Yet Plotinus displays a subtle aversion from it. There is in him none of that hatred of the world as essentially evil that characterises oriental religions but nonetheless he has a longing to turn away from it. Despite his friendliness in his private life, he recoils from the multitudes of mankind. People fall into three types: the sages, 'intent upon the sublimest, upon the realms above'; a class of people reminiscent of good and 'therefore not without touch with good', and the rest, 'mere populace, serving to provide necessaries to the better sort'.

Evidently, Plotinus had no regard for the humdrum virtues of ordinary folk; but, despite this attitude, he delighted in the loveliness of people. He rejoiced in physical beauty as he did in the beauties of nature and of art but was not so carried away by it as to fail to recognise that it is only skin deep. What he really admired was the inner beauty of a well-proportioned, virtuous personality. It was not superficially good appearance or prettiness that he valued but the kind of refined appearance that excellence of character and high spirituality produced, the faces of the saints. Such beauty is to be loved with heart and mind; but more especially with mind.

But what is it that awakens all this passion? No shape, no colour, no grandeur of mass: all is for a Soul, something whose beauty rests upon no colour, for the moral wisdom the soul enshrines and all the hueless splendour of the virtues. It is that you find in yourself, or admire in another, loftiness of spirit; righteousness of life; disciplined purity; courage of the majestic face; gravity; modesty that goes fearless and passionless and tranquil; and shining down upon all, the light of godlike intellection.

All these qualities are to be reverenced and loved; but what entitles them to be called 'beautiful'? Contrast the ugliness of the vile and vicious person. The soul has become ugly by falling into matter and mingling with the material, just as gold is degraded by becoming mixed with earth. But let the soul become isolated from all that is foreign to it and cleared of the desires that come of too intimate association with the body, let it be emancipated from the passions and regain its solitariness, and in that moment the ugliness that came from the alien is stripped away and the soul appears in its true beauty.

When a person falls in love with someone possessed of this interior beauty he is irresistibly reminded of his state in the celestial sphere from where his soul came to inhabit the body. From love of the individually beautiful he comes to an appreciation of the beauty in which all things participate and his love becomes broader and more comprehensive.

The born lover has a certain memory of beauty from the time before the soul became embodied but he is severed from it and no longer comprehends it. At first he is fascinated by physical loveliness but he must discipline himself to see beauty everywhere and to recognise the beauty of the immaterial and the spiritual. From this he will be led to the Intellectual-Principle, treading the upward way.

But if love for a particular person is the first step in the ascent to the heights, it is our innate recollection of, and tendency towards, the highest that originally inspires our love for the individual. This is true even of the higher manifestations of sexuality, which is the desire to beget in beauty. The lower forms of sexuality are content with mere physical attraction but we should look for more than that.

> Now if the sight of beauty excellently reproduced upon a face hurries the mind to that other Sphere, surely no one seeing the loveliness lavish in the world of sense – this vast orderliness, the form which the stars even in their remoteness display – no one could be so dull-witted, so immovable as not to be carried by all this to recollection, and gripped by reverent awe in the thought of all this, so great, sprung from that greatness.

Like so many of his contemporaries, Plotinus was mainly interested in personal salvation. The whole of his system, with all its refinements and complexities, centres on that. Salvation for him comes through aesthetics. While it is untrue to say that he is not interested in the will, because he is much concerned with virtues and vices which require the exercise of will, he lays more stress on release; the emancipation of the soul from contamination. This, rather than a redirection of the will is what he requires. The righteous man is valued because his personality is harmonious, symmetrical, unified and true to itself. Salvation begins with love of this beauty which sends the soul winging back to the eternal and infinite beauty, the source of its being, in 'the flight of the alone to the alone'. In all this there is no morbid sense of guilt and no evangelistic call to repentance, but there is discipline and struggle.

It appears, then, that a man no sooner falls in love than he turns his back upon the beloved to reach for more exalted glories. Plotinus often writes as if this were so; yet his antagonists charged him with binding men down to the earthly. In reply, Plotinus is at pains to make clear that his system implies neither repudiation of the earthly nor inextricable involvement in it but more a kind of detachment. Certainly, in his own personal life he did not turn his back upon his friends but enjoyed them until the end. Yet his finest moments were those in which he was wholly absorbed in contemplation of the divine. This is like the musician who still takes pleasure in the singing of children while finding his deepest fulfilment in the works of Chopin and Liszt.

In this scheme of salvation what rôle does the beloved play apart from the passive one of being lovable? The notion of a mutuality in which each is lost in the other seems to have eluded Plotinus. What impresses him more is that in the experience of love a person becomes conscious of his own separateness. The 'flight of the alone to the alone' is a solitary experience. No less characteristic is his insistence that we do not generate beauty from within ourselves but discover it in the external world and enter into it. When we have found it we realise that it coincides with something in ourselves, which Plotinus thought was recollection. Beauty is not 'in the eye of the beholder' and is not a matter of taste but is objective. There are eternal standards to which both persons and things must approximate if they are to be regarded as beautiful. Herein lies the discontent of the artist, always aware of a perfection of which he has fallen short. Our appreciation of the aesthetic is not a passive pleasure but an intense activity which ultimately carries us beyond ourselves to the contemplation of the absolute beauty.

Instead of suddenly lilting into myth as Plato used to do, Plotinus first constructed a coherent system and then recapitulated it in terms of myth. One of the problems that baffled Greek philosophers was that of showing how the divine, eternal infinite, immaterial and perfect, could have any relation at all with the world of time, space, change and evil. To do this they ingeniously devised graded hierarchies linking the two. Plotinus follows this tradition.

He begins by personalising the higher love under the name, 'Eros', who was born on the day of the heavenly Aphrodite's birth. This heavenly Aphrodite was the daughter of Ouranos (Heaven) or of Kronos, the son of Ouranos. She was identified with the Intellectual-Principle and was Soul at its most divine. Incapable of looking toward the lower things she was uncontaminated by the material. Authentic Being, she was directed wholly toward Kronos or Ouranos, and was therefore unmothered. It was this relation of love that Plotinus personalised as Eros, through whom she continued to look toward Kronos (Ouranos).

Below the Intellectual-Principle is the Soul of the All. This is the Secondary Aphrodite, the daughter of Zeus and Dione, who moves toward the material world and presides over earthly marriages. She also has an upward look, which is how she mediates between the two realms. She, too, has to have a love with which to look upward and this, also, is personalised as Eros. This upward striving stirs and leads upward the souls of young people and all those with a recollection of, and therefore a desire to return to, their divine origin.

Plotinus then asks whether the soul of the individual human

being contains such a love and answers that it must be so, not only with humanity, but with all that has life. This is the spirit that walks with every being, the affection dominant in every nature. Each individual has his own Eros which, in a returning movement, clings to the All-Love.

This love, like that of the All-Soul, is twofold. First is the Eros who is a god, leading the particular soul to the Divine. Second, there is the Eros in the Soul that enters into the world of the senses. This does not rank as high as a god but is a celestial. The celestial Eros is the child of Penia (Poverty) and Poros (Possession). Penia stands for undirected striving; Poros for self-sufficient reason. The distinction of the celestials is that, although they are eternal, they are also capable of experience and of passion. They are brought to birth by each individual Soul as it enters the world. They are in a perpetual state of need that can never be satisfied. All loves that serve the purposes of nature are good: those that do not are accidents attending on perversions and are in no sense Real Beings. They are the accompaniments of a spiritual flaw.

To sum up: on the human plane Eros is desire. All human love includes an element of desire, but what the higher Eros desires is union with beauty and divinity. It is not a possessive desire in the exclusive sense of grasping to ourselves and depriving others. Beauty is a non-competitive good. The more we have of it the more we make available to others. The lower Eros is immersed in the world of the senses and of the material. Its desire is for exclusive possession and bodily satisfaction. This is the Eros that in Piccadilly Circus perpetually aims its permanent arrow at the passers-by. The Eros of Piccadilly Circus has a relatively minor part to play in the grand scheme of Plotinus, well aware though he is of the damage it can wreak.

Chapter Three

The Latins

CICERO

Cicero (106–43 B.C.), orator, philosopher, literary man and statesman, differed from the Athenian thinkers in that his were no sequestered meditations. He was deeply involved in the passions and the violence of Roman politics. An admirer of the ancient Roman virtues and a dedicated supporter of the Republic, he died by the executioner's hand not long after Republicanism had given place to Caesarism. His attitudes were those of the Stoic philosophers; his literary style so pure and lucid that it became the standard for the language. The *De Amicitia*, which is reckoned among the noblest of his works, was written in 44 B.C.; ten years after Caesar's second invasion of Britain.

Following a literary convention of his time, Cicero puts his thoughts on friendship into the mouth of a certain Laelius, whose discourse he claims to have heard repeated by his tutor, the aged lawyer, Scaevola. Laelius had had it from his intimate friend, Scipio Africanus the Younger (185–129 B.C.), the conqueror and destroyer of Carthage, himself a literary man and patron. Laelius discusses the ideas of Scipio with his sons-in-law and another friend. Using this convention, Cicero does not so much set out a metaphysic or a theology of love as offer his reflections on the practice of the art of friendship.

Laelius admits to his grief at the death of Scipio but confesses that it is a selfish grief. Unless he had wished to live forever, what reason is there for feeling sorry for Scipio? He was successful both in politics and in war and is known to everybody for his charm and integrity. What advantage would he have gained from a few more years of life? Besides, Laelius is of the same opinion as Socrates;

that after the death of the body the soul returns to the heavens and that, for the virtuous man, the journey is easy. Grief for such a man as Scipio is therefore more a sign of envy than of friendship. But, if the opposite view were correct; if it were true that soul and body perished together, as there was nothing good about death neither was there anything bad about it and they should content themselves with gratitude that Scipio had lived at all, that they had enjoyed the happiness of knowing him and that he would continue to live in their memories.

Friendship can exist only among good men; those who in daily life are loyal, upright, fair and generous, free from passion, caprice and insolence and of strong character. There is a natural tie between all men which strengthens with proximity; but friendship is more than mere relation. Goodwill can be eliminated from a relation without destroying it but goodwill is of the essence of friendship. How much more is friendship than mere relation appears from the fact that, whereas the ties uniting the human race are infinite, the bonds of true friendship unite only a few people.

In what, then, does friendship consist?

Friendship is nothing else than an accord in all things, human and divine, conjoined with mutual goodwill and affection, and I am inclined to think that, with the exception of wisdom, no better thing has been given to man by the immortal gods. . . . For friendship adds a brighter radiance to prosperity and lessens the burden of adversity by dividing and sharing it.

All other objects of desire are adapted to a single end; but friendship covers innumerable ends. It is never in the way and no barrier shuts it out. We may understand the power of friendship by considering the results of its opposite because the consequences of enmity are always divisive and destructive. So widely is this recognised that the whole world unanimously approves and applauds any signal display of sacrificial friendship.

Is it true that friendship originates in weakness and want, which may be relieved by the giving and receiving of favours? On the contrary: love comes first and the mutual exchange of favours follows the cementing of the friendship, which is not a pretence put on for the sake of advantage but springs rather from nature than from need. It comes by inclination rather than by calculation. If among animals this bond exists between parents and their offspring how much more does it exist between human persons? Friendship is, indeed, akin to the affection between parent and child that only the most execrable conduct can destroy. It arises when we meet someone of congenial character and habits in whom we see the epitome of virtue. For there is nothing more lovable than virtue. In this spirit we may feel a sentiment of friendship for people whom we have never even seen when we admire them from a distance. If the friendship arising from close proximity to someone we admire is further strengthened by evidence of reciprocation, then there does indeed spring to life a burning greatness of goodwill.

Were friendship in truth the child of poverty and need, the worse off a man was the more ready he would be for friendships; but this is not so. What could Scipio possibly have wanted from him! Of course material advantages did ensue from their friendship but what was of more serious importance for both sides was the love itself. If friendship depended upon advantage it would break up as soon as the advantage ceased; but true friendships are eternal.

It is hard for a friendship to last a whole lifetime. Sooner or later the parties themselves change or else some kind of rivalry comes between them. Among average men, desire for money is usually the poison of friendship while, among the nobler sort, it is rivalry for preferment or honour. Friendships sometimes come to an end because one party wants the other to join him in a dishonourable line of conduct.

This raises the question as to the nature of the obligations of friendship. Do they extend to partnership in wrong-doing? For example, ought the friends of Coriolanus to have supported him in resorting to arms against his own country? No: friendship is originally proffered in response to virtue and if virtue is repudiated the friendship is forfeited.

Therefore let this be ordained as the first law of friendship: ask of friends only what is honourable; do for friends only what is honourable and without even waiting to be asked; let zeal be ever present, but hesitation absent; dare to give true advice with all frankness but, if the occasion demands, even with sternness, and let the advice be followed when given.

There are those who teach that friendship should not be deep or binding but that we should sit loosely to it for, otherwise, we should be involved in the cares of the friend and add his worries to our own. This is a poor way of arguing. It means that a man should be attached to possession or honours, which cannot respond to him, and miss the best attachment of all, namely, that to responsive people from whom we receive as much as we give and with whom we can share our own cares. A man's virtue is the magnet that attracts friends to him. When we respect and admire a man for his goodness, friendship toward him is almost involuntary, a necessity from which there is no escape. Good men are inevitably drawn to each other in respect and affection. But, in any case, what is life worth without friendship? It is not a matter of expediency or calculation. Nobody on earth wishes to be surrounded even by unlimited wealth if it is conditional upon being unloving and unloved. Such is the life of the tyrant who is suspicious of everybody and is himself suspected and feared by everybody.

Wealth and power can be barriers to friendship when they uplift a man in pride and arrogance. Such a man procures for himself everything except what is worth most of all. But for whose benefit he toils to amass material possessions he does not know.

Friendship has neither limits nor boundary lines. The notions that we should think of our friends as we think of ourselves, that our goodwill toward them should correspond with theirs towards us, or that we should place upon a friend the value he places upon himself, are the thoughts of mean and calculating men. So, too, is the discreditable saying that 'We should love as if at some time we were going to hate'. Love does not think in terms of a neatly measured less or more but is self-giving and holds nothing back. The harmony and agreement between friends should be complete.

This implies that friendship is a deeply serious matter. Hard work is involved both in selecting and keeping friends. Rivalry in public affairs or competition in business can so easily wreck friendships that to rush into them heedlessly is unwise. Better by far is it to feel our way toward friendship and give the other partner opportunities of showing his true worth. The rock upon which friendship is built is loyalty, without which there can be no satisfactory relation. The man chosen as a friend must be frank, sociable and sympathetic, for these qualities are the pre-requisites of steadfast loyalty. Feigning and hypocrisy are incompatible with it.

Friends should conduct themselves as equals. It may well be that one partner is superior to the other either in personal qualities or in fortune but he should not make a point of it. Similarly, the other should not show consciousness of inferiority. Both should be natural and unaffected in manner. Friendships made after the attainment of maturity are likely to be the finest and most durable. It is foolish to expect that the companionships of boyhood and youth should last because characters change during the transition to maturity.

Care in the selection of friends is particularly important because of the calamities that can arise out of the breach of friendship. If one partner so behaves that continued friendship with him becomes undesirable, or if his attitudes alter, it is better to let it die away gradually than to end it suddenly. If the breach is hasty the old affection too easily switches to the bitterness of present hatred. That is why it is so important to ensure that our friends are similar to ourselves in character, tastes and attitudes.

We need friends. Even such a one as shuns and loathes the society of men still needs someone to whom he can pour out his bitterness of spirit. Man is social by nature and cannot find true fulfilment in loneliness.

None of this implies that there should be no disagreement or criticism or that there is friendship in flattery. The part of a friend is often to advise and even to point out faults. Were it otherwise, enemies would be more valuable than friends for they would at least give us the truth. Advice offered in the spirit of friendship is to be heard with respect and taken to heart. Flattery and hypocrisy do not for long deceive even the crowd listening to the rhetoric of an orator. How much less do they deceive the man of virtue who alone is worthy to be a friend. Cicero ends by putting into the mouth of Laelius a eulogy of virtue as the creator, the preserver and the bond of friendship. Everything rests upon virtue.

LUCRETIUS

In his philosophical poem, *De Rerum Natura*, Titus Lucretius Caro (*c*.99–*c*.55 B.C.) takes over and develops the atomic theory as propounded by Democritus and Epicurus. He anticipates remarkably the conclusions of modern scientific research, even in eugenics, and speculates on the origins of human society. Not the least value of his work is its cathartic quality. Since the universe as we know it came into existence as a result of the chance concourse of atoms, and since the soul itself is material and dies with the body, such gods as are allowed to remain can be relegated to a minor and ineffective rôle. Nobody need be afraid of them or take the trouble to propitiate them. As there is no survival after death, conscience need no longer make cowards of us all. The poem, elegant and of singular charm, is a purgative of superstition and fear.

In the middle of this wide ranging and brilliant discussion, Lucretius suddenly breaks into a violent tirade against passionate love, which he treats as if it were a disease of adolescence, centred on the genitals. It is a madness that grows and increases and that brings tribulation with it as well as pleasure. It is folly because the pleasures of Venus can be had without any of this painful emotion.

Passion may be temporarily exhausted in the process of love-making but it quickly returns and is never fully satisfied. By reason of this insatiability it takes the fun out of sex. The lover knows neither how to start nor how to continue and the pair on the bed are left pawing each other's bodies inconsequentially. In the meanwhile, each is at the other's beck and call. Even a wealthy man finds himself squandering his resources. All this could be avoided if men would only look at women objectively; but they permit themselves to be so blinded by passion that even the most unattractive becomes irresistible to them. Men make fools of themselves and women are just as bad because they hanker after sex and give way to passion just as much as men do.

Scientific as always, Lucretius tries to trace a law of heredity and notices that family resemblances often skip a generation. Apart from that, children tend to take after whichever partner is the stronger in the sex act. The child of an equal partnership shares in the qualities of both. A childless couple should not delude themselves that superstitious practices will solve their problem. The reasons for sterility are purely physical and with a different partner children might appear. The passage concludes with a few sentences of advice on posture in the sex act.

Lucretius appears mainly to be concerned that, in the sexual relation, passion should be minimised and pleasure maximised, and so anticipates certain Christian writers. This dictum turns cold-blooded lechery into a virtue.

OVID

Ovid (43 B.C.–A.D. 18) was nothing if not a philanderer. He was also a landowner with an adequate, but not large, patrimony and a poet. He was the type of man who flourishes in those social groups, which seem to exist in every advanced civilisation, whose members are financially provided for and have nothing to do except amuse each other. His profession was poetising and his hobby womanising; not with the crude promiscuity of a Don Juan but with discrimination and fastidiousness. The fact of having three wives in succession did not deter him from concurrently having a succession of mistresses. Indeed, he recommended having at least two mistresses at the same time so that none should be indispensable.

That last remark catches the light-hearted and light-headed tone of Ovid's erotic poems, more particularly the *Ars Amatoria*. Their intention was to entertain rather than to edify but they reflect attitudes in the more pleasure loving circles. Literary quality apart, they read like a manual for philanderers in the style of Dale Carnegie (*How to Make Friends and Influence People*) with his books for callow youths in search of social poise. They make no attempt to set a standard or state an ethical point of view. Disturbed by the declining morals of Rome, the Emperor Augustus exiled Ovid for having written these verses, which he evidently thought to be corrupting. It was a pity he had so poor a sense of humour.

Ovid's advice to philanderers can be classified under the following heads: where to look for your woman, how to make passes at her, how to get her, how to keep her and how to be rid of her when tired of her. He is in favour of passionate love but the passion must not be overwhelming. Reason and commonsense must remain in control. He wishes his mistress's husband would watch her more jealously because when he is tolerant and indulgent there is less fun in cuckolding him. At the same time he agrees that there is precious little point in husbands guarding their wives, who will manage to give them the slip whatever they do.

A lover should avoid visiting his mistress on her birthday because this would give her an excuse for expecting a present; and women are rapacious enough without gratuitous encouragement. Women over the age of thirty-five are to be preferred because experience is more amusing than naivete. A man can find his way to the heart of his *inamorata* by ingratiating himself with her maid. He might then be able to enjoy the maid as well as the mistress and will have a thoroughly trustworthy go-between. Discretion is vital: all written correspondence should be destroyed. At heart Ovid was conventional: without the element of danger and intrigue philandering would lose its attraction. Perhaps this is the one moral thought that emerges: moral judgment evokes the very conduct it most condemns.

Women also could benefit from Ovid's advice. In terms

resembling television commercials he warns them against body odour, halitosis and bad teeth if they want to keep their lovers. They are to be careful about their appearance but should remember that inexpensive clothes can be just as attractive as the costliest. Why wear a fortune on their backs when they can obtain their ends just as well without? They should be careful not to let their lovers see them at their toilets for that would spoil the effect. He recollects surprising one of his mistresses when she was adjusting her wig, which fell askew, making her feel ridiculous. One poem instructs women how to greet their lovers when waiting for them on their beds. They should so arrange their limbs as to display their better points and conceal their blemishes. Their choice of posture in the act should be made with the same purpose. If they do not feel rapture in the act they should simulate it for the sake of their lovers.

In a word, Ovid's erotica are a *jeu d'esprit* of little significance but indicative of the way of life of the gilded socialites. There is always a hint of mockery; but what Ovid mocks is not so much the genuine article as the travesty of it that passed for love in his own circle.

BOETHIUS

Last of the classical philosophers and first of the Mediaevals, Boethius (A.D. 480–525) lived when the Roman Empire was disintegrating and its former culture had fallen away. Seventy years before his birth the barbarian troops of Alaric the Hun had sacked Rome itself and in 476 the last of the Emperors, Theodosius, finally lost his authority and Rome came under the rule of Odoacer. In 493 he, in turn, was displaced by Theodoric who then became King of Italy and the Ostrogoths. It was not to be long before the wars of the Lombards destroyed Italian civilisation and reduced Rome to the dimensions and importance of a country town, a vestigial remnant of her former grandeur.

But Theodoric, although illiterate, was a wise and civilised man and an able ruler who welcomed to his inner circle the cultivated Boethius, a Roman patrician of the old school. His father had been

Consul and he himself was a consul in A.D. 510. Two years before his death his sons were joint consuls. But after a brilliant career in public affairs he came under suspicion of conspiracy and was exiled and imprisoned. While awaiting the death sentence he wrote the work that has perpetuated his name, *The Consolations of Philosophy*.

There has been much discussion as to whether Boethius was a Christian. The true authorship of the few short theological treatises that are attributed to him has been a matter for debate. But while the *Consolations* contains nothing incompatible with the Christian faith it savours far more in spirit of the Graeco-Roman tradition. In manner of life, in his concern for public affairs and in his intellectual attitudes Boethius was an old Roman through and through.

His value lay in his transmission of Platonic and Aristotelian thought to later centuries. He attempted a reconciliation between the two and, although he did not complete the task, he undertook to translate and comment upon the whole of Aristotle's writings. His industry must have been truly remarkable.

The theme of the *Consolations* is that through devotion to philosophy we attain the blessedness which is synonymous with absolute good, namely God himself. Although there is only one God, we ourselves can share in that Godhead by participation. An essential means to this end is detachment from terrestrial concerns. Certainly we must work for the public welfare and enjoy glory, pleasure and wealth; but only in so far as these contribute to the absolute good and not for their own sakes. Friendship and family are sacred but even these must not be allowed to obsess us. The way of salvation is a lonely way; some might even say a selfish way, although self-centredness is not a charge that has been laid against Boethius.

He is still revered. In his *History of Western Philosophy* Bertrand Russell remarks of him: 'During the two centuries before his time and the ten centuries after it, I cannot think of any European man of learning so free from superstition and fanaticism. Nor are his merits merely negative; his survey is lofty, disinterested and sublime. He would have been remarkable in any age; in the age in which he lived he was incredible.'

The *Consolations* is written alternately in prose and poetry, both of great dignity, and consists of a dialogue with Philosophy, personified as a woman. While in prison Boethius has beguiled his mind with the muses when, one day, he finds Philosophy standing near him. Philosophy bids him dismiss the muses and attend to her, which he does. There is nothing new, Philosophy begins, about lovers of wisdom being exposed to dangers by wicked men. But it is the part of wisdom to deride and expose them.

But why, Boethius expostulates, since in public life he has always followed justice and compassion, should there not have been those at hand to protect him from vicious men? The fact that the innocent are deprived of security and defence calls in question the just government of the universe. He agrees that the world is governed by reason but bewails that men alone are void of God's care.

Philosophy accuses Boethius of having forgotten whither all things tend and what the truth of his own nature is. He has been in love with Fortune and now feels let down. But, in fact, Fortune is only following her usual habit in being mutable. If we yield to Fortune as our best friend and our mistress we must accept her conditions. What injury has she done him? She has not robbed him but has merely ceased to lavish her gifts on him. Wealth, honours and the like are hers to bestow wherever she pleases or to withhold. However she heaped riches upon us we would still be discontented. Let him recollect all the benefits he has enjoyed! Yet it is the everlasting law that all things should fade. It is Philosophy, not Fortune, that he should make his friend.

When Boethius objects that the worst adversity of all is to have known happiness and lost it, Philosophy breaks in again to bid him recollect what benefits he still enjoys. His loyal wife is still alive and so is her noble father whom he so greatly respects. He himself still lives in his children. Even his place of exile is to some people their much loved home. Nobody can expect everything to go right with him all the way round all the time. To such a person the least setback would seem complete overthrow. Nothing is miserable unless it is thought to be.

The chief goods cannot be anything that can be taken away; for otherwise all men would fall into misery at death. How can that be happiness the loss of which does not cause misery? The gifts of Fortune are competitive and are most satisfying in the process of being expended. But the deepest satisfactions are in non-expendable and non-competitive goods, such as natural beauty. Philosophy then discusses, one by one, the gifts of Fortune men most desire and shows their inadequacy: wealth, status and dignities, power, glory and fame. Pleasure is dismissed in a stanza:

> All pleasure has this property,
> She woundeth those who love her most.
> And, like unto an angry bee
> Who hath her pleasant honey lost,
> She flies away with nimble wing
> And in our hearts doth leave her sting.

Family happiness is no better:

> That pleasure which proceedeth from wife and children should be most honest; but it was too naturally spoken, that some tormentor invented children, whose condition, whatsoever it be, how biting it is, I need not tell thee, who has had experience heretofore, and art not now free from care. In which I approve the opinion of Euripides, who said that they which had no children are happy by being unfortunate.

Bodily strength and fleetness of foot do not raise men above the animals, which have them in greater measure. Physical beauty is of the surface only: the beauty even of an Alcibiades looks faded when we think of his intestines.

None of these goods of themselves leads to happiness. Mainly they are competitive goods and only fragments of the true good. Fortune is most friendly when she lets us suffer adversity for then she shows herself in her true colours, no longer dissembling, and forces us back on the authentic grounds of happiness. That, indeed, is what all men ultimately seek. It is the chief of goods and inclusive of all other goods. All men want the true good but most are deceived as to what it is and how it is to be found.

But is there extant in the world a supreme good that is the fountain of all goodness? The answer is affirmative; for the sovereign God is most full of sovereign and perfect goodness and in him is most perfect blessedness and happiness. Since he was at the beginning of all things all blessedness necessarily proceeds from him and nothing evil can originate in him or have his sanction. Evil arises when, through their self-deception, men lose sight of his sovereign goodness as the purpose of their living and so suffer the privation of goodness. Men do not consciously will the evil. In the last resort all things are desired in respect of goodness, which means that all desire is for God. We obtain this blessedness and achieve divinity for ourselves by participation in the goodness of God.

Boethius wrote his *Consolations* in the time of his extremity. Friends had turned against him; he was disillusioned with human nature and with life itself. Yet, whereas most men in such circumstances would rail against mankind in bitterness and despair, he made Philosophy his friend and, learning from her, embarked on the lonely voyage to sanctity, detached from the world of men and affairs. We are bound to agree that the man and his achievement were incredible.

Chapter Four

The Hebrews

EDEN AND ALL THAT

Since the influence on interpersonal relations of the Christian scriptures has been profound and far-reaching, and since ultimately it merged with the Greek tradition to create the spirit of mediaeval and modern Europe, it would be absurd to omit reference to it, however familiar the ground.

Much in the earlier chapters of the Book of Genesis is pure dream material and much of the rest is legend; but from the dreams and legends a society has thought worth preserving we can learn much about them. Even so, the interpretation must necessarily be speculative. Can we not, for example, see in God's gift to Adam of dominion over the earth the reflection of the transition of the Hebrews from a nomadic to a more agricultural society? Is it fanciful to see in the reversal of the order of nature by the birth of Eve from the rib of a male a reflection of the transition from a matriarchal to a patriarchal society with its concomitant devaluation of womanhood? The Eden story has raised perplexities for theologians who, in centuries passed, debated learnedly how the defloration of Eve could occur without spoiling the painless bliss of the Garden, and whether the sexual act was pleasurable or purely rational. More sophisticated students regard it as the reflection of adult nostalgia for the paradisial pleasures of the mother's breast.

More to the point is the reason given for the creation of Eve. The passage indicates, at the same time, the kinship that men felt with animals. Unhappily, they were not quite adequate as companions :

Then the Lord God said, 'It is not good for the man to be alone. I will provide a partner for him.' So God formed out of the ground all the wild animals and all the birds of heaven. He brought them to the man to see what he would call them, and whatever the man called every living creature, that was its name. Thus the man gave names to all cattle, to the birds of heaven, and to every wild animal; but for the man himself no partner had yet been found. And so the Lord God put the man into a trance, and while he slept, he took one of his ribs and closed the flesh over the place. The Lord God then built up the rib, which he had taken out of the man, into a woman. He brought her to the man, and the man said:

> 'Now this, at last –
> bone from my bones,
> flesh from my flesh! –
> this shall be called woman,
> for from man was this taken.'

That is why a man leaves his father and mother and is united to his wife and the two become one flesh. Now they were both naked, the man and his wife, but they had no feeling of shame towards one another.

So Adam was delighted with his new companion and the episode has provided the standard and the ideal for marriage in the western world ever since. But we are not told why it should be thought remarkable that a husband and wife were unashamed of their nudity. It has been popularly thought that because they covered themselves immediately after the first disobedience, sexuality was at the root. Nothing in the story seriously points to this and St Augustine and others following him attributed the sin to pride. The serpent had played upon Adam and Eve by promising them equality with God if they ate of the tree of knowledge of good and evil which, he implied, this all-too-human God had forbidden them only out of jealousy. God revenged himself by turning them out of the garden into the vale of sorrows.

This idea that the evil of the world had its origin in some primaeval choice that caused man to fall from the state of grace into that of sin has had disastrous consequences. The implication is that the unspeakable travail through which mankind has passed is due solely to his own wilfulness and is no more than he deserves. No doctrine could be better calculated to poison the springs of compassion and this it has, in fact, done. Man is regarded primarily as sinner and this has been held to justify aggressive intolerance and to excuse the neglect of social reform. The history of Christianity could be rewritten as the story of the conflict in the depths between the compassion of Christ and the bitterness of moral judgment. On the evidence, man should be regarded primarily as sufferer, for surely his sin arises out of his agony.

One of the most sinister evils of the present century, for instance, is the reintroduction of torture as an instrument of inquisition. We ask with horror how a human interrogator can deliberately inflict upon a helpless man or woman the extremity of pain. It can be only because he and his masters are relieving their agony by projecting upon the victim the contortions and writhings of their own souls. A normal and happy person urged under duress to perpetrate these deeds, ordered, perhaps, to be a Belsen guard, would and should commit suicide rather than comply, if that were the only way out. The extreme case illuminates the rest. From the standpoint of the interpersonal relation, it is said that a vile kind of attachment comes into existence between the torturer and the tortured.

What must be one of the earliest love affairs of which we have records, that of Jacob and Rachel, also occurs in the Book of Genesis. The events out of which the legend grew probably occurred about the beginning of the fourteenth century B.C. Jacob had fled from the Negev to stay with his uncle, Laban, a man of some wealth. As he neared Laban's home he saw Laban's daughter, Rachel, and fell in love with her immediately. An agreement was made that Jacob should serve Laban for seven years in return for Rachel in marriage; but when Jacob had completed his side of the agreement, Laban surreptitiously substituted Rachel's elder sister in the marriage bed, because it was considered wrong for the younger to be married first. Jacob had to work another seven years for his Rachel.

Polygamy, it is interesting to note, is nowhere explicitly

condemned either in the Old or New Testament and is actually tolerated in the Old. There was nothing unconventional about having two wives at a time.

Not unnaturally, Leah was jealous because Jacob preferred her prettier sister and, by way of compensation, God enabled her to have three children. Rachel now had reason for jealousy and her solution was to give Jacob her maid, Bilhah, as a mistress, to bear children for her, as it were, by proxy. Bilhah had two sons by Jacob and so Rachel was beginning to catch up. Leah replied by giving Jacob *her* maid, Zilpah, and she, also, had two sons by him.

While going through the fields Leah's son, Reuben, found some mandrakes, a plant in the potato family whose fruit was believed to have aphrodisiac properties. Rachel wanted them and, when Leah tartly refused, offered in return to let Jacob spend the night with her. So Rachel had her mandrakes and Leah had another son. Indeed, she went on having children; and then God delighted Rachel by letting *her* have a son.

Such were family relations in Jacob's home. His years of toil for Rachel 'had seemed like a few days because he loved her', but this did not deter him from regularly enjoying three other women as well. Neither of his wives appeared to mind about this. Leah was hurt because her sister was Jacob's favourite as a person, while Rachel was hurt because she had no children, which was a reflection on her womanhood. But there seems to have been no jealousy on the grounds of Jacob's promiscuity. The women did not imitate him in this but shuttled him between themselves at will. It was they who dominated the domestic scene. Rachel did not try to end her sterility by taking a lover, which was the obvious way out. In a society in which inheritance was through the males of the line this would have been intolerable. Nobody would have known who the father of the children was or whether the children were entitled to inherit.

Although it has no ethical or religious value the story of Ruth has always been a favourite for its sensitiveness to loyalty. It seems likely that the events recorded occurred between 1220 and 1020 B.C., the period of settlement after the conquest of Canaan, and has interest as a picture of the relations that existed between people in a very ordinary, decent family. It hinges on the custom that if a man's brother died childless he was expected to marry the widow. His first son by her was to inherit the dead man's name. Should the man refuse, the widow was to hale him before the elders of the city and spit upon him and curse him in their presence. The intention of this was to discourage mixed marriages and to preserve the family property.

There was a famine and a man of Bethlehem, Elimelech, with his wife Naomi and his sons, Mahlon and Chilion, migrated to Moab to escape it. Shortly afterwards Elimelech died and the sons married wives from among their new neighbours. After ten years the sons also died, leaving Naomi with her daughters-in-law, Orpah and Ruth. Both women had by this time developed a deep affection for Naomi and when she decided to return home Ruth insisted on going with her:

> 'Do not urge me to go back and desert you,' Ruth answered, 'where you go, I will go, and where you stay, I will stay. Your people shall be my people, and your God my God. Where you die, I will die, and there I will be buried. I swear a solemn oath before the Lord your God: nothing but death will divide us.'

On arrival at Bethlehem the two were warmly welcomed and Naomi (meaning 'amiable') asked her friends to know her as Mara (bitter) since she had returned bereft of her husband and sons.

Naomi had a wealthy relative by marriage named Boaz. Ruth went gleaning in his fields during the harvest. Seeing her there, Boaz looked on her with favour and gave her a special position among the reapers, shared his meal with her and ensured that she had plenty of grain to take home in the evening. On her mother's advice, Ruth went to him as he lay down to sleep by his winnowing floor. When he awoke in the night he was surprised to find her there. 'I am your servant, Ruth,' she told him, 'now spread your skirt over your servant because you are my next-of-kin.' But Boaz knew someone still more closely related to Ruth who had the prior right to marry her. They agreed between themselves that the nearer relative would forgo his right in favour of Boaz, who then bought Naomi's property and married Ruth.

THE LAW AND THE PROPHETS

While some of the laws of the Torah seem to us trivial and unnecessary and some, such as the law that enjoined the stoning of adulterous wives, actually cruel, many more are gentle and humane. The poor are made the responsibility of their fellow townsfolk, who must lend them enough to tide them over their difficulties. Slaves are to be freed in the seventh year of their service and must be given generous 'redundancy' payments. If the slave had grown so fond of his master and the household that he did not wish to leave he was to be bound for life. If a man saw cattle or sheep astray, or came across lost property, whether it belonged to his brother or to his enemy he must ensure restoration to the owner. Hired servants, whether local men or strangers, were to be treated with kindliness and their wages were to be paid before sunset on the same day as they were earned. When harvesting, farmers were to leave some of the crop for poor people and strangers to pick up for themselves. Concern is shown for the poor, the widows and orphans, the deaf and the blind and respect for old age is enjoined. In a period and a region that made the blood feud obligatory these laws forbade it categorically:

> You shall not nurse hatred against your brother. You will reprove your fellow-countryman frankly and so you will have no share in his guilt. You shall not seek revenge, or cherish anger towards your kinsfolk; you shall love your neighbour as a man like yourself.

The feeling of kinship with the animals reappears. The ox is not to be muzzled when treading out the grain because it would be inconsiderate to have the animal aware of the corn but unable, as the day wore on and the work became tiring, to take a few mouthfuls for itself. There is no reason, either culinary, dietetic or even humane, why a kid should not be boiled in its own mother's milk; but this is forbidden because the idea of it is repulsive and unnatural. Animals have their own dignity, which should not be offended.

We have to wait for the prophet Hosea, who began writing about 750 B.C. before love, in the fullness of majesty and power, became the dominant theme in Hebrew religion. His entire message dwelt on the strength and endurance of love and on this he grounded his interpretation of the character of the Deity and the meaning of life. In this he contrasts with his predecessor, Amos, who was the unforgiving prophet of law and justice. Under a great king, Jeroboam II (died 743 B.C.), the country had enjoyed a period of military success and economic prosperity; but the people had not responded well. They attributed their fortune to the favour of the local fertility gods and it was to them they gave their allegiance. Jehovah had to be content with perfunctory ritual observance. Moral decay had bitten deeply into the nation as a consequence and it was in danger of falling before the Assyrian armies that were on the move again. Defeat and captivity lay ahead. The people had rebelled against the law of God and His justice would overtake them. Such was the message of Amos and he offered no hope of pardon or restoration.

Hosea came as the prophet of invincible love. Like other Hebrew thinkers, he based his message on experience, proclaiming it in a series of passionate outbursts. Because of this some critics have found his prophecy lacking in coherence; but the main outlines of his story and of the conclusions he drew from it are clear enough. We shall be doing no violence to the text if we try to reconstruct them.

Hebrew writers tended to ignore the immediate causes of events in the natural world and in history and to attribute them to the direct intervention of God. We are therefore not surprised when Hosea begins by saying that God instructed him to marry a prostitute. He is reading back into the years the experiences that moved him in the depths later on. We may imagine him to have been a man of profoundly passionate nature, of wonderful generosity and kindliness and of the utmost sensitivity. But his sensitivity was protected by an integument of reserve that he broke through only when feeling had so accumulated in him that he could no longer contain it. Such men may appear to the outside world to be morose or over-serious, perhaps even dull, while inwardly they are in ferment. Often they are attracted to women of vitality and light-heartedness whose out-going cheerfulness compensates for their own brooding introspection. If Hosea and his wife were such as these the following story would be explained.

Hosea married a woman named Gomer; but it was not long before he began to suspect her of infidelity. She may well have been the type who wanted to spread her wings and enjoy herself; who may have found life with Hosea did not provide the gaiety she wanted and who was drawn to look for her amusement to those who were ready to offer her a spurious promise. By the time the first child arrived Hosea's suspicions were deepening. His anguish dragged from him his first message. The son that had been born to Gomer was to be called Jezreel, for the storms were gathering about Israel and their fate would be decided on the historic battleground, the Valley of Jezreel. His prophetic message was, 'I will break Israel's bow in the Vale of Jezreel'.

By the time the second child was on the way, Hosea's suspicions were confirmed. The second child, a daughter, was to be called Not-Loved. Gomer's infidelity was a parable of the disloyalty of Israel to God. In his deepening agony the message he had for his countrymen was, 'I will never again show love to Israel, never again forgive them'.

When the third child, another son, was born Hosea was quite sure that it was not his and he repudiated him in words, if not in fact. The son was to be called, Not-My-People. The message on this occasion was that the waywardness of the people was such that God could no longer accept them as his own.

Gomer left home to live with her lovers; but not without a tumult of pleas and warnings from Hosea. Through all this his love for her had not diminished and he was concerned for her. He besought her children to intercede with the wife who was no wife to him. He threatened to shame her publicly as an adulteress. He warned her of the coming time when her lovers would not want her any more; she would chase them and they would avoid her. Yet all along he made sure that she was supported and he sorrowed only because she attributed her continued well-being to the generosity of men who were, in fact, exploiting her. Here again is the parable of Israel attributing their prosperity to the Ba'als of the land instead of to the true God. Punishment would come upon the people as a result and they would be shamed before the nations.

Finally, Hosea's fears were verified: Gomer reached the same point as that to which the prodigal son came, when she realised she had played the fool. Afraid to return home, she sold herself as the bought woman of a paramour.

Even now, Hosea's love was not exhausted. He so far humiliated himself as to redeem her as if she were a slave. 'So I got her back for fifteen pieces of silver, a homer of barley and a measure of wine.' But Gomer was not immediately to be restored. First she was to spend a period in seclusion so that she could break completely with her old life. Hosea wanted reassurance that the change in her was no ephemeral remorse. When he was sure, Gomer would again be his wife in the fullest sense of the word.

Love such as that is rare; but it does occur. We cannot say that the story of Hosea is unrealistic. The experience was a revelation to him. If he, as a man, could love like that, and restore his wife after all she had done to him, what must be the love of God for his people? Surely it could not be less than his. The divine love would follow the people through all the bitterness and, when they came to their senses, would be ready to receive them back as his own. Love was the supreme authority, above justice and law, and its gifts were pardon and peace.

Entirely different in spirit is the Song of Songs. Some critics, because of its contents, attribute it to the period of Solomon, dating it to the latter part of the tenth century B.C.; but the advance in sophistication over any other literature of the time suggests a later date. Other critics, looking at it from the linguistic point of view, assign it to a date as late as the third century B.C. when Greek influence in the Middle East was strong.

Studied academically the Song of Songs disintegrates into fragments. Some critics have thought it to be a collection of short love songs, others a dialogue between two lovers, others a drama. For many centuries it was thought to be an allegory of the divine love. In this spirit St Bernard of Clairvaux delivered a famous series of sermons upon it which are still extant. The translators of the Authorised Version took this view. But it is a view that is not seriously held nowadays.

When read simply as an erotic poem these difficulties fall away. It is rich in sexual symbolism and uninhibited in its extravagant display of passion. The man and woman addressing each other show no self-consciousness. Their love is not a prelude to marriage, of which there is no mention. No distinction is made between the physical, the emotional or the spiritual. The two personalities are totally engaged in mutuality and reciprocity. There are no reserves. What kind of man and woman they are is left to the imagination: here their whole nature is drawn into their love and nothing is left. We are presented with them solely in their capacity as lovers. Here are two examples:

> I am an asphodel in Sharon,
> A lily growing in the valley.
>
> No, a lily among thorns
> is my dearest among girls.
> Like an apricot-tree among the trees of the wood,
> so is my beloved among boys
> To sit in its shadow was my delight,
> and its fruit was sweet to my taste.
> He took me into the wine garden
> and gave me loving glances
> He refreshed me with raisins, he revived me with apricots;
> for I was faint with love.
> His left arm was under my head, his right arm was round me.
>
> I charge you, daughters of Jerusalem,
> By the spirits and goddesses of the field:
> Do not rouse her, do not disturb my love
> until she is ready.

Hark! My beloved! Here he comes,
Bounding over the mountains, leaping over the hills.
My beloved is like a gazelle
or a young wild goat:
there he stands outside our wall,
peeping in at the windows, glancing through the lattice.

> Wear me as a seal upon your heart,
> as a seal upon your arm;
> for love is strong as death,
> passion cruel as the grave;
> it blazes up like a blazing fire,
> fiercer than any flame.
> Many waters cannot quench love,
> no flood can sweep it away;
> if a man were to offer for love
> the whole wealth of his house,
> it would be utterly scorned.

THE NEW TESTAMENT

When Christians speak of Jesus as the incarnation of love this is
not so much because he theorised about it as because he lived it.
His character revealed itself in his relations with the people
around him, in his acts of compassion and in the manner of his
death. There was little that was original in his teaching. Most of
it had already been said by the rabbis or was contained in the
Torah. But he gave the word greater fullness by insisting that all
humanity was to be taken in its scope, nobody excluded. What
was new was the recklessness of the love he recommended. Love
was to be without qualification and was not to depend on mutuality or reciprocation:

You have learned that they were told, 'Love your neighbour, hate
your enemy'. But what I tell you is this: Love your enemies and pray
for your persecutors; only so can you be children of your heavenly
Father, who makes his sun rise on good and bad alike, and sends the
rain on the honest and the dishonest. If you love only those who love
you, what reward can you expect? Surely the tax-gatherers do as

much as that. And if you greet only your brothers, what is there extraordinary about that? Even the heathen do as much. There must be no limit to your goodness, as your heavenly Father's goodness knows no bounds.

Reciprocal love was no different from a commercial bargain: what you receive you pay for. Human love was to be a reproduction under the conditions of this world of the infinite and eternal divine love. The kind of love that is withdrawn in reply to injury is not the love that Jesus taught. It is evident that Jesus was not thinking in terms of a particularised emotional involvement with individuals but rather of an attitude or a disposition. He himself responded in a special way to chosen individuals, even among the twelve disciples. At the Last Supper, 'One of them, the disciple he loved, was reclining close beside Jesus'. Whether he was ever 'in love' we are not told. The Gospels, after all, amount to little more than biographical notes. For no obvious reason some people find the thought repulsive, which suggests that they imagine there to be something discreditable about being 'in love'. But, on the evidence, Jesus had several close friends among women and surely it would enrich his humanity to have been 'in love' with one of them. Could it have been Mary Magdalene, who was deeply devoted to him?

We see Christian love at its height in the confrontation between Jesus and Judas Iscariot. The question is often asked how Judas could have brought himself to his act of betrayal, since the money he gained by it does not provide a convincing enough motive. Several theories have been worked out by novelists and others, notably by Scholem Asch in his *The Nazarene*. But the really fascinating question is why Jesus, who knew what was in the hearts of men, ever accepted Judas as one of the Twelve. It may be that he saw in him great potentialities for loyalty and self-committal and leadership. Could it be that he was marked as the future administrator or theologian of the society Jesus would found? Or would he have undertaken the missionary enterprise that subsequently fell to St Paul? However that may be, Jesus did accept him and must have hoped to win his allegiance. Yet St

John's Gospel reports him as saying, 'Have I not chosen you, all twelve? Yet one of you is a devil'. To know that someone in his circle is bent on his destruction is for any man a disturbing experience and not one that engenders friendship. The usual reaction is to destroy him before he has his chance. It occurs regularly wherever ambitious men are associated with each other.

Knowing this, Jesus still accepted Judas. Even at the Last Supper he showed him signal marks of honour and affection before despatching him on his fatal errand. There can be no question that to the last he hoped to win Judas by the power of friendship. It was not until Judas saw the results of his treachery that he came to himself and was so overcome with shame that he could not survive. He committed suicide. In the moment of his own death Jesus had won the battle of love. That was a triumph of the cross.

Against the ecclesiastical authorities of the time, Jesus saw the sterility and lovelessness of institutionalism and legalism in religion. That was what came under his lash. Love and compassion must always take precedence over law. Love, not law, is central to religion. If we have that we know all we need to know because God himself is love. St John in his Epistle writes:

Let us love one another, because love is from God. Everyone who loves is a child of God and knows God, but the unloving know nothing of God. For God is love; and his love was disclosed to us in this, that he sent his only Son into the world to bring us life. The love I speak of is not our love for God, but the love he showed us in sending his Son as the remedy for the defilement of our sins. If God thus loved us, dear friends, we in turn are bound to love one another. Though God has never been seen by any man, God himself dwells in us if we love one another; his love is brought to perfection in us.

To this there has to be added St Paul's definition and analysis in his famous Hymn to Love. For St Paul love is a charisma, a gift, and the greatest of gifts. Without it, even faith and hope are sterile. The characteristics of love are patience, kindness, modesty, self-effacement, respect, courtesy, sensitiveness. Love is never irritable or resentful. It is never malicious and finds its happiness in the happiness of the beloved. Love is of immeasurable strength and everlasting endurance. Thus love in the New Testament is far more than a generalised goodwill toward mankind at large. It is a compendium of the virtues. It is not passive but is active and outgoing toward mankind as individual persons. We need different words to distinguish this from the strong emotion mutually felt that we experience in friendship or in being 'in love'. The New Testament has it in *agape*. In English the word 'charity' could be used, but is not inclusive enough in its popular connotations. Confusion and misunderstanding arise from the use of the word 'love' to cover all cases.

Two other aspects of the New Testament teaching on interpersonal relations call for discussion. The first is its teaching on marriage. The tendency of the Gospels was to revalue womanhood. There is nothing in them to which even the most ardent feminist could object. The attitude of respect Jesus took towards all the women in his own circle, and also to those of notoriety he encountered, was notable. Indeed, he was much less severe with the sins of the flesh than with those of the spirit. He virtually repealed the law that the adulterous wife should be stoned. The fact that a woman had a bad reputation did not affect his attitude toward her in the least but he was angry with those who passed facile judgment upon her.

Interpreting the law with unwarranted freedom, the rabbinical schools of the time were casual in their treatment of marriage. It was gravely to the disadvantage of women in the social circumstances of the time that a husband was allowed to divorce his wife for trivial reasons. Jesus set a much higher standard. What he intended in legal terms, if anything, is a matter much debated. Since he repudiated the absoluteness of law, and set the requirements of love and compassion higher, it is unlikely that he intended to legislate absolutely in this instance and to prohibit divorce altogether. But everybody would agree that the effect of his statements was to afford protection to women and enhance the respect in which they were held.

St Paul's pronouncements on marriage have been the subject of endless, and often futile, discussion. He is sometimes held

responsible for that devaluation of womanhood and marriage, and
that fear of sexuality, that blemished the thought of many churchmen for centuries. Certainly the tone of his writing on the subject
differs from that of the Gospels. His legalist cast of mind did not
entirely desert him on his conversion. He might also be thought
of as a celibate pontificating on a subject of which he had no
experience.

These views are over-simplified and unfair. The confusion
arises because St Paul expresses so strongly his sense of the dis-
unity of the human personality. For him, spirit and flesh are in
perpetual conflict. Sexuality belongs to the flesh. He could never
understand sexuality as the spontaneous and natural expression of
affection between a man and a woman. He could not see it as
an element in a totality. Rather was it an independent appetite
that demanded satisfaction. So he argues that, while perpetual
celibacy is preferable to marriage, because single persons can
dedicate themselves more wholly to service, if this means that the
flesh will gain the upper hand and a man will be obsessed with
lust, then it is better to marry. Once married, husband and wife
should render to each other their due on a basis of equality:

> It is a good thing for a man to have nothing to do with women: but
> because there is so much immorality, let each man have his own wife
> and each woman her own husband. The husband must give the wife
> what is due to her, and the wife equally must give the husband his
> due. The wife cannot claim her body as her own; it is her husband's.
> Equally, the husband cannot claim his body as his own; it is his wife's.
> Do not deny yourselves to one another, except when you agree upon
> a temporary abstinence in order to devote yourselves to prayer;
> afterwards you may come together again; otherwise, for lack of self-
> control, you may be tempted by Satan.

At first sight this looks more like a counsel of mutual exploitation
than like a truly unitive mutuality. Take into account that St
Paul was protesting against the folly of entering into purely
spiritual marriage with the repudiation of sexuality and it has a
different look. St Paul now is telling his readers not to be silly or
sentimental about sexuality, which is a powerful force seeking its

proper outlet and not to be treated arbitrarily. St Paul recognises that men and women alike have instinctual desires and needs. There is nothing about them to be ashamed of provided they are fulfilled in the proper way. It is also interesting that St Paul insists on union and fulfilment rather than on procreation as the true purpose of sexuality. Otherwise, the idea of a man demanding his 'rights' and the woman giving in to him as a duty, or vice versa, would be barbarous.

But it would not do to leave the Pauline treatment of the subject at this point. While it is true that St Paul thought that women should not play a public rôle in church affairs, and while he thought that domestically the wife should be subordinate, yet there is much in his writing that removes the sting. His own relations with women were marked by affection and respect. He had no wish to put them in purdah! Like the prophets before him, he was much concerned to safeguard the emerging Christian community from the moral contagions that threatened it. He believed the manner of life he enjoined to be the best way of doing this. Anybody who knows what St Paul thought of the relation between Christ and his bride, the Church, will seize the tremendous significance of the following passage:

> Husbands, love your wives as Christ also loved the Church and gave himself up for it. . . . In the same way men also are bound to love their wives, as they love their own bodies. In loving his wife a man loves himself. For no one ever hated his own body: on the contrary, he provides and cares for it; and that is how Christ treats the church, because it is his body, of which we are living parts. Thus it is that (in the words of Scripture) 'a man shall leave his father and mother and shall be joined to his wife, and the two shall become one flesh'. It is a great truth that is hidden here. I for my part refer it to Christ and to the Church but it applies also individually: each of you must love his wife as his very self; and the wife must see to it that she pays her husband every respect.

While the New Testament does not explicitly condemn polygamy it is certainly incompatible with thoughts such as these.

The second type of interpersonal relation that calls for mention is that between master and slave. It has often been held as a reproach against the New Testament that it nowhere denounces the institution of slavery or proposes an alternative. We have seen how the legislators of the Old Testament handled the problem. The slave was for them more a domestic servant on a contractual basis than a 'chattel'. At the end of his term he was to be sent away generously loaded with gifts. He was in a totally different position from that of the miserable wretches working in chain gangs on the latifundia of the Roman Empire.

In his letter to his friend, Philemon, St Paul recommends the Torah attitude. Onesimus, a slave of Philemon, had run away to take refuge with St Paul, then imprisoned in Rome awaiting trial. While they were together St Paul came to regard him as a son, and wanted to keep him, but felt in duty bound to return him to his master. So he begs Philemon to take him back, 'no longer as a slave, but as more than a slave – as a dear brother . . . welcome him as you would welcome me'. In the atmosphere this generated, slavery lost much of its repulsiveness and ultimately withered away. While the Christian record has often been blotted since then, it was in the spirit of the Epistle to Philemon that Wilberforce secured the abolition of the slave trade.

A GUIDE TO THE THEORIES OF LOVE

We have now traced to the end the development of two traditions. Hebrew experience has reached its culmination in the New Testament: Platonism has received its most systematic formulation in the work of Plotinus. At this point it may well be fruitful to break off and to compare the two and to see whether, from these roots, any principles can be derived that will enable us to bring order into the numerous conflicting theories that will be presented in the rest of this book.

First, we must dismiss out of hand the attempt made by Anders Nygren, Bishop of Lund, in his *Agape and Eros*, to set Hebrews and Greeks in polar opposition to each other, for it has confused thought about this issue for over forty years. Nygren was deeply impressed by the comment of St Paul: 'Even for a just man one of us would hardly die, though perhaps for a good man one might actually brave death; but Christ died for us while we were yet sinners, and that is God's own proof of his love toward us.' Accordingly, he writes:

> But in Christ there is revealed a divine love which breaks all bounds, refusing to be controlled by the value of its object, and being determined only by its own intrinsic nature. According to Christianity 'motivated love is human'; spontaneous and 'unmotivated' love is divine.

God does not love man because of the infinite value of human personality, continues Nygren, nor for any other reason of the kind. On the contrary, it is the divine love that confers value upon the human personality or creates value in it. The redeemed man's love is patterned upon this divine love and participates in it, sharing its quality, but does have the motive of wanting union with God. By contrast with *agape*, thus conceived, which is theocentric and altruistic, *eros* is egocentric and acquisitive.

Nygren's assumption that because man is sinful he is entirely destitute of value and wholly and utterly unlovable seems unwarranted and gratuitous. Even the most extreme doctrines of total depravity recognise in him the potentiality for redemption and this, according to St John's Gospel, is the justification for the Incarnation: 'God loved the world so much that he gave his only Son, that everyone who has faith in him may not die but have eternal life'. In other words, agape does have an objective, namely, that everyone shall realise his full potential. In this it does not differ from eros, for even the most cursory reading of Plato makes clear that this is precisely what eros wants for its human object.

But what does Nygren mean by 'unmotivated love'? Love is always, in fact, itself the motive. Take, for example, a characteristic statement: 'Any man worth his salt will go through fire and water for the woman he loves'. Here, the motive that drives a man through his ordeal is none other than his love. It is this that makes the thought of the woman's death intolerable and the hope of her rescue worthy of his effort. 'Unmotivated love' is a contradiction in terms.

Moreover, love between persons is always prior to the recognition of value. Otherwise, it is no better than the friendship between Aristotle's businessmen, which lasts only for so long as they are useful to each other. It is not love so much as interest, or a bargain. If we delude ourselves that we love people for their qualities it is not the person we are loving but the qualities. A young girl may be flattered when a young man sings:

> I'll go and court her for her beauty
> Till she do say 'yes' or 'no'.

or she may realise that it is not herself that he loves but her appearance; and how many marriages have collapsed when the love has faded with the beauty! Were the young man to sing:

> I'll go and court her for her money

the girl would be flatly insulted. Eros goes far deeper than that. One point we shall have to clarify later on with as much precision as possible, although I doubt whether a high degree of precision is possible, is what it is in the human personality that attracts love.

On the other hand, it is no less a misunderstanding to treat eros as egocentric and acquisitive than it is to treat agape as unmotivated. Writers are apt to overlook the clear distinction between the heavenly eros and the earthly. It is the latter that wants exclusive possession. The divine beauty, which attracts the higher eros, is not available for acquisition. In practice, the more I enjoy it in contemplation the more it is likely to be available for others. In Wordsworthian terms it is that

> Presence that disturbs me with the joy
> Of elevated thoughts: a sense sublime
> Of something far more deeply interfused,
> Whose dwelling is the light of setting suns . . .

Like agape itself, it originates in the heavenly places, the recollection of which, stirred by earthly loveliness mirroring the divine, impels the soul to longing for its first home:

> Our birth is but a sleep and a forgetting:
> The soul that rises in us, our life's star,
> Has had elsewhere its setting,
> And cometh from afar:
> Not in entire forgetfulness,
> And not in utter nakedness,
> But trailing clouds of glory do we come
> From God who is our home.

We recognise with sadness how the visions of youth die away under this-worldly pressures until later, in the dreaming of dreams, we learn again to find the deepest satisfactions in the rediscovery of eternal values, the true, the honest, the just, the pure, the lovely and the things of good report. This experience does not differ essentially from that of the Christian who sees the glory of God in the face of Jesus Christ and who, through the Christ, seeks knowledge of God. Agape and eros are not the downward and upward escalators but there is reciprocity in both.

Nygren's error arises partly out of misplaced emphasis on such words as 'egocentric' and 'theocentric' which, in this context, are meaningless theological jargon. Other writers have lost their way for similar reasons. The most notable recent example is Robert G. Hazo who, in his *Idea of Love* presents the thinking on the subject of the American Institute for Philosphical Research. Hazo makes a bold attempt to classify the leading theories of love, both classical and modern, under three heads: love as acquisitive desire, love as benevolent desire and love as wholly or primarily judgment. Severe manhandling is required to fit the various theories of love into these categories and, in the process, most of them are impoverished. Whether by accident or design I do not know, Hazo omits some of the most enlightening theories that could not by any squeezing be fitted into his scheme, such as those of Buber and Macmurray, while admitting to difficulties with Max Scheler. What has gone wrong?

No treatment that does justice to so rich a theme as this can be fitted into a neat pattern. For authors such as these, love is something that one self, or *ego*, does to another, across a gulf of separation. The unrecognised assumptions underlying critiques such as those of Nygren and Hazo are quite astonishing! If the first self is lucky the other will do the same by way of return. It is a most superficial concept of any interpersonal relation beyond those on a merely business or technical level, as described by Aristotle. Ordinary experience, and the colloquial language in which it is expressed, give the lie to the notion. Love, whether of a sexual character or what normally nowadays we think of as 'friendship', is always a relation we enter into, not one that we project from ourselves. In the extreme instance we talk of 'falling into' it, as if it were an unfenced pool awaiting the unwary. The relation takes possession of the selves involved in it. Young people tell each other, 'This thing is bigger than both of us'.

In treating of Plotinus, the late W. R. Inge made the point persuasively and with force that, in the western world, philosophers have, from the beginning, laid far too much weight on the ego and the consciousness of self, especially since Descartes taught us to regard the ego as external to the world of appearance. 'I think, therefore I am', is for him the starting point of all knowledge and it has to be proved that anything else exists at all outside the thinking self. This, wrote Inge, tends to set us over against the rest of society and over against the cosmos itself. Yet, in fact, we are totally involved in society and the self is no more than a point of reference. We shall not enter into the deeper meaning of love until we can escape from this concept of a mechanical giving and receiving between isolates which, at the best, is to be likened to the flickering of a spark between terminals. When we come to the study of Sartre we shall see that this is the concept of love that arises out of an unmitigated atheism or secularism. That we should be so proud of our self-consciousness, as the distinguishing characteristic of the human race, is the more incomprehensible because we spend at least two-thirds of our time trying to be rid of it: in sleep, alcohol, the crowd, in frenzy, the dance, sexual orgasm, music, or drugs. The burden of it is intolerable. Many people feel themselves to be truly alive only when they are free of it.

Primitive societies, as far as we know, have known nothing of this isolation of the ego. For them, interpersonal relations have been tacitly accepted as undifferentiated participation in community. The community itself has not, for them, in any sense been separate from, or over against, the transcendent organic unity of the cosmos. Human society has been as much an integral part of it as the spirits of the trees and the hilltops. At the time of sowing, husband and wife have gone into the field together to lie in the furrow so that the earth could be infected with their fertility. So intimate was this unity.

Civilisation has suffered from the loss of it, and we are always in search of surrogates. But among the Greeks the sense of unity with the cosmos was still strong and there found philosophical expression. Plato's world soul was no *deus ex machina* but permeated and illuminated the whole, a pantheism bringing all things into coherence, including the mind of man. Such is the background against which we have to understand eros at its highest; not an appetite engendered by the glandular secretions that craves to possess and to devour but the fine flowering of the universal spirit, an endowment and a grace of which sexuality ought to be, and sometimes is, the sacrament. Eros is the way of salvation.

By contrast, Christianity devalues the cosmos in relation to man. The early chapters of the Book of Genesis, as we have seen, give man the dominion over nature, almost as if man came into existence first and was given the cosmos solely to be his instrument or his plaything. But I cannot go all the way with Max Scheler (*The Nature of Sympathy*) in emptying the Christian scriptures entirely of this sense of unity with the cosmos. In the Old Testament Jehovah dwells in the mountain tops and speaks to man through the thunderstorm. The movements of nature and the nations are his activities and his instruments. The prophets go into the desert to commune with him. The Psalmist sings:

> Praise the Lord from the earth,
> you water spouts and ocean depths:
> fire and hail, snow and ice,
> gales of wind obeying his voice;
> all mountains and hills;
> all fruit trees and all cedars;
> wild beasts and cattle,
> creeping things and winged birds . . .

St Paul writes that 'the created universe waits for God's sons to be revealed . . . because the universe itself is to be freed from the shackles of mortality and enter upon the liberty and splendour of the sons of God . . . the whole created universe groans in all its parts as if in travail of child-birth'. And, if we regard the Incarnation itself as the expression of universal love, which is a legitimate interpretation from any point of view, instead of thinking of it as the descent of the Crown Prince 'out of his ivory palaces' into an alien world, do we not find the same significance? The great Christian sacrament, with the representative elements of bread and wine as the means of grace, is often taken to be symbolic that 'the earth is the Lord's'.

For present purposes the important difference between the universes of the Greeks and of the Hebrews is that whereas the former was an *emanation* the latter was a *creation*. According to the Bible the world was deliberately uttered by divine fiat. It had a beginning and its history was moving towards a grand climax when righteousness would reign and the wolf lie down with the lamb. The world originated with the act of a God who was personal, living and dynamic, a God who spoke and who guided the destinies of men both as a collectivity and as individuals. He was a developing God, who 'grew up'. The genocidal, arbitrary, temperamental God of the early books of the Old Testament became the mature Deity of the New. This was a dynamic God governing a dynamic universe.

Nowhere in Greek philosophy do we find anything comparable, certainly not in Platonism. In that other great tradition, Stoicism, God is material, the providential reason immanent in nature, the active principle of the universe. He is creator; but he creates the world only to reabsorb it into himself in a great conflagration, after which he recreates it again exactly as before. Man is governed at every step by the laws of nature, his freedom consisting of the supreme privilege of knowing that he cannot do other than he does. In Platonism, too, time and history are not progressive but cyclical. The cosmos of the Greeks was static, its God impersonal and impassive. It is the God of the philosophers, a very different being from that of the prophets.

In two such widely different universes it is not surprising that the conceptions of love were different. Eros encourages a more intellectualist, more contemplative attitude to life. Agape is a more dynamic, active concept. It is tempting to compare the two by their fruits. While eros may not have produced great men of adventure, reformers or men of deep compassion for their fellow men, neither has it given rise to the aggressiveness or to the desire for domination that has so often discredited Christianity. Yet, without institutions, hierarchies or missionaries, it has spilled over the whole world and exercised a civilising influence. It is sometimes charged with being uncreative; but this is unjust. Plato is explicit on the point and all Greek culture belies it. On the other hand, in its degeneracy it can lead to passivity and world-rejection.

Some writers tend to confuse eros with the excesses of the Dionysiac cults. These have not distinguished adequately between the earthly eros and the heavenly. It is true that the heavenly eros inebriates with the glories of the aesthetic; but this is a very different inebriation from that of the Dionysiacs who, in their frenzies, were finding outlets for the dark forces which, in any society, must find acceptable channels if they are not to do limitless damage. There may have been some relation between these and the lower eros but not with the heavenly. Even in these days, Dionysius still has a rôle to play and great Pan himself is not yet quite dead whatever they may say.

Because eros and agape are different does not imply that they are incompatible. Indeed, for their enrichment they need each other as complements. The Christian Fathers, as we shall see, undertook the enterprise of bringing about a marriage. Nygren thinks that this was the great, strategic error of Christian thought. How mistaken he is we shall realise as we go along.

In the meanwhile, we must not overlook the delightful *philia*, a word that occurs in the New Testament as well as in the philosophers. In some authors it conveys the suggestion of kissing one another. It has the meaning of mutuality. In Empedocles it has a wider meaning than that of interpersonal mutuality and has the significance of the eternal Harmony which, in response to the challenge of Discord, is the creative activity in the natural world. Shelley catches the spirit of it:

> The fountains mingle with the river
> And the rivers with the ocean,
> The winds of heaven mix forever
> With a sweet emotion;
> Nothing in the world is single,
> All things by a law divine
> In one another's being mingle –
> Why not I with thine?

Max Scheler is of the opinion that the failure of the Christian tradition in the appreciation of man's unity with the cosmos, and the acceptance of his unchallenged dominion over nature, affected the whole development of the theme of personal relations. St Francis of Assisi provided the one happy interlude and the Renaissance, too, recovered for a time something of the Greek spirit. 'Christianity,' he writes, 'brought with it a non-cosmic personal love-mysticism of universal compassion; though it no longer looks down, for it is directed upwards, and welded into unity with the love of Jesus.' He may have overlooked the part played in popular devotion by the Virgin Mary, as Queen of Heaven, and all the ranks of angels and archangels, saints, martyrs, spirits and demons, who had replaced the nature gods and spirits of paganism. The mediaeval universe was well populated.

We can understand Scheler better when he comes to deal with the consequences of the Reformation, he himself being a product of German Protestantism. He writes:

Protestantism has a bearing on our enquiry in four main aspects: (i) it excludes love in any form, whether benevolence, love of our neighbour, or the love of God as a mystical reality, from among the means necessary to salvation. (ii) It rules out any kind of pagan identification with Nature, therefore powerfully reinforcing the primary Judaeo-Christian tendency to subjugate Nature into an exclusive preserve for human *control and activity*. (iii) It arrests the development of a spiritual eros by rejecting both the practice and the ideal of other-worldly asceticism (monasticism). (iv) It deflates and domesticates the emotional relationship between the sexes (in complete contrast to the Renaissance).

Here, again, Protestant devotion is occasionally better than its theology. In hymns and prayers there are sometimes glimpses of a less austere outlook and, in their little books of prayers children are allowed to indulge their friendship for animals and flowers.

The theme reaches its contemporary phase in the 'general benevolence' of the positivistic schools which think in terms of the solidarity of living mankind in material need, and which tend to ignore the higher values and the development of the individual in favour of the values common to the masses, an average of mediocrity. It is a fair enough criticism of contemporary egalitarianism that it often seems as much concerned to destroy excellence wherever it is to be found as to raise the general standard.

Between the technological industry that has arisen out of the Protestant subordination of nature to man, and the administrative system required by the positivistic schools, the individual is suffocated, interpersonal relations are impoverished and the surface of the earth is devastated. With a tempering of eros mankind would not so thoughtlessly have wrought these evils. But technological advance has now attained such increasing momentum that nothing can stop it. In its application to practical affairs, the scientific method seems almost to have acquired an independent life and mind of its own which knows nothing of humane values. Even medical science brings curses in the wake of its benediction. It may be that the recoil from all this that is now becoming evident will compel the men of power to recover some sense of loyalty to Nature, their mother, and turn the instruments at their disposal to the purposes of praise instead of destruction.

We shall hear more of this. The intention of this section has been to sum up what has gone before and to indicate the general direction of development in such a way as to provide a theme to which subsequent theories can be related and which will assist in recognising where they have gone wrong. The authors presented have been so selected as to shed light from different angles on the many-faceted diamond that is our theme while keeping in sight the historical development.

Chapter Six

St Augustine

With the development of the Early Church the focus of interest changes. There is now relatively little discussion of friendship and its meaning; that is taken for granted as something to be cherished, although we are warned of the mutability of the human affections. Two new interests take possession of the minds of philosophers and theologians.

First and most admirable of these is sympathetic pity, benevolence or compassion, inculcated not as a stern duty or as a law that had to be obeyed, but as an indispensable element in the Christian character and a natural expression of faith. This was one aspect of respect for human dignity; but it was more than a mere recognition. It involved warmth and tenderness of feeling; an outgoing of sympathetic emotion when in contact with human suffering and a self-identification with the sufferer. It was not confined to a small circle of friends but, ideally, took the whole of humanity in its sweep.

The classical thinkers knew nothing of this. The Stoics actually warned against emotional involvement with the miseries of others. As they cultivated fortitude for themselves and despised self-pity so their philosophy had no room for altruistic identification with the sorrows of the world. It is hard to imagine Platonism encouraging the sacrificial life. Plato might well have backed the establishment of the welfare state but it would have been more in the interests of justice than out of compassion for the deprived and underprivileged. The tendency of the Classics would have been to insulate themselves from such considerations while they continued their pursuit of truth, justice, beauty and the virtuous.

For Christians, the central theme of the Gospels is the coming of the Kingdom of God, a utopian society under the divine monarchy, to be inaugurated by cataclysmic intervention at some unpredictable moment in an unknown future. It is not, like the republic Plato described, an ideal state to which human societies should endeavour to conform. Indeed, apart from the divine monarchy, we are given little indication of the structures and mores to which we should try to conform. The ethic of the New Testament is an ethic for a world in which evil has free rein; not for one from which evil has been abolished. This kingdom has singularly little substance if regarded as an ideal that mankind should strive to actualise. For ordinary folk, whose anguish is here and now, this undated promissory note is of minor significance. It is no more than a vague expectation that in the long perspectives of history the righteous will turn out to have been on the winning side, despite present appearances. The concept has been seized on by cranks, faddists and escapists who try to predict from the signs of the times when the world will end.

What in the Gospels has influenced ordinary men and women has been the example and precept of compassion. Although there have been periods when the flame has flickered low it has never quite died away. At present it burns as brightly as ever. To ordinary folk, the main justification for the continued existence of the Christian Church is its work of mercy and its provision for living as a community. This same 'caritas' has entered into Humanism and, through that movement, qualifies our politics and our conduct of public affairs. Once this New Testament theme had gained hold, human attitudes could never return to the old indifference. It has been unfortunate that it has had to compete with the implications of the doctrine of original sin.

Self-identification with the suffering of mankind is the Incarnation principle. As the creator and ruler of the universe took upon himself human form and shared the experience of mankind, so Christians are expected to follow this example and to share the sufferings and sorrows of their fellows. Whether or not the generality of people nowadays are able to accept this as objective truth, most will acknowledge that the concept is magnificent and has been deeply influential.

The second new theme was a concern for, not to say an obsession with, sexuality. The seed St Paul sowed germinated rapidly. Sexuality became identified with the world, the flesh and the devil – more especially the flesh. One consequence was the devaluation of womanhood. The western world is only now recovering from this.

Since womanhood was the epitome of sexuality, the evil associated with sexuality brushed off onto women in general. Woman was the temptress, the *fons et origo* of sensuality, something to be avoided if possible; even to be abhorred. So we have Origen (A.D. *c*.185–*c*.254) having himself castrated for fear of contamination. He wrote: 'Marriage is unholy and unclean'. Tertullian (A.D. 160–220) frowned heavily on second marriages after first partners had died. For some of the Fathers, marriage was at best a *pis aller*, a means of avoiding loss of self-control and promiscuity when all else had failed. Virginity was the loftiest way of life for the Christian, whether man or woman. Tertullian wrote: 'Woman! You are the gateway of the devil. You persuaded him whom the devil dared not attack directly. Because of you the Son of God had to die. You should always go dressed in mourning and in rags.' Elsewhere he describes woman as 'a temple built over a sewer'. Jerome (A.D. 342–400) one of the finest scholars of the Early Church, the translator of the Bible into Latin and thus the author of the Vulgate, still the official version of the Roman Church, could not bear to look at women for fear of the lascivious thoughts and longings the sight of them aroused in him. He took to the hermitage and the monastery to escape the pollution of the world. He wrote: 'Marriage is a vice'. Pathological, perhaps, but if so the disease must have been contagious for it laid firm hold upon the Church.

As to how the Christian community would be sustained if all its members followed this counsel of perfection there were several easy answers. In the first place, the end of all things was not far away and this made the question irrelevant. Apart from this, any child had to undergo spiritual rebirth as a qualification for entry into the kingdom and parents could not guarantee this for their children. The Church would be recruited in the future, as it had been in the past, from converted pagans. In any case, salvation did not abide by the hereditary principle but was a matter of selection and predestination from before the foundation of the world.

We may well ask how it was that an attitude so remote from the spirit of the Gospels could ever have gained ground. The Gospels are characterised by tender reverence for womanhood. While not in the least condoning them, Jesus displayed a kindly understanding of the sins of the flesh, which he appeared to think much less serious than the sins of the spirit: hypocrisy, arrogance, vainglory, pride. There was, of course, the association of womanhood with the wickedness of Eve, which cannot entirely be dismissed as irrational, given acceptance of the historicity of Genesis. In those days the person was not individualised to anything like the extent that he is now. In the second or third centuries it would not seem outrageous that womanhood in general should be deemed to have participated in the guilt of Eve. Hereditary guilt would be regarded as a psychological fact rather than as an ethical one. To us it is monstrous that the sins of the father should be visited upon the children. The fact that in the natural order this is inescapable leads us to question whether there is any moral order at all. The notion that this should be divinely willed as a penalty for the sins of the fathers calls in question the justice of God. Yet, until recently, it was thought perfectly consonant with justice that the whole of mankind should be held guilty and confined to eternal limbo because of the sin of Adam. It was considered an astonishing mark of the divine mercy and compassion that God should at random pick out a few here and there for salvation.

It has been held that the attitude of the Early Church to sexuality was due to the influence of Eastern dualism with its world-rejecting attitude. In the teaching of the Persian, Zoroaster, the powers of light and of darkness were locked in deadly antagonism until such time as a Saviour should appear; Ahura Mazda and Ahriman, the spiritual and the material, in timeless conflict. The powerful Gnostic and Manichaean sects were under this influence. There must also have been an osmosis between

Greek thinking and the Easterns. But a clear dualism such as that of Zoroaster was never characteristic either of the Greeks or of Christian orthodoxy. The Stoics, believing that wisdom consisted in conforming to the laws of nature because they were the thinking of the divine mind, were pantheists. The Platonists saw evil as remoteness from the divine enlightenment, the deprivation of good, rather than as an independent, active force. Christian orthodoxy was not committed to any of these positions, although none of them was entirely without effect. A more likely explanation of the Church's attitude to sexuality is that it was the recoil of Christian leaders from social conditions in the Roman Empire of the time.

These men were the true successors of the noble Romans of the Republic, with their austere morals and their stern self-discipline. They saw, and deprecated, the slow disintegration of the Empire but there was nothing they could do to halt the process. Except for those wealthy enough to sustain prominence at the imperial court, the political system offered no scope for the public spirited private citizen. The Church was the one institution where the abilities of such people could find a satisfying outlet. There they were occupied in constructing an ecclesiastical system that would project into the future the values for which Rome had stood in the past: good administration, justice, the rule of law, orderliness and lofty ethical standards. How well they built we can still see.

In these circumstances, the Church became a community within a community; not so much a semi-autonomous institution in a pluralist society as a community in a polemical relation with contemporary society. For the sake of order it gave its obedience to the State but it had its own government, its own social arrangements and its own mores. Withdrawn from public affairs, churchmen turned from the social life of the times with nausea.

What the truth is about that social life we can only speculate. In the absence of accurate techniques of observation we have to rely on personal impressions, which are notoriously unreliable. A distinguished ecclesiastic describes the British as, 'a sex-ridden nation of drug addicts, gamblers and thugs'. He probably believes it! From the Old Testament onwards exaggeration has been the special prerogative of prophets. It is so charmingly spine-chilling to generalise from a few small cliques to a whole nation. Did we but know, the majority of Roman citizens probably lived in much the same humdrum way as the majority always have lived. But the elements of licentiousness and violence were more ostentatious. The pornography and savagery of stage and colosseum knew no restraint. Some men of sensitiveness and dignity found themselves fascinated by it in spite of themselves. That fastidious and principled men were revolted by it all is hardly surprising: the pity is that their disgust became permanently institutionalised.

One outcome was the monastic system. Now whatever the achievements of monasticism, and they are not inconsiderable, what cannot be claimed is that it makes any contribution to interpersonal relations. Like President Coolidge's clergyman and sin, it is against them. It does not, for instance, set an example of marital bliss. At one time my duties led me for a succession of week-ends to be the willing and appreciative guest of a number of monasteries. One of these was a closed order of contemplatives in which the rule of silence was rigorously maintained. But on the Sunday afternoon the rule was relaxed for a half-hour of 'recreation' in which I was invited to participate. I went to the 'recreation' room where a large circle of chairs had been arranged. At the appointed moment the monks filed in and took their places in the circle – and remained in complete silence. This was broken only by myself and the monks on either side of me. Having expected that, after a week of restraint, there would be an immediate outbreak of eager talk I wanted to know why nobody started a conversation. I was informed that after a week of restraint nobody had anything to say. Yet, I was assured, the monks experienced a sense of community among themselves deeper than any that could be achieved by verbal communication. For myself, I can confirm that in the silence I did not feel in the least lonely.

That this might be true is credible among an isolated group of men dedicated to scholarship, to the precision of religious ritual and to the cultivation of the life of prayer. But that this should have been the predominant ideal for many centuries is another question. It meant that the men who were the most qualified to exert a civilising influence on human relations were withdrawn from society and acted upon it only indirectly. What is unmistakably clear is that the monastic contribution to marriage and to interpersonal relations generally was not merely neutral; it was negative.

These various strands of thought and experience came together in the life and work of St Augustine of Hippo (A.D. 354–430), one of the most massive intellects, the greatest of all some would say, in the history of Christendom. With him the development of the Early Church came to a head and he, more than any other, launched the Church into the Middle Ages. His influence was deep and lasting. Such diverse minds as Aquinas, Luther and Calvin were indebted to him. The life and writings of this fascinating personality are worth more than a cursory glance.

Born at Tagaste in North Africa into a middle class family of moderate means, he received a Christian education and afterwards studied rhetoric at Carthage University. His father, a choleric man, was pagan. He reserved a special reverence and affection for his mother, Monnica, who was a Christian and must have been a woman of unusual character and intelligence. Augustine describes in his *Confessions* how, by a combination of acquiescence and dignity, she handled her obstreperous husband and so won his respect that he ultimately came to share her faith and amend his manners.

Augustine's reflections on his schooldays have a contemporary flavour. At first bored, and slow in the uptake in learning the rudiments of grammar, his teachers had no better idea than to beat knowledge into him. In this beating they apparently showed more efficiency than they did in their teaching. Time after time he showed his parents the weals they had raised, while they, in their turn, had no better idea than to make a joke of it. Then he came to the study of great literature; his imagination quickened and his brilliance revealed itself. But, despite his later admiration for Greek authors, he was never able to learn their language. He concludes that the only satisfactory way of teaching is to arouse the pupil's curiosity and so stimulate an eagerness to learn. No modern educationist would quarrel with that.

As a youth Augustine was lively and mischievous. An incident that affected him occurred when he and a gang of unruly friends stripped a neighbour's pear tree and then wantonly threw away the fruit. He was struck not so much by the magnitude of the offence as by its meaningless stupidity, which came to epitomise for him the destructive absurdity of sin.

His parents were hard pressed to finance his education. Realising, while at the university, that his social status and lack of means debarred him from the kind of career in the public service that would have matched his abilities, he devoted himself to literary pursuits and to teaching. Passionately interested in philosophy, he so absorbed the influence of the Platonists that their attitudes became as if bred in him. Deserting orthodox Christianity at the age of nineteen, he became a Manichaean, remaining faithful to his sect for ten years, and leaving it when he found that its most learned doctor, one Faustus, could not answer his questions.

During this period, prevented by social circumstances from marrying, he lived with a mistress by whom he had a son, Adeodatus. After fifteen years conscience impelled him to break the association, but he found himself unable to live the celibate life and took another mistress. That he must have been a man of great charm and attractiveness is evidenced by the affection that both these women had for him and by the filial relation between him and his son.

At the age of twenty-nine Augustine moved to Rome, where he set up a school of rhetoric, but shortly afterwards moved to Milan, where he came under the influence of the great bishop, St Ambrose. A famous passage in the *Confessions* tells how the turning point of his life came at the age of thirty-two. Walking in a garden in a condition of agonised spiritual turmoil he lay down under a fig tree:

So was I speaking, and weeping in the most bitter contrition of my heart, when, lo! I heard from a neighbouring house a voice, as of boy or girl, I know not, chanting and oft repeating, 'Take up and read; take up and read'. Instantly my countenance altered, I began to think most intently, whether children were wont in any kind of play to sing such words: nor could I remember ever to have heard the like. So checking the torrent of my tears, I arose; interpreting it to be no other than a command from God, to open the book, and read the first chapter I should find. I seized, opened, and in silence read that section, on which my eyes first fell: 'No revelling or drunkenness, no debauchery or vice, no quarrels or jealousies. Let Christ Jesus himself be the armour that you wear; give no more thought to satisfying the bodily appetites'. No further would I read; nor needed I: for instantly at the end of this sentence, by a light as it were of serenity infused into my heart, all the darkness of doubt vanished away.

Following this experience, Augustine and Adeodatus were baptised together. Augustine separated from his mistress and returned to Africa. On the way Monnica, overjoyed at her son's conversion, died. For a while Augustine lived in community at Tagete with some friends, engaging in the study of philosophy. In A.D. 396 he was consecrated Bishop of Hippo and ruled over the diocese until his death. He was also a magistrate for the district in secular cases.

Such was the life's experience of this great man. At least he was no dry academic or sequestered monk. When he wrote about sex and marriage he did so on the basis of warm-hearted personal knowledge and he was of too powerful intellect to let himself be led into absurdities and extremes. What he wrote on the wider issues of loving and life and the meaning of life was the precipitate of a profound inner struggle and a thorough acquaintance with the thought of his time. Yet he was no more free than the rest of us from the limitations of his times.

As a Christian, Augustine remained Neoplatonist; which meant that he had to hold together both the Platonist idea of the cosmos and that of the Hebrew tradition. Professor Burleigh (*The City of God*) remarks, quoting Gilson: ' "He passes constantly from the one perspective to the other, rather with the feeling of their profound unity than by virtue of an explicit doctrine elaborated to unify them'', and without apparently perceiving the necessity for one!' It would be presumptuous to suggest that a man of such intellect did not know what he was doing. This is a rather startling example of the truth that it is possible to hold apparently incompatible hypotheses at the same time without losing either consistency or integrity. Since this is done in physics, why not in metaphysics? The Church of England does so to the present day. While the Thirty-nine Articles maintain the doctrine of the *Deus impassibilis* every hymn and prayer in the book denies it. Consistency is the vice of the feeble-minded.

In his non-Platonist dress Augustine took the Genesis myth to be literal truth. He believed that when God had created the heavens and the earth, and had crowned his work by giving Man the dominion, he looked out on his creation and saw that it was good – all of it. What God had made could not be less than good, and nothing existed that did not owe its existence to God. There is no sign here of dualism. Evil entered into the world through the sin of Adam. Once the virus had taken hold it was ineradic-able except by the redemptive work of God in Christ, mediated by the divine grace. But the grace was available and the potenti-ality for redemption was present. This means that evil is a phenomenon of history only; it is not embedded in the nature of the cosmos.

For Augustine, the conflict between good and evil is epitomised in the two cities, the City of God and the Earthly City. The former is the Communion of Saints and is the abode of love, rationality and peace. It includes both the saints still on earth and the saints in glory. While not coterminous with the Church, the inevitable tendency is to identify the two. The Earthly City, on the other hand, is the loveless abode of unrighteousness and law-lessness, the realm of anarchy and chaos. Augustine sums up the situation thus: 'Two loves made two cities: love of self to the contempt of God made the Earthly City: love of God to the contempt of self made the Heavenly City' (*De Civitate Dei*). Organised societies such as those of Greece and Rome belong fundamentally to the Earthly City; but, in so far as they ad-minister enough of order and justice to make social life livable at all, they have a little bit of the Heavenly City. To the extent that they provide the framework for satisfactory living they participate in the values of the city of God.

So much, at least, of the background is essential to an understanding of Augustine's doctrine of love in its various forms. Although he did not unroll his thought systematically as, for instance, Aquinas was later to do he was, in fact, an architectonically systematic thinker and all the components of his teaching form parts of a massive whole.

In this, as in much else, Augustine looked to St Paul. He turned to the famous passage in I *Cor.* 13: 'In a word, there are three things that last forever: faith, hope, and love; but the greatest of these is love'. This was the love denoted by the word *caritas*, the Latin root of our own word, 'charity', which fell into disrepute when it came to signify the offensive condescension of the comfortably-off to the deserving poor. Since the birth of the welfare state removed the need for charity of that kind the word has recovered some of its former greatness. Even now it has not recovered the full wealth of meaning it had for Augustine. In this word eros and agape are brought into a unity that is virtually a new concept. There is no question of any incompatibility between them. One difficulty remained unresolved: Augustine could not understand how God could love because he needed nothing.

Through grace, the soul is caught up into the love of God and is absorbed into mystical union with him. But mankind and, indeed, the entire material world as well, are God's creation and are in essence, good. Through the Incarnation, God had become identified with mankind in a new way. To love God and fail to love mankind is a contradiction: it is impossible. The one love necessarily flows from the other. To grasp this it is far better to browse through Augustine's sermons on the *Epistles of St John*, and to catch the spirit of them, than to quote particular passages. Love of mankind comes from the love of God as heat from the fire. Augustine does not think of mankind as an abstraction but as a multitude of living, individual persons. Despite their declension from their primitive state of perfection, men are to be cared for. The good of others is to be our own good. We are to love our

neighbours as ourselves, certainly, for if we do not respect ourselves how will we know what love of neighbour means and how
will we be able to love at all? That having been said, self is to sink
into insignificance and self-love is to be transferred to others so
that we shall gain our own fulfilment in promoting the good of
others. We are to lose our lives to save them.

Such was caritas for Augustine, and it is as well to have a special
name for it because there is no necessary connection between that
and interpersonal relations of a warmer and more intimate kind.
In practical terms, caritas is more a creative goodwill, a desire for
the good of others that is strong enough to stifle envy, hatred and
malice and that promotes, as St Paul says, patience and kindliness.
There is nothing about it of the passion or warm affection that
comes into existence between two persons who are deeply
attached to each other. It is remote from that passionate longing
for the obliteration of separateness that unites a man and a
woman who are 'in love'.

Augustine was never able to dissociate this kind of love from
concupiscence in the pejorative sense of the word. In Christian
circles 'concupiscence' itself is a pejorative word, as if there
never could be a good desire for wordly things or a wholesome
lust. It is a surmise, although not a wild one, that under the
influence of guilt feeling Augustine misinterpreted his own
experience. What seems mainly to have upset him was the
independence of the male genitals. Precisely when a man most
clearly and intelligently wills them to operate they perversely
refuse. When he most wants them to be quiescent they most
obstinately assert themselves.

There can be few normal males who have not, on occasion,
mourned with the Saint this sad phenomenon, but for different
reasons. Augustine did not write this with a lugubrious smile. For
him this experience epitomised the human predicament. Men, he
says, are at their happiest when they live according to reason;
which is only a rather technical way of saying the obvious, that
people are most likely to be happy when they live intelligently,
instead of allowing themselves to be torn by conflicting compulsions. Yet here is a powerful appetite, sexuality, essential to the

continuance of the race, that is beyond rational control. In the sex act itself reason is in abeyance and people are entirely dominated by pleasure and passion. That is why they always want privacy for their indulgence: they do not want others to observe them when so devoid of self-mastery.

In the state of primal innocence before the Fall reason did have the upper hand: the appetites and drives were the servants of intelligence instead of its masters as they subsequently became. That is why Eden was a garden of perfect bliss. Certainly, Adam and Eve could have procreated had they wished but their residence in Eden was too short. In that event they would have exercised their sexual powers solely for the sake of procreation, without thought for the pleasure of it, and would have done so under conditions of full self-control. Reason would then have been responsible for the propagation of the species. The most ardent eugenist could not ask for more!

With the Fall, reason lost its pre-eminence and concupiscence entered into human nature. That was the essence of the Fall. With reason supreme, man would voluntarily have accepted the will of God as his own. In a glorious servitude he would have enjoyed perfect liberty and perfect happiness: 'in whose service is perfect freedom'. For the religious man that is the paradox at the heart of life. With the Fall, the appetites and compulsions take over and reason becomes the instrument of their indulgence. In his fallen state, man does not ask what reason requires of him but, rather, how he can use his reason to satisfy his desires. From thenceforward it was not reason but concupiscence that was responsible for the propagation of the species and it was through concupiscence that the sin and guilt of Man were perpetuated.

It is difficult in these days to enter into such a scheme of things as this. The myth of Eden and the Fall upon which it is based is alien to our way of thinking and corresponds to nothing in our interpretation of human evolution. We look for psychological explanations of it. For Augustine and his contemporaries the myth was as factual as are the deliverances of modern science to us.

Considering the background Augustine's practical teaching on marriage was, by the standards of his day, surprisingly liberal. It is summed up in his treatise, *The Good of Marriage*, which was written in A.D. 401 as a reply to a certain Jovinian, whom Pope Siricius and St Ambrose had recently condemned as a heretic for maintaining that the married state was equal in spiritual status to that of virginity. Augustine chose a positive title as a rebuttal in advance of the charge of Manichaeism. He wanted to make clear from the start that his views on marriage were not dictated by a hatred of the flesh as necessarily and inherently evil in itself.

The marital virtues, says Augustine, are procreation, fidelity, its sacramental quality of relation and the companionship it provides. Marriage is good because it channels concupiscence into the service of procreation. The Patriarchs of the Old Testament were allowed polygamy because, in their situation, it was necessary for the propagation of the People of God; what they did was done rationally and with full self-control and not incontinently. Monogamy is the law of God. Intercourse between husband and wife for the sake of procreation is good: with any other motive it is sinful, although venially so. Even incontinence is dignified by marriage if directed to procreation: 'The concupiscence of the flesh which parental affection tempers is repressed and becomes inflamed more modestly. For a kind of dignity prevails when, as husband and wife, they unite in the marriage act, they think of themselves as father and mother'.

Yet in marriage it is better to refrain from intercourse than to indulge, even for the sake of procreation. When a family has been brought into the world it is better for husband and wife to refrain from intercourse voluntarily than to wait until advancing years forces continence upon them. Evidently Augustine had no notion of the unitive function of sex in marriage. Sex, to him, meant either procreation or concupiscence.

Thinking, no doubt, of his discarded mistresses, Augustine goes on to say that a woman who has intercourse with fidelity, but knowing marriage to be impossible for social reasons, is not adulterous. If she has intercourse with a view to bearing children she is better than the wives who force their husbands to have intercourse with them for pleasure only. The one redeeming feature of such women is that they are, in fact, married.

Married people owe it to each other to support each other in their human weakness; so that, if one partner is inflamed with frustrated desire, and likely to be driven to adultery for satisfaction, it is not for the other partner to withhold, even for the sake of virtue. The husband, it is true, has authority over the wife's body, but this is reciprocal; the wife also has authority over her husband's body. The marriage debt is binding on both partners.

Second marriages are permitted but signify a decline from the highest standard. The marriage of the faithful is better than the virginity of the unbeliever but the ideal is Christian virginity. It is better not to marry at all. Virginity and marriage are both good but virginity is the higher good. The future of the human race is no problem. That can safely be left to the incontinent.

Husband and wife are to love each other 'as Christ loved his spouse the Church'; but this must be a spiritual love. Augustine may not have thought the flesh to be evil in itself but he evidently thought the dichotomy between soul and body was such that a purely spiritual marriage could be undertaken without detriment to either side. Sexuality means concupiscence, and concupiscence has the nature of sin. It must be hedged around. While Augustine was not insensitive or inhumane it is hardly surprising that, in the hands of lesser men, the doctrine he propounded to provide for this, the most intimate of human relations, should have become destructive of womanhood and that sex should have been degraded to a mechanical apparatus for the production of babies. It goes without saying that the prohibition of contraception was absolute.

The Mediaevals

SOCIAL BACKGROUND

There are still educated people who imagine the centuries between the fall of Rome and the Renaissance to have been a period of unmitigated blackness, a dark age in which culture was dead and the people of Europe, having forgotten their heritage, lived as barbarians. Their illiterate overlords spent their days and nights in fighting and feasting while the dull peasantry endured a harsh serfdom.

If that is what they learned at school, so much the worse for their schooling. Fascinating works of history are available to disabuse them. Certain aspects of contemporary society would be incomprehensible if that were true. What is fact is that the centre of European culture moved to Byzantium, where the glories of Greece and Rome were perpetuated in luxurious isolation. While Byzantium may have been an animated museum, rather than a living and developing culture, it did, nonetheless, produce great architects, artists and scholars. When the city fell to the armies of the Sultan Mohammed II, in A.D. 1453, it still retained enough vitality to be able to hand over some remnants of its inheritance to western Europe and so instigate the Renaissance.

In the meanwhile, western Europe was for centuries the prey of marauding barbarian hordes and battling barons. Enlightened men had a severe struggle to maintain any vestige of civilisation. But their light was never completely extinguished. There were still towns where standards could be upheld and castles whose lords provided protection for men of learning. Along the fringes, as in Moorish Spain and Celtic Ireland, the flame burned brightly. Of the humbler crafts, the vellums produced in the monastery libraries were an art form in their own right. In the towns and villages of England and elsewhere, carving and the ceramic arts flourished. While the soil was uncongenial for the emergence of great names or outstanding works of literature, it was kept well tilled so that, when the right seed was available, it had the potentiality for a good crop.

From the time of the monk, Alcuin, and his patron, Charlemagne, crowned Holy Roman Emperor in A.D. 800, and in the England of Alfred the Great (A.D. 849–99), despite wars and invasions, the European system acquired new virility and began to thrive. Great names and great intellectual enterprises slowly multiplied. All along there had been the monasteries where scholarship had been pursued, not merely as a religious duty, but for sheer love of it. These now became prolific breeding grounds of theologians and philosophers. From them, also, came encouragement for the architects and builders who constructed the many splendoured abbeys and cathedrals which are still the glory of Europe. Such greatness did not spring suddenly from nowhere.

To imagine that the Church entirely dominated the situation is just as mistaken as it is to imagine that there was no civilisation at all. The soul of Europe was not easily, and never wholly, converted to Christianity. The paganism that survived from Roman imperialism did not evaporate at the wave of an episcopal staff. The barbarian invaders themselves had brought with them other myths and superstitions and other customs and ceremonies. They did not vanish at the command of Charlemagne with his mass conversions and hosepipe baptisms. Europe at that time, and for long afterwards, was well-stocked with the ingredients of Frazer's *Golden Bough*. The pleasanter as well as the darker elements, although in many instances driven underground, survived in witchcraft and alchemy and in such rituals as those of the maypole, the Christmas tree and the Hallowe'en festival. With them there survived also the uninhibited pagan attitude to personal relations and its robust attitude to sexuality. Pagan gaiety and vitality survived, too. The preaching friars could frown their features into fretwork, the villagers still danced and still made love.

There was guerilla war in the soul of Europe and often in the souls of individuals. The moral discipline of the Church struggled with the spirit of paganism and, while a disciplined force was bound to win in the intellectual and administrative spheres, in the life of feeling it was less effective. This situation was reflected more in poetry and in song than in the thought of the period.

From John Scotus Eregina (A.D. 810–77) to the last of the great mediaeval scholars, Nicholas of Cues (A.D. 1401–64), was a period of intensive intellectual activity. Jewish and Arabic thinkers contributed to the stream. This was the time of the foundation of the universities, each with its own specialisation: Salerno (ninth century) and Montpellier (thirteenth century(in medicine; Bologna (A.D. 1088) in law; Paris, Oxford and Cambridge (twelfth century) in theology. As the administrators of the period had the Roman Empire as their only model and so organised the Church and the Holy Roman Empire on that pattern disregarding, in some measure, the realities, so the scholars looked for inspiration to classical antiquity and carried forward that tradition. In this they were assisted by the Arabs, who had preserved the Aristotelian tradition. In their work we hear strong echoes of Greek and Roman thought. The index to Gilson's *History of Christian Philosophy in the Middle Ages* lists the works of some three hundred or more philosophers between Eregina and Nicholas.

THE SCHOLASTICS

In general, the Scholastics take self-love as their starting point in dealing with interpersonal relations, whether with other human persons or with God. That every human person loves himself and seeks his own good they regard as self-evident. But, as we have seen before, owing to the difficulty of definition the term can be misleading. We have to distinguish between self-love and selfishness, which is its opposite. The man with self-love accepts himself as he is and wants to develop such gifts as he has. The selfish man tries to attach everything and everybody to himself because he is not content with himself as he is but is conscious with shame of his inadequacies. His desire is insatiable: he wants more and more of more and more, for he can never compensate himself enough. The Stoics had realised this and sought a solution in the extinction of all desire. A third type, the Narcissist, is pleased with himself to the point of infatuation. He is incapable of loving anybody else because he can find nobody worthy of his love.

But the self-love of the Scholastics means that a man places a right valuation upon himself as a human person. It is as such that he cares for, and respects, himself rather than as a particular individual. Another way of putting the point is that he loves life and must, therefore, love the life within himself. He is glad to be alive. He loves the human nature that he shares with every other living person. So far is this from cutting him off from others that it is precisely what enables him to care for others with a similar nature. One of the puzzles of the Scholastics was how this self-love could be reconciled with that disinterested, unreserved love of God that religion requires.

In the writings of the mystic, St Bernard (A.D. 1091–1153), the starting point is this self-love but it is considered realistically and pragmatically. Bernard wrote from experience. Not an intellectual, in the sense of being a systematic thinker, in the manner of an Augustine or an Aquinas, he was still a man of superb ability and became one of the most influential men of his time, the trusted adviser of kings and popes. This he owed to his profound piety and rigorous asceticism, not unalloyed with arrogance, and his personal force. One of his talents was that of being able to influence men of power. He was as much a states-man as a religious. He was also the unshakeable friend of the underdog and an implacable foe of cruelty and oppression in any form. He was the author of the hymn, *Jesu dulcis memoria*. His thoughts on love are contained in his *Sermons on the Song of Songs* and his *De diligendo Deo*.

We have, he writes, to take man in his self-love as we find him. The exigencies of the realities of life oblige him to concentrate his attention first of all on himself and his own needs. That is a condition of survival and is also at the back of his insatiable desire. But this is true only on account of the Fall. In the Garden of Eden it was not so. As a result of the confusion into which his fallen condition has brought him he is unable to see where his true good lies, until the grace of God enlightens him. From this polluted self-love the soul rises by stages until it comes to ecstatic unity with God and, ultimately, to the beatific vision.

This can occur because the ultimate basis of self-love is the image of God in man. His desire as a fallen man is insatiable because really it is God that he wants and no amount of fulfilment of worldly desires will compensate for lack of Him. That is why human desires often take such strange and extravagant forms. Man is made in the image of God whether he knows it or not and it is this that he really loves. This means that the more his own will is conformed by grace to the will of God, the more nearly he becomes his true self. At the last stage the difference between himself and God is obliterated. That does not mean that he becomes absorbed into God to the loss of his own identity. He is not God and never becomes either God or part of God. He is still always a creature. Indeed, as he develops in the spiritual life his personal identity is strengthened and enriched because he is more nearly his true self instead of being distorted and defiled. In his unity with the divine he is still separate. At this stage, the more he loves God the more he loves himself because he was made in the image of God. By converse, the more truly he loves himself the more he loves God. This solves the dilemma as to how anyone can love God with a completely disinterested love, without hope or expectation of reward, and still retain his self-love. Yet the fact that his love is disinterested does not imply that he is to find no fulfilment in his love for God. He does not seek that fulfilment but he finds it none the less. It is a question of losing his life to gain it; a glorious side-effect.

Gilson states the matter in this way:

Love seeks no recompense: did it do so it would at once cease to be love. But neither should it be asked to renounce joy in the possession of the thing loved, for this joy is co-essential with love; love would no longer be love if it renounced its accompanying joy. Thus all true love is at once disinterested and rewarded, or let us say it could not be rewarded unless it were disinterested, because disinterestedness is its very essence. Who seeks nothing in love save love receives the joy that it brings; who seeks in love something other than love, loses joy and love together.

(The Spirit of Mediaeval Philosophy)

The person now loves himself as God loves him because he is entirely at one with God. For the same reason he also loves other people as God loves them. And he also loves them as he loves himself. He loves his neighbour as himself.

This is sometimes known as the 'ecstatic theory' because it involves the outgoing of the personality to another person. The alternative theory, which is really complementary, is that espoused by St Thomas Aquinas (A.D. 1225–74) and known as the 'physical theory'. Gilson points out that the distinction between them does not involve much significant difference.

Thomas, 'the Angelic Doctor', contrasts strongly with Bernard both in temperament and in way of life. A scholar and professor to his finger tips, he played no part in public affairs apart from joining in a few ecclesiastical controversies. Indeed, contemplating with awe the profundity of his erudition and the volume of his writings, it is clear that he can have had little time for anything else in his forty-nine years of life. It is not as if his writing were hasty or verbose: it is compact and lucid with scarcely a loose sentence anywhere. While clarifying the distinction between the two, he was the great synthesiser of reason and revelation, theology and philosophy. What distinguishes his thought is to be so highly systematic, with each theme integrated into the whole and related to all the rest. It has the architectonic quality of a Gothic cathedral or the quality of a symphony, moving with a deceptive inevitability through each phase to its climax. Whether present day philosophers accept his system or not and, outside the Roman Catholic Communion, not many do, they still reckon his work to be one of the outstanding products of the human intellect. In 1879, Pope Leo XIII, in his encyclical, *Aeterni Patri*, re-established him as the official philosopher of the Roman Church, describing him as 'towering' above his contemporaries, and as 'that peerless man', and enjoining his study on all theological students.

To abstract from such a system for the present purpose, without distortion or loss of perspective, is exceptionally difficult as it is, indeed, difficult to enter into the mediaeval way of thinking. With the aid of commentators I shall try to present a free interpretation.

Our point of departure is that all our knowledge begins with what we discern by means of our five senses. Our intellects work with these perceptions and sort them out but cannot unshackle themselves from them. We are completely earthbound creatures. This means that, without grace, which we know by revelation and which is the subject matter of theology, we can have no direct knowledge of God. We are left to infer even his existence from what we observe and experience in the world around us. This Thomas does in a series of five proofs, arguing, for example, from our perception of causality and movement. Without recapitulating the long trains of ratiocination associated with them, these arguments point to the existence of a being that is eternal, infinite, invisible, indivisible, in which is nothing material and no corporeality, no change, no movement, no potentiality but only existence (pure act) and will. At this stage all that we can predicate of this being are negatives : for example that it is *not* finite and *not* corporeal. It wants nothing and needs nothing.

That may be all very well but this being is more a logical conclusion or a mathematical symbol than a God who will appeal to the love and worship of the believer, a cold and comfortless God little resembling the God of the prophets or of the New Testament. But Thomas does not leave us with this celestial iceberg. There is another way by which we can arrive at a richer understanding of God than that, namely, the way of analogy. To explain what is not an easy concept we can use analogies of our own. By studying a work of art we can infer much about the artist. If we listen to a symphony we can learn, without further enquiry, something of the mood of the composer when he wrote it; what kind of musician he is and what his skill and knowledge, the depth of his emotions and his talent as an innovator. With only minimal biographical knowledge, the critics have been able to trace the spiritual development of Shakespeare by studying his plays in depth. Can we not apply the same principle in our thought about God?

Thomas believes that we can. Now the gap between the infinite and the finite is much greater – infinitely greater – than that between Shakespeare and the characters he created. But by observing the perfections of the creature we can, none the less, gain some faint indication as to what is included in the perfection of the Creator. By analogy we can infer that he is personal, and that he is the ultimate in wisdom, rationality and justice – and love. Our finite minds cannot grasp what is implied in these concepts on the scale of the infinite but we can grasp a little bit of it; enough to give us confidence. The late Archbishop William Temple used a somewhat similar argument when he said somewhere that God must be good to have produced even one superlative person, Jesus Christ.

Yet it is in this gap between the infinite and the finite that the weakness of the argument lies. We may well believe that there is justice in God and that it is in some way analogous to human justice. But, if it is away beyond our comprehension, it can have no meaning for us. Outside churches there used to be a wayside pulpit proclaiming in large letters, 'Right will prevail in the end'. I could not help asking, whose end – that of the children enslaved in the coalpits of the Industrial Revolution? And when will the end be? If the divine justice unrolls only over millions of light years, or in a future life in a heaven which is opaque to our imagination, it means nothing to us. But Thomas saw the matter differently.

Reasoned argument has now brought us to an understanding of God very close to that given in *Revelation*. God is not only timeless and infinite but is also wisdom, love and justice. Yet still he has neither wants nor needs and nothing can be added to him. Why, then, did he will creation into existence? The answer Thomas gives is that God loves his own goodness. He does not mean that the Holy Trinity is a mutual admiration society. It is more that the love and goodness of God require each other. God willed creation freely, because of love. We could put it that love willed creation for goodness's sake or that goodness willed it for love's sake. Creation therefore has both its origin in God and God as its true end and purpose. This, again, does not mean that God created a terrestrial claque to applaud his mighty acts, like a television studio audience. A better simile would be that of lovers willing a child into existence for the sake of love. They do not need a child. They are content with each other; but it is the nature of lovers to objectify their love in a child.

Every created thing, therefore, from the grains of sand on the seashore upward, in some small measure reflects the nature of God. Man, at the apex of creation, is made in the image of God. Thomas visualises the universe, not as a static structure, but as a continuing movement toward the divine. This movement is love. Mankind always seeks the good. Does this contradict the saying of St Paul, 'when I want to do the right, only the wrong is within my reach', or that other saying, 'The best I see and approve, I follow the worse'? Not at all: because of the Fall, men are often unable to recognise the good and, if they do, are too torn by worldly desires to follow it. Whatever we may think in moments of calm reflection, in the moment of decision whatever we are going to do presents itself to us as the good. The vindictive man, for example, seldom tells himself he is doing evil for the sake of evil: he is always teaching the other fellow a lesson. I overheard a man say to an associate: 'You and I will make him crawl and then we shall gloat'. He was finding a perverse satisfaction in the other man's forthcoming humiliation. It is the same with the alcoholic; each glass is just what he needs, whatever he may foresee for the next morning. When Mao Mao terrorists killed an Englishman and took out his eyes and brains what they wanted was the White Man's enlightenment, but because they had been humiliated by white men they could not accept it by the normal way of education and had to seize it for themselves. Even the villains of history have to delude themselves that they are pursuing some kind of ideal, however twisted and shabby. None of this excuses or condones the evil. There is always a reason why people are evil but they come under judgment none the less for that.

Always seeking the good, men seek their own good first. This is taken to be axiomatic. They also love themselves first. Just as our knowledge of ourselves is prior to our knowledge of others, so our self-love is always prior to our love for others. It is, indeed, the greatest love because it is the love from which all other loves derive. But this is not a selfish love, for what a man loves in himself is that humanity which he shares with everybody else. As a consequence, he tends to love this same humanity in others; which does not imply that he may not select particular individuals either for special friendship or for dislike. A person's self-love is greater, also, because it is unitive, whereas love between two or more people makes a union but not a unity.

Love goes with similarity. Two people are friends because they share a common nature or common interests. Such people can communicate with each other and this communication is basic to the friendship, a way of appreciating in each other what they have in common. They will each other's good as they will their own because they love in each other what they love in themselves. Self-love therefore becomes the measure and criterion of all other loves. We test our love for our neighbour by our love for ourselves. If we sacrifice ourselves for our friends it is because we love the virtue that is in us.

The limited good that is in us is perfect in God; therefore the love with which we love ourselves is directed with still more strength toward God and we love God more than we love ourselves.

What, then, is the true end of man? Not, certainly, to attract as many people and possessions to himself as he can in the delusion that this will provide a fulfilment he can find only in God. This is concupiscence. The answer Thomas gives coincides with that of the Scottish catechism: 'to glorify God and enjoy him for ever'. In the last resort, man finds fulfilment only in the beatific vision when, freed from the bonds of corporealty, the soul can meet with God, as it were, face to face. By grace a man may enjoy glimpses of this while still in the flesh. While we are here on earth our blessedness is to be found in withdrawing our attention from the affairs of this world and meditating on the divine truth. Truth is the highest of the values and the noblest occupation of man is the pursuit of it. Philosophy is therefore man's loftiest activity and we are left with the impression that, for Thomas, the philosopher is the saint.

In his ethical theory, Thomas follows Aristotle closely, teaching the doctrine of the golden mean. This is not a synonym for 'mediocrity'. Virtue in excess can be as deplorable as vice. Humility, for example, becomes in excess a repulsive servility. Even truthfulness can become the instrument of spite. A person who insists on blurting out the truth at the wrong moment may be merely a figure of fun; but he may also be more dangerous and detestable than an outright liar.

But what of chastity? If we observe the golden mean must we not say that virginity and celibacy, to which Thomas himself was vowed, are chastity to excess and therefore to be condemned? St Thomas would have agreed that, for the majority of the human race, that is true; but not when vows of virginity and celibacy are conformable to reason, as in the circumstances of those who experience a vocation to a way of life that is inconsistent with marriage. The monastic life and the priesthood are, for Thomas, obvious examples.

Before the Fall procreation would have occurred, not for the preservation of the species, but for the multiplication of individuals. It is evident that Eve was created for this purpose. The somewhat odd grounds that Thomas finds for this statement are that: 'We are told that woman was made to be a help to man. But she was not fitted to help man except in generation, because another man would have proved a more effective help than anything else'. In other words, since women are useless for anything except child-bearing, Eve must have been created for that purpose! But virginal integrity would have been preserved because, the sexual powers being completely under the control of the will, the membrane would not have been broken in intercourse. Purity of soul would have the consequence that the pleasure of intercourse was more intense and refined than it has been since the Fall. Since the sexual powers were under the control of reason, continence would not even have been praise-worthy. As it is, people are so much under the domination of pleasure and passion during the act that they become brute beasts. Continence is therefore praiseworthy in man's fallen state.

ABELARD AND HELOISE

Study of St Thomas Aquinas follows naturally and easily upon that of St Bernard of Clairvaux because he provides the philosophical counterpart of St Bernard's mystical insights. To treat of Peter Abelard (A.D. 1079–1142) here is to depart from chronological order; but he is so far outside the main stream of development both in his personal experience and in his writing that it seems better to discuss him separately. His experience and the light it sheds on the period is as important as his philosophy from the present point of view.

Born the son of a landowning knight in the Breton village of Le Pallet, this Abelard was the intellectual wonder of his age. Although expected to follow his father in the military pro-fession, he became so dedicated to learning that he determined to make scholarship his career. At the age of twenty-one he went to Paris and there became a master of dialectic. It was his mis-fortune that he was of divisive personality. His intellectual precocity would, in any case, have aroused the jealousy of the teachers whom he so quickly surpassed and of the distinguished professors who, as an upstart youngster, he so easily defeated in the public debates that were then the delight of the academic world. But Abelard increased this hostility toward himself among his colleagues by an arrogance such as brilliant young men often assume as a defence when they are thrown, as they inevit-ably are, among people of greater experience than themselves. As Abelard left behind one teacher after another, and humiliated one dialectical opponent after another, he made no attempt to conceal his scorn for them while they, in their turn, reacted as anybody else would. It is hardly surprising that Abelard was sur-rounded by enemies during most of his life and that they con-tinually hounded him.

Academic and ecclesiastical bickering were as virulent and as squalid then as they have ever been. Abelard was always in the centre of the whirlwind. Twice his works were condemned: by the Council of Soissons in 1121 when he was compelled to burn his own treatise on the Trinity; and by the Council of Sens in 1141, as a consequence of which he incurred the Papal condemnation. St Bernard himself was active in the latter event. It was one of Bernard's less admirable characteristics that he was unsympathetic toward theoretical thinking and apt to be afraid of it. His suspicion of Abelard was therefore natural to him; but at Sens he allowed his prejudices to lead him into unworthy intrigues. The only redeeming feature of the affair is that he was afterwards reconciled with Abelard, and the papal condemnation was rescinded, at the Abbey of Cluny, where Abelard spent the last months of his life in hard-won peace.

Fair-haired, slight of build and with handsome features, Abelard was a man of strong personality. This, allied with his mastery of his subject, his talent for exposition and his amazing originality, drew students to him in droves from all over Europe. Unlike his professorial colleagues, these students were devoted to him personally and he returned their affection ardently. Yet his success served only to deepen the ire of his enemies. His penalty for transcending his period was to be the victim of it.

To recount his tumultuous career in detail and to outline his philosophy here is impracticable. Already, this has been more than adequately done by various authors. The fine novels of Helen Waddell and George Moore are not to be missed. The originality of his philosophy was such that the scholars of his day, already settling into a traditionalist groove, could not accept it; but he adumbrates ideas that became current centuries later. His doctrine of the atonement enjoyed a restoration at the hands of Oxford's outstanding liberal theologian, Hastings Rashdall, in the early twentieth century and an attenuated version of it informs much popular religion at the present time.

What determined the course of his career was a love affair that began in his thirty-eighth year. Until then he had been too preoccupied with his work and his thought to have had time for adventures with women. Perhaps that had not prevented unful-filled needs and desires from simmering under the surface. Normally, he liked the company of women and women took to him more than men did. As far as is known he had not been on terms of sexual intimacy with any woman previously.

There lived in Paris with her uncle, Fulbert, who was a canon of Notre Dame, a young woman named Heloise, sixteen years of age, whose loveliness and intelligence made her famous through-out the city. These qualities, together with vitality and zest for life, made her unusually attractive. In France women were not, then, at a disadvantage intellectually. It was said of Heloise that she surpassed all women in beauty and most men in brilliance. Hearing of her on all sides, Abelard determined to make her acquaintance. He approached Fulbert, asking him for lodging in his house. So flattered was the Canon by this request from so eminent a man that he not only readily agreed but also entrusted the education of Heloise to him. That, in doing so, he authorised him to use corporal punishment on the young woman shows Fulbert's character in a poor light. Hardly had they come to know each other than Abelard and Heloise became lovers, dominated by an increasing passion.

The obvious, man-of-the-world, simplistic explanation is that Abelard, twenty-one years her senior and a man of experience, had cold-bloodedly planned the seduction of a naive young woman and had then found himself caught up in an emotional storm. But the simplistic answer is seldom right. There is nothing in his record to suggest that Abelard was a cynical lecher. Subsequent events suggest a far more plausible explanation.

He had been devoted to his parents, both of whom had taken vows as soon as their children had grown up, but was especially fond of his mother. Although he had suppressed it for so long, he felt a deep need for feminine companionship and affection. Most men do; but he, in particular, was far from being the self-contained person he liked to believe he was. He needed this complement to himself more than most. But neither the Church nor the academic world, which to all intents and purposes were the same, made any provision for the fulfilment of such a need.

Had Abelard been a don at a modern university, or a Protestant clergyman, his course of action would have been clear. He would have sought an introduction to Heloise and proposed marriage. At the time he was probably still in minor orders and could have married but to have abandoned the outward show of celibacy would undoubtedly have prejudiced his future. No alternative remained but a clandestine affair. Only an exceptional woman would have been adequate for this exceptional man and Abelard felt drawn to Heloise by what he had heard of her superb gifts. 'A meeting of eagles', is how George Moore described their encounter. To have attached himself to a less talented woman would have been, for a man of his sensitivity, to exploit her as an instrument of his desires.

Although there were plenty of churchmen of the period whose lives were not what they pretended them to be, few would have understood this situation and still fewer would have sympathised. As we have seen, Aquinas says explicitly that women were created for exploitation and were of little use for anything else. The Church, as such, would have passed the harshest judgment and made the cruellest recommendations without stopping to consider what the consequences might be on this earth for the two persons concerned. The Church was primarily interested in the world to come. The ascetic principle was supreme.

Looking back from the secularised world of the twentieth century, it seems as if a wave of masochism swept over Europe during the mediaeval period. But the disgust and contempt with which we in these days read of the self-tortures of the ascetics would have surprised and bewildered the people of the time. Heavy iron chains worn for years round the waist, next to the skin, until they bit into the flesh, flagellations before the altar, endless fastings: these were thought a small price to pay for eternal bliss. These were the mortification of the flesh. As for the renunciation of personal fulfilment, that was the main purpose of celibacy. Was not the contemporary, Peter Lombard (A.D. 1100–60), to write in a standard textbook that passionate love even between a husband and wife was adulterous? The only fulfilment worth having was the beatific vision. In a case such as that of Abelard, the fact that the renunciation would not be of his own choice was of no significance. The tragedy was that Heloise and Abelard rightly belonged to the twentieth century. The results of their conflict were agony, frustration and destructive crises of conscience.

So deeply was Abelard engrossed that he began to neglect his lectures and to offer repeats of old ones. He composed love lyrics that became the rage of Paris. The name, Heloise, was on all lips. Everybody knew about the affair except Fulbert. At length, the pair were discovered together and Abelard had to leave the house. But they still managed to meet and, finally, Heloise became pregnant.

As might be expected, Fulbert was enraged. All his ambitions for Heloise were destroyed. Abelard secretly took her away and sent her to his sister in Britanny where a boy, Astralabe, was born. Then he placated, or thought he had, Fulbert by marrying her. With what motive is unknown, he then had her go immediately into a convent at Argenteuil. But Fulbert was not placated. Entering Abelard's room with some thugs one night he had him assaulted and castrated. When he had recovered, Abelard himself took vows. Some time afterwards the turn of events was such that he took Heloise from Argenteuil and made her Abbess of a house founded by himself, the Paraclete. There she achieved fame both for herself and her order.

It was not long before Abelard's career resumed its former turbulent course. The story is fascinating but not directly relevant. During this period there seems to have been little correspondence between him and Heloise. Then, in 1132, Abelard wrote an autobiography in the form of a letter to a friend, *Historia Calamitatum*, which came into the hands of Heloise, who was wounded by its tone and grieved for the sake of Abelard. His castration, and the flood of troubles that followed it, had driven him into himself and filled him with the spirit of despondency and despair. He had, for instance, been appointed Abbot of a monastery that had fallen into degeneracy and disrepute. In view of his record the monks thought he would be an indulgent superior. When they discovered him to be a man of integrity, intent upon the restoration of discipline, they turned against him and tried repeatedly to murder him. The mood of pessimism born of experiences such as this showed through his writing and coloured his account of his relations with Heloise and his marriage.

Deeply hurt, Heloise writes him a long and profoundly moving letter which, while reproaching him for his inconsiderateness, reminds him of the glory of their love for each other. She tells him of the depth of love she still has for him. Even now, she says, she hankers after the days of their happiness. During the day she remembers their love making and at nights she dreams of it. She tells him of the reverence and affection her nuns have for him as their founder. All through the letter she is trying with feminine skill to challenge his despair and restore his confidence in himself and in her. She writes of the nobility of love. Blaming herself for his misfortunes, Heloise writes that, although she does not believe in free love, she would gladly have remained his mistress if to marry would have damaged his career. The world must not be deprived of the intellectual riches he could contribute to it. For a woman, to love was to give herself wholly and to put her lover always first.

There followed a remarkable correspondence between the two. Abelard assures Heloise that while they are husband and wife in fact and in feeling, in Christ they are brother and sister and he acknowledges her spiritual superiority. Heloise confesses that she took the veil for love of him and not with any sense of vocation to the religious life. This troubles her conscience because she realises that her love for Abelard is more of a reality to her than her love for God. Yet for his sake she serves God. Little by little she draws him out of himself, disperses his sense of failure, and impresses upon him that he is one of the world's greatest philosophers. She complains of the unsuitability of the rule of St Benedict for a convent of women and has him draw up a new rule for the Paraclete. Gradually, a change comes over Abelard's letters. His capacity for satisfactory human relations returns to him and he becomes himself again, but qualified now by profound experience both of love and suffering. What was unusual in a churchman of the time was the deep respect, amounting to reverence, that Abelard displayed for a living woman and his recognition of equality in mutuality.

When he died in a daughter house of Cluny, at St Marcel, the Abbot of Cluny himself, Peter the Venerable, removed his body secretly, by night, and took it to the Paraclete where, twenty-two years later, the body of Heloise was laid nearby.

The correspondence does not theorise or philosophise about love but expresses it perfectly. It provides the materials with which philosophers can work. Had these two lived in the twentieth century, their relation would have been recognised as ideal. In the twelfth it was calamitous.

Abelard's experience in depth of the interpersonal relation affected his thought. Legalism was excluded from his ethics. Motive was all-important. A man was not to be judged by his deeds but by his intentions. If a man aimed at a bird that he could see and killed a man that he could not see he was not on that account to be adjudged a murderer, because he had not consented to the death of the victim. Yet mere good intentions were by themselves no warrant of morality. Self-delusion was too easy for that. The good intentions must coincide with the will of God for him. At the same time, he could not be condemned for ignorance of the will of God unless that ignorance was wilful. Knowledge of the will of God was available even to those who were strangers to revelation. Their diligence in the search for truth had earned even for pagans a glimpse of enlightenment.

In Abelard's theory of the atonement this theme is still more apparent. His answer to the perennial question, *cur deus homo* (why did God become man?) was that man's salvation depended on providing him with a motive. Abelard cut away unnecessary and misleading elaborations: that the sacrifice of the cross was the payment of a purchase price to the devil for the souls of mankind; that Christ's sacrifice satisfied the divine justice on behalf of the sin of mankind. It was enough that the love of God, made manifest by Christ's willingness to go to the utmost length, was sufficient to draw mankind to him and thus win his redemption.

Other theologians of the period interpreted the crucifixion in the light of their experience of the justice of princes, who ruled by fear and whose laws were backed by sanctions. Man sinned and therefore deserved retribution. Christ took the penalty upon himself and so God let the sinners off. Abelard put this forensic rubbish aside and interpreted the crucifixion in the light of his experience of the power of love, which could inspire mankind with a new motive and therefore bring about their salvation. The purpose of the crucifixion was to pour charity into human hearts.

Abelard sums up his thought in his *Expositio*:

It seems to us that we are justified in the blood of Christ and reconciled to God in this, that through the singular grace manifested to us in that his Son took our nature and that teaching us both by word and example he persevered even unto death, Jesus bound us closer to himself by love, so that, fired by so great a benefit of divine grace, true charity would no longer be afraid to endure anything for his sake.

Every man is made more just, that is more loving toward God, after the passion of Christ than he had been before, because men are more incited to love by a benefit actually received than by one hoped for. And so our redemption is that great love for us shown in the passion of Christ which not only frees us from the bondage of sin, but acquires for us the true liberty of the sons of God, so that we should fulfil all things not so much through fear as through our love for him who showed toward us a favour than which, as he himself says, none greater can be found: 'There is no greater love than this, that a man should lay down his life for his friends'.

(Quoted from J. G. Sikes, *Peter Abelard*)

THE TROUBADOURS AND AFTER

For some centuries after their deaths, Heloise and Abelard, their works, their writings and their love, were half forgotten. In the seventeenth century they began to fascinate the literary imagination of Europe again. It can hardly be accidental that the contemporary ideal of love between the sexes, involving mutuality, freedom, equality and respect, resembles so closely as it does that between Heloise and Abelard. But to claim, as some have, that they were the first passionate lovers in the modern sense, is to rate even them too highly. Surely the relation between Pericles and Aspasia was in the same order, although not as tragic. Ovid may have travestied and Lucretius devalued passionate love; but to be travestied and devalued it must have existed. To the mediaevals it may have appeared to be new because the Church would have none of it. Passionate sexuality of any kind was, as we have seen, suspect to the Scholastics because it seemed to them to mean the suspension of reason. The trouble with the Scholastics was that, if they had any sexual experience at all, it could be only with a guilty conscience. Even Heloise and Abelard were too much the product of their own time to be free of it – at any rate after the disaster had occurred.

But, just as scholasticism was asserting its intellectual ascendancy, a parallel movement with a wholly different outlook was gaining ground. This was the Troubadour movement that had its rise in Provence in the late eleventh century with the writing of William, Count of Poitiers. From Provence it spread over Italy, Spain and Portugal and touched Germany and England.

No historian has claimed to provide an adequate explanation of its rise. Because it came to life in the same region as the dualist Catharist heresy which bore strong resemblances to Manichaeism and the ancient mystery religions, some writers have postulated a connection between the two and have treated the troubadours and the Catharist heresy as a last outburst of the old cults. This is to take the continuities of history too seriously. Similar conditions give rise to similar consequences and it does not follow that one set of consequences derived from another merely because that other appeared earlier. The troubadour phenomenon appears almost to have been a case of spontaneous combustion. Perhaps the severity of the Church and the hypocrisy that flowed from it called into existence their opposites. It would be pleasant to think so. Some churchmen became troubadours and some troubadours took to the monastery in later life. This coming and going between the two suggests a dialectical connection.

Apart from that, the materials for combustion existed in plenty. The courts of feudal Europe were partly staffed by landless knights, their lances at the disposal of any who could pay for them, too penurious to marry according to their status and apt for little else but the tournament and the chase. These far outnumbered the ladies of the court for whose approval they competed in manly sports. Add to this that marriage, in the upper classes, was based entirely on interest, the barons bartering lands for wives, and sealing their alliances with weddings that could be cancelled as easily as they were made when interests changed, and we have a highly inflammatory situation.

The unruly steed of which Plato wrote was running spare. The Church had baptised some of the old pagan festivals but had failed to baptise pagan sexuality and love of freedom. To those it could oppose only an unconstructive negative. There were archetypal forces in human nature that could find no outlet through the mores and religion of the time.

A precedent for the new movement was already in existence. Since Roman times a class of wandering entertainers had travelled from court to court, earning their way by their talents as raconteurs and singers. We have nothing analogous at the present time, unless it be the popular idols who travel the world, serving at the courts of King Demos wherever they are to be found. But these are more stellar than aristocratic. The troubadours, the successors of the old minstrels, now due on the scene, were definitely aristocratic. They included such men as our own Richard Coeur de Lion and Alfonso II, King of Aragon. Most of them were neither as exalted nor as powerful as that but they belonged to the nobility. The movement never recovered from the Albigensian Crusade, launched against the Catharists by Pope Innocent III, in A.D. 1208, in which the nobility of Provence were annihilated. The names of some five hundred troubadours are known, seventeen of them women. Some of their works, in the Langue d'Oc dialect are still extant. Jongleurs attached themselves to the troubadours and popularised their works. These must have been talented men. They had to be skilled enough musicians to play seven or eight instruments well.

Written in highly stylised verse, the appeal of the troubadours' compositions is more that of virtuosity than of poetic inspiration. Some are written in an allegorical mode that has long ceased to be congenial. Yet their influence was far-reaching and has lasted well into modern times. Mediaeval churchmen had little reverence for womanhood. The Blessed Virgin Mary stood surrogate for their mothers and to her they sublimated the regard they owed to them. In any case they had no wives. Many of the troubadours had to do without marriage but to the ladies of their choice they offered an exaggerated reverence. That was the central core of their message.

The troubadours lived by the theory of courtly love, whose pillars were humility, courtesy and the religion of intersexual love. The objective of the love was not marriage because it was always love for another man's wife. But, theoretically and by profession, it was not an adulterous love. The story of Tristan and Isolde in various versions was, for instance, a favourite. This may have been either out of deference to the Church or the result of Catharist connections. The Catharists were rigorously anti-sexual. Where the prohibition of adultery was, in fact, taken seriously it was a reversal of the psychology of the Church. The devotion due to the Blessed Virgin Mary was sublimated to the lover's lady. The probability is that, in most instances, the repudiation of sexuality was fictitious. C. S. Lewis, one of the most brilliant of critics, says bluntly but surely with truth: 'Any idealisation of sexual love in a society where marriage is purely utilitarian, must begin by being an idealisation of adultery'. Since there was no prospect of a satisfactory consummation of the relation, and in the last resort it had always to be furtive and clandestine, there was a miasma of despair hanging about troubadour poetry.

Lewis quotes Chretien de Troyes as describing how, when Lancelot visited Guinevere, he first kneeled at her bedside in adoration of her, and on leaving her he genuflected. The modern reader will find this amusing or nauseating according to taste; but to Chretien it was a proper expression of the right relation between a lover and his lady – adoration before copulation. Will-

subjection was the key to the relation: the lover had to acquiesce abjectly in his lady's wishes.

These affairs were governed by a strict ritual and are not in the least to be confused with a general permissiveness or promiscuity. The lover had to pass through four stages, those of aspirant, suppliant, suitor and accepted lover. The relation was sealed by an oath of allegiance and a ring. When Elizabeth II was crowned the scene in Westminster Abbey was strongly reminiscent of this. The nobility of the realm kneeled before the Queen and vowed:

> I . . . do become your liege man of life and limb, and of earthly worship; and faith and truth I will bear unto you, to live and die, against all manner of folks. So help me God.

Thereafter, the lover had to strive to be in every way worthy of his lady.

C. S. Lewis remarks that the courtly sentiment was an escape, a truancy from vulgar reality and commonsense; but that it was a noble truancy. He points to the continuity with it of the poetry of the later Middle Ages and of the present day. It has, he says, left no corner of our ethics, imagination or daily life untouched and it erected a barrier between ourselves and our classical past and our oriental present.

C. S. Lewis wrote prior to 1936, when the influence of which he speaks was trailing out in the trivialities of Ethel M. Dell and Dornford Yates and the authors of women's magazine serials. Romantic love was bogged down in oleaginous sentimentality. There is little evidence of the tradition in contemporary literature. But the influence on our habits and mores cannot be welcomed without reserve. If it issued in old-fashioned courtesy and gave women the respect that is their due, it also led to that false idealisation of women, and that artificial deference, that Mary Wollstonecraft was later to deprecate so fiercely. Where the romantic tradition was in the ascendancy, womanhood was put on a pedestal. She was too exalted to be allowed to share in the rough and tumble of the world and, in the upper classes, she tended to oscillate between the boudoir and the ballroom. Lower down the social scale she was merely left with the household chores. She received ostentatious deference but little real respect. When, in the emancipation movement, women rebelled against this they encountered obscene ridicule. Whoever is on a pedestal invites the attentions of the cartoonist and the carica-turist. Not even Nelson on his column is safe. While women insist on special privileges they will never attain true equality.

At the close of the period of the troubadours, the theory of courtly love underwent a twofold development. In the work of the great Florentine, Dante Alighieri (1265–1321), love was entirely spiritualised. This was a dead end. When love becomes a purely spiritual relation an ultimate has been reached. No further progress is possible. This is not to say that Dante's work was sterile; nothing could be further from the truth. His wonder-ful use of language and his invention of the *terza rima* poetic form would be enough in themselves to save him from that. But his *Divina Comedia* was the culmination of a phase of European literature rather than the beginning of a new one. His treatment of the love theme derived in part from his personal experience. He had met his Beatrice at the age of nine and they had loved each other; but theirs must have been more than the usual boy and girl friendship because it lasted and deepened until Beatrice died sixteen years later. Afterwards, Dante formed another attachment and married; which he later recognised to be a declension from the ideal and bitterly regretted. Although a real person, in the poem Beatrice is used as an allegorical figure.

To attempt to put into a nutshell Dante's masterpiece would be absurd. Not only is it a highly allegorical work, with more than one level of meaning, its subject matter is no more separable from its structure and presentation than is light from a lamp. The phrase '*Il dolce stil nuovo*' to describe the loveliness of Dante's use of the loveliest of languages; and *terza rima*, have become the nameplates of perfection. The best that can be done is to indicate the lines of his thought.

The key to the whole poem is not provided until the final canto. A modern journalist trying to convey the same message would have put this canto at the beginning. But that would not have

suited Dante's purpose. He builds up his vision of the supernatural realm stage by stage until he reaches the summit of holi-
ness. His way of salvation, which is the theme of the poem, lies
through all the stages of man's descent into evil and his ascent to
the holiest. An architect does not build the topmost pinnacle of
his temple first. Through the *Inferno*, the *Purgatorio* and the
Paradiso, Dante has passed from deepest Hell to highest Heaven.
Now St Bernard is with him, praying to the Virgin that he might
be vouchsafed the ultimate vision:

> Thenceforward, what I saw,
> Was not for words to speak, nor memory's self
> To stand against such outrage on her skill . . .
>
> Here vigour failed the towering fantasy:
> But yet the will rolled onward, like a wheel
> In even motion, by the Love impelled,
> That moves the sun in Heaven and all the stars
>
> (Carey's translation)

Aristotle's 'unmoved mover' is here identified with love and so
the movements of the celestial spheres and the cycle of nature
form a cosmic symphony under the inspiration of love. To do evil
is not so much to breach a moral law as to sin against love itself.

Love does not stand in contrast to reason: the two are in this
context virtually the same. In Canto 5 of the *Inferno* lust is condemned, not because it is a perversion of love or a misdirection
of the natural powers, but because it subjects reason to appetite.
Authentic love does not do that. In this canto, the lustful are con-
signed to the second circle of Hell where they are incessantly
tossed about by gales and hurricanes:

> I learned that to such sorry recompense
> are damned the sinners of the carnal sting,
> who make the reason thrall to appetence.
>
> (tr. by Melville R. Anderson)

We may find it easy enough to understand why Semiramis, Helen

of Troy and Cleopatra should be thought deserving of such a fate:
but surely not poor Francesca and Paolo. Francesca was married
to a nobleman, deformed from birth, whom she did not love. She
was drawn to his younger brother, Paolo, and surrendered herself
to him, which seems a relatively venial offence to incur so dreadful a retribution. The incontinent and those of indeterminate
sexuality had opportunity of renewal in Purgatory.

Until he approached the frontier of Paradise, the poet Virgil
had been Dante's guide. Suddenly he becomes aware of the
presence of the spirit of Beatrice, vested in faith, hope and
charity and crowned with wisdom. He is seized with the same
thrill she had inspired in him in youth:

> there moved
> a hidden virtue from her, at whose touch
> the power of ancient love was strong within me.
>
> (Carey)

But before there can be renewal of their old union at a higher
level, Dante has to repent of his infidelity. Beatrice is unsparing in her reproaches:

> for I showed
> My youthful eyes, and led him by their light
> In upright walking. Soon as I had reached
> The threshold of my second age, and changed
> My mortal for immortal; then he left me
> And gave himself to others. When from flesh
> To spirit I had risen, and increase
> Of beauty and of virtue circled me
> I was less dear to him and valued less.
>
> (Carey)

Cleansed in the waters of Lethe, Dante passes over into Paradise
where he is reunited with Beatrice.

The other strand of the tradition of courtly love went through
Chaucer and Spenser and had a long future ahead of it. Geoffrey
Chaucer (A.D. 1340–1400) carried it forward in his *Troilus and*

Criseyde, in which he retold the sad tale of the famous Trojan pair. A born teller of stories, Chaucer told this one with his tongue in his cheek, for none of the *dramatis personae* had quite the dignity or nobility of character that true courtly love demanded. His poem is not a lampoon but it is not written with deadly seriousness either. Nor is it allegorical; it is pure Chaucer.

We begin with Troilus, son of Priam, King of Troy, love-lorn and moaning for Criseyde, whom he has seen but not met, and who knows nothing of his longing. Because of his good appearance and his prowess on the battlefield, Troilus is a popular hero. He is, in fact, the typical schoolboy captain of games: charming, everybody's favourite, not blessed with a superabundance of brains, and an oaf. Criseyde was, of course, one of the loveliest of Troy's lovelies, widowed and lonely, the daughter of Calchas the seer who, with more self-interest than patriotism, had defected to the Greeks.

Moaning and groaning for the lady he was doing nothing about, Troilus was discovered by his beloved's uncle, Pandarus, who was of a very different type, the wheeler-dealer who can arrange anything. He arranged for Troilus to meet Criseyde and, later, to be secretly in bed with her. Criseyde fell as much in love with Troilus as he was with her and they vowed eternal fidelity.

But the time came when the Greeks, egged on by Calchas, insisted that Criseyde be sent to them in exchange for prisoners of war. Here was heartbreak indeed. The two swore that, whatever came to pass, they would remain faithful to each other. Criseyde promised with tears that she would find the first opportunity of making her way back. In due time the handsome battle-veteran, Diomede, came to fetch her to the Greek camp. At first she sat sullen and disgruntled in her tent; but Diomede was an experienced lady's man. No Troilus to need the intercession of a Pandarus, he conducted the affair himself. It was not long before Criseyde had bestowed upon him all she had sworn to reserve for Troilus alone. In the meanwhile, Troilus was standing day after day on the walls of Troy, vainly awaiting the sight of Criseyde slipping unseen by the Greeks across No-Man's-Land, back to his arms. Instead, while examining a coat plucked from the back of

Diomede in a skirmish, he finds on it – the brooch he had given Criseyde as a pledge of loyalty. The last we see of Criseyde, she is in the arms of Diomede, to go down to history as the prototype of feminine inconstancy and fickleness, the scorn of women. Chaucer ends the story with the pious thought that, if the un- happy couple had only set their minds on higher things, none of this would have happened. So, in his cynical hands, the tradition of courtly love becomes a cautionary tale with a moral.

EDMUND SPENSER: POET OF THE RENAISSANCE

At the Renaissance there was not, in speculative thought, the clean break with the past and the fresh start that we find in art and architecture. The scholars of the period were far too deeply engaged in resurrecting and disseminating the Classics to be creative in their own right. They gloried in the recovery of what had for so many centuries been submerged. But, in doing so, they also restored to life the old *eros* theme and disentangled it from the accretions that had been built around it. The influence of this is unmistakable in the works of the Great Masters, not only in their choice of robes for their models and in their use of land- scape but, also, in their mythological subjects. People learned again, too, to rejoice in nature and its beauty.

One of the profoundest consequences was a new respect for the individual. In Italy, where it all began, the change this brought about in the social mores was quite startling. Hierarchy and status lost much of their importance: personal worth and achievement replaced them as criteria. There were people of the highest distinction, enjoying public adulation and reverence, who had the support neither of ecclesiastical background nor of noble birth. This was the period of the great *condottieri*, soldiers of fortune who had often risen from the lowliest social origins by their cleverness to the command of their own, independent, armies. Some of them learned with their success to achieve a new greatness as patrons of culture while a few even carved out little principalities for them- selves and became enlightened rulers. It was the period of dis- tinguished families, of which the Sforzas and Medicis are the most obviously famous, who, whatever their vices and their crimes, won their renown principally by their encouragement of the arts. The ideal was the well-rounded, cultivated gentleman who was what he was by his own right and not by right of descent or by the favour of the Church. They could use their minds freely and independently.

Women achieved a new independence and dignity. Those of well-to-do family had their schooling with the boys of the family, from the same tutors, and in the same subjects. When they grew up, they would often form their own literary circles and their own salons. Among the upper classes, marriage was an equal partnership and a cultivated man looked to his wife for companionship on his own level.

This period saw the rise of a new type of business man, more in the style of the modern entrepreneur, who approached his affairs more systematically and scientifically than his predecessors had done. The invention of accountancy and statistics belongs to the Renaissance and with it we have the beginnings of modern methods of administration. The rulers of the cities could now know what was happening within their domains.

Seldom, if ever, in world history has there been such an astonishing outburst of creative and civilising activity. Perhaps it was too explosive to last. However that may be, the creative energy drained away with the spread of the Reformation and the answering Counter-Reformation. New preoccupations dominated Italy and Europe.

We see the Renaissance yeast strongly at work in Shakespeare, with his evident admiration for self-reliant and high-spirited women and his uninhibited attitude to sexuality. But I take as typical Edmund Spenser (A.D. 1552–99), who was more explicit on the points at issue. His poetry is a natural development of the theme of courtly love but his thought is undoubtedly that of the Renaissance.

The setting of his masterpiece is the Land of Faerie and the climate is preternatural, a permanent English June. On first acquaintance, the *Faerie Queen* is a much convoluted narrative of the adventures of knights and their ladies with wicked witches and dreadful dragons and all the other denizens of a child's imagination. When the pink and white ladies with their gorgeous tresses are good they are very, very good but when they are bad they are awful. The knights in their shining armour are either the exemplars of chivalry, *sans peur et sans reproche*, or are vile villains with no redeeming feature. Were it not for the splendour of the language, and the almost psychedelic quality of the description we might easily dismiss all this as naivete. But the poem is allegorical. These knights and their ladies, and the foul friends and monsters they encounter, are personifications of the deeper forces of the human psyche and of the cosmos, or are representations of high ethical principles or their opposites. C. S. Lewis says that, in this poem, we are dealing with the stuff and substance of life. This becomes clearer the deeper we search into it. We need a Lewis to introduce us to the multitudinous personifications and to guide us through the labyrinthine imagery. Otherwise, in these prosaic times, we might be baffled.

For present purposes the important parts are Books 3 and 4, which deal ostensibly with chastity and friendship but at a deeper level with the nature and ideal of interpersonal relations. To begin with, Spenser holds womanhood in high esteem and wants women to be thought the equals of men. Only the envy of men has deprived them of the honour that is rightly theirs and held them in subjection:

> But by record of antique times I finde
> That women wont in warres to bear most sway,
> And to all great exploites them selves inclind,
> Of which they still the girlond bore away;
> Till envious Men, fearing their rules decay,
> Gan coyne streight lawes to curb their liberty;
> Yet sith they warlike armes have laid away,
> They have exceld in artes and policy,
> That now we foolish men that prayse gin eke envy.

Spenser anticipated by three centuries the women's emancipation movement.

Britomart was Spenser's own heroine in this respect. Until she

unfastened her armour to let her tresses fall in uncontrolled
splendour over her shoulders she was unrecognisable as a woman.
There was quite a scene when the Lady of Delight, mistress of the
Castle Joyous, fell in lust with her and went so far as to slip into
bed with her, unaware of her true sex. The smart evasive action
Britomart took was such as to bring the castle guards running.
Britomart personified marriage. In a magic mirror she had seen
the image of a knight whom she instantaneously loved, without
having met him face to face. At once, she took a suit of armour
from her father's collection and rode forth with her elderly hand-
maid, disguised as her squire, to search the Land of Faerie for her
beloved. During her wanderings she performed valorous deeds
and maintained impregnable chastity. Her magic spear, that
nobody could withstand, might be thought to have given her an
unfair advantage; but chastity had its own proper authority,
which this spear symbolised.

Not the least of Britomart's mighty acts was the rescue of the
fair Amoret from the dungeon of a magician who had used every
available blandishment, spell and torture to seduce her, but in
vain. Through it all, Amoret remained true to her husband.

Spenser believed in marriage as the appropriate consummation
of the love relation between a man and a woman. A Protestant
Christian by personal conviction, he had no word to say in praise
of renunciation or of perpetual virginity. He had none of that
distrust of sexuality, and certainly none of the fear of it, that we
have noted in so many previous writers. But sexuality was to go
with chastity and fidelity. Under these conditions, sexual passion
was to be welcomed. So far was it from suspending the operation
of reason that it exercised a purgative effect on the emotions and
released the reason and the energies for noble purposes; for that
service to the will of God which is the life of reason itself. Amid
the oceans of prejudice that have drenched the subject, this
thought stands out like a lighthouse:

> Most sacred fyre that burnest mightily
> In living brests, ykindled first above
> Emongst th'eternal spheres and lamping sky,

And thence poured into men, which men call love!
Not that same, which doth base affections move
In brutish mindes, and filthy lust inflame,
But that sweet fit that doth true beautie love,
And choseth vertue for his dearest Dame,
Whence spring all noble deedes and never dying fame:

Well did Antiquity a God thee deeme,
That over mortall mindes hast so great might,
To order them as best to thee doth seeme,
And all their actions to direct aright:
The fatall purpose of divine foresight
Thou doest effect in destined descents,
Through deepe impression of thy secret might,
And stirredst up th'heroes high intents,
Which the late world admyres for wondrous moniments.

Neither philosopher nor theologian since Plotinus could have
written in that vein. Love is God-given and is the inspiration of
greatness. And Spenser is not referring to love for the divine
but to intersexual love. It is also remarkable that love is here conceived of as an independent influence that takes possession of the
lover. It is 'ykindled first above emongst th'eternal spheres and
thence poured into men'. Even so, love can be perverse:

Wonder it is to see in diverse mindes
How diversely love doth his pageaunts play,
And shewes his powre in variable kindes:
The baser with whose ydle thoughts alway
Are wont to cleave unto the lowly clay,
It stirreth up to sensuall desire,
And in lewd slouth to wast his careless day;
But in brave sprite it kindles goodly fire,
That to all high desert and honour doth aspire.

Within these provisos, Spenser is in no doubt about the reasons
why sexuality was ordained. It was not primarily for procreation;
but for enjoyment and happiness. Spenser delightfully describes
the Garden of Adonis, where springtime and harvest continually

reign, for both meet together at the same time. There Venus has a private bower to which she repairs for relaxation; her *lieblings-platz*. That Spenser approves of the garden is evident from the fact that everything in it is natural. Lewis observes that in this poem the environment of vice is always artificial, but this arbour was:

> not by art
> But of the trees own inclination made,

and so is the rest of the garden. This is Spenser's earthly paradise:

> But were it not that Time their troubler is,
> All that in this delightfull Gardin growes
> Should happy bee, and have immortall bliss:
> For her all pleasure and all plenty flowes;
> And sweet love gentle fitts emongst them throwes,
> Without fell rancor or fond jealousy.
> Franckly each Paramor his leman knowes,
> Each bird his mate; ne any does envy
> Their goodly meriment and gay felicity.

Jealousy, that 'hateful, hellish Snake', is the enemy of love:

> Fowle Gealousy! that turnest love divine
> To joyless dread, and makst the loving hart
> With hatefull thoughts to languish and to pine,
> And feed it selfe with selfe-consuming smart?
> Of all the passions in the mind thou vilest art.

For Spenser, then, sexual passion is to be accepted and affirmed; its rites celebrated with glad abandon. But it must be a sexuality grounded in integrity and qualified by love. Otherwise, sexuality becomes undirected lust, perpetually longing and for-ever unfulfilled, all spontaneity gone. It is a definition of Hell that would have satisfied Dante himself. Spenser's description of the Castle Joyous, which is virtually a temple of voyeurism, is not unamusing. No action is possible because everybody is all the time jealously scrutinising everybody else. This is reminiscent of those night-clubs where guests, members and staff are alike so conscious of sex that the actual behaviour is impeccable.

After Book 3, the Fourth Book, with friendship for its theme, comes as something of a disappointment. True, it contains excellent narrative and fine lyrical passages; but it adds little to our insight into the subject. Spenser, indeed, appears to be more interested in the influences making for the disruption of friendship than in studying its nature. His description of Ate, the witch of discord, is surely a classic:

> Her face most fowle and filthy was to see,
> With squinted eyes contrarie ways intended,
> And loathly mouth, unmeete a mouth to bee,
> That nought but gall and venim comprehended,
> And wicked words that God and man offended,
> Her lying tongue was in two parts divided,
> And both the parts did speak and both contended;
> And as her tongue so was her hart discided,
> That never thoght one thing, but doubly still was guided.
>
> Als as she double spoke, so heard she double,
> With matchless ears deformed and distort,
> Fild with false rumours and seditious trouble,
> Bred in assembles of the vulgar sort,
> That still are led with every light report:
> And as her eares, so eke her feet were odde,
> And much unlike; th'one long, the other short,
> And both misplast; that, when th'one forward yode,
> The other backe retired and contrarie trode.

A charming creature! Unfortunately, we can often discern her lineaments.

These, then, are the thoughts of a literary man of insight, who was also a close observer of human affairs, and who lived during the reign of the first Elizabeth. Since the time of the troubadours, with their self-abasement before womanhood, and the Scholastics, with their sour attitude to sexuality, a revolution has occurred. Abelard and Heloise have at last come into their own. Dante stands in solitary magnificence in the distance. A gleam of spring sunshine has broken upon a wintry world and the climate has become more wholesome. Here we have a statement of the ideal of the man-woman relation that may need elaboration and development but which cannot be set aside. For centuries after Spenser little of importance was added to what he wrote on this subject; but his insights were developed in practice and this or that element emphasised as outlooks changed for better or for worse. During the nineteenth and twentieth centuries, existentialists and psychologists have brought to bear new ways of thinking and new approaches: but they have not discredited Spenser.

Chapter Seven

Post-Reformation

LUTHER AND CALVIN

In 1517, Martin Luther (1483–1546) took the first initiatives in ridding the Church of the evil legacies of mediaevalism. Every schoolboy knows into what a state of degeneracy and corruption ecclesiastical institutions had fallen. It was through these grimy windows that Luther saw the great thinkers of the mediaeval tradition and his vision was distorted. Anglican and other Protestant theologians who have recently been in dialogue with Roman Catholic leaders for oecumenical purposes have not found the differences between them to be as clear-cut and insurmountable as their predecessors of a century and more ago. Luther saw them in the harshest possible light and turned from Rome with abhorrence. The situation needed an explosive personality to blow away the accumulations of cobwebs.

Whatever savoured of Platonism had to go. Luther would not hear of the upward movement of caritas to God. There was no upward movement from the human condition. Man's salvation began and was completed by the divine condescension as manifested on Calvary. Man was justified before God by his faith alone, which was his response to the grace of God. His depravity was total: he could not by his own efforts gain merit or make any progress in the way of salvation. This faith was not formed, or qualified, in any way by love, as the Scholastics had said; it was faith alone that was of importance for salvation. The Christian's love for his neighbour was the Christian becoming a channel for the generous outpouring of the divine love. This left no room for self-love, which Luther equated with the grossest selfishness. The great commandment he interpreted to mean that we should take our self-love when in the state of sin as the pattern of our love for neighbour, which was to recognise no difference between one person and another.

Although Luther was never able to divest himself of the shame associated with sexuality, he handled the subject with a compassionate realism that, in some respects, went far beyond what Christians of his own, or any other, period could tolerate. Since the Fall sexual desire had been irresistible by any except a few people. Celibacy was therefore to be rejected. Marriage was not in any respect an inferior way of life to that of the celibate. It was the divinely ordained means of directing and controlling desires that would otherwise defeat even the finest of Christians. But he would not have marriage hedged about by masses of pettifogging regulations. He took his stand on Christian liberty and referred contemptuously to the Romanists with their 'misleading and vexatious canons and decretals, together with all the crawling maggots of man-made laws and regulations, which by now have eaten into the entire world'. He spoke of the blundering inhumanity of the penance imposed for incest, that the penitent must sleep with his wife without having intercourse with her; as if anything could be better calculated to drive a man into further sin.

If a woman's husband were impotent, and if it would be embarrassing to seek a nullity decree, he advised that the woman, preferably with her husband's consent, should take his brother or some other close friend as a lover. If a man's wife were frigid, then let the maid take her place with him. Luther hated the thought of having people humiliated by dragging their intimate affairs through the courts. Since the Scriptures nowhere forbade polygamy, which was practised by the Patriarchs, he saw no reason for forbidding it either, in extreme cases. He recommended Henry VIII to extract himself from his divorce entanglements with Katherine of Aragon by marrying Anne Boleyn bigamously and he advised a similar course for the Landgrave Phillip of Hesse, whose wife was unattractive and frigid. While subscribing to the ideal of lifelong partnership in marriage, and while reluctant to sanction divorce, except in the case of adultery, he thought that a long period of desertion should also be ground for divorce. Since marriage was ordained for the control of desire, similar reasoning applied also to remarriage after divorce, which he recommended. Taken together, these recommendations constitute a powerful plea for realism in providing for sexuality, one of the most powerful and uncontrollable of human urges. He was also anxious to safeguard the individual from emotional cruelty and actual hardship. It must be admitted that circumstances can be visualised in which Luther's solutions to marriage problems would cause less suffering and less breach of the conventions than those that have since been found in most Western countries. In Moslem countries they are practised with success. He did acknowledge that there were advantages in celibacy for the few who were suitable for that state.

John Calvin (1509–64) was the systematiser of Protestantism. In general, he agrees with Luther; but his emphasis on the arbitrary sovereignty of God and on the doctrines of predestination and human depravity are such as to deprive his religion of all its graciousness. His *Institutes of the Christian Religion* comprises some 700,000 words. The word 'love' appears only twice and the word 'charity' only seven times. What are we to think of a man who is capable of writing of newborn babies before baptism: 'Nay, their whole nature is, as it were, a seed of sin, and, therefore, cannot but be odious and abominable to God,' (*Inst.* IV, Chap. 15, Para. 10), and who elsewhere describes with relish how God occasionally allows those predestined to damnation to feel as if they are among the saved, just so that they shall realise what they are missing when they are thrust back into despair! What odious mind could write this: 'Let it stand, therefore, as an indubitable truth, which no engines can shake, that the mind of man is so entirely alienated from the righteousness of God that he cannot conceive, desire or design anything but what is wicked, distorted, foul, impure and iniquitous; that his heart is so thoroughly envenomed by sin, that it can breathe out nothing but corruption and rottenness; that if some men occasionally make a show of goodness, their mind is ever interwoven with hypocrisy and deceit, their souls inwardly bound with the fetters of wickedness.' (*Inst.*, II, Chap. 5, Para. 19).

It would be impossible to take this monstrous stuff seriously were it not that, historically, it became a desperately serious matter. Such an outlook, such manifest hatred of the human race, led necessarily to ethical legalism, to the dogmatism of prudery, to the extent that, in practice, Calvinism was a hard, bitter and loveless moralism that cast a blight over society wherever it touched.

But Calvin reacted against mediaevalism in much the same way as Luther and, in general, his views on marriage are the same. Virginity is to be admired only in the few who have a special gift for it. Clerical celibacy is a grave evil imposed by a tyrannical Pope. There is scarcely a convent anywhere, writes Calvin, that is not to all intents and purposes a brothel. By far the majority of men have a clear duty to marry, not only for the sake of companionship, which is rated as a highly important aspect of marriage, but also as a means of controlling sexual lust, which would otherwise wreak havoc. Any union outside marriage is an abomination and accursed in the sight of God. Men have also to beware of exploiting their wives sexually, for this is no different in essence from fornication itself. Marriage is intended to be life-long but Calvin sanctions divorce on the same ground as Luther.

For a Reformation valuation of womanhood we may turn to Richard Hooker (1554–1600) founder theologian of the Church of England:

> And for this cause they (brides) were in marriage delivered unto their husbands by others. Which custom retained hath still this use, that it putteth women in mind of a duty whereunto the very imbecility of their nature and sex doth bind them, namely to be always directed, guided and ordered by others.

Which sentiment can hardly have ingratiated the judicious Hooker with his gracious Queen, Elizabeth I.

THE FEMININE RÔLE

At least the Reformers sloughed off the old valuation of womanhood as merely imperfect man and the source of concupiscence and sensuality and all the sins of the flesh. At least they accepted sexuality, even if only as a regrettable inevitability. Marriage ceased to be the last resort of the incontinent. These were considerable improvements. But the tendency in Protestant households, especially the more Puritan of them, was for the father to be undisputed master and his wife and daughters to be meek and submissive. No doubt, many Puritan families had dignity, gentleness and courtesy, but they were firmly patriarchal. The vocation of the wife was to be the bearer of children and her husband's helpmeet. The notion of her having a life of her own would never have occurred to them. A woman's sexual errantry brought upon her the vilest public obloquy and social ostracism. It was one of the most vicious by-products of the system that, when a woman most needed friendship and help, she was thus driven out. Two lives, that of the mother and the blameless child, had to be sacrificed to atone for the sin. Nobody was so unrighteous as to spare a kindly thought.

Not even Cranmer, who was no Puritan, could rise much above this. In the 1552 Prayer Book the causes for which matrimony was ordained are said to be three:

> One was the procreacion of children, to be broughte up in the feare and nurtoure of the Lorde, and prayse of God. Secondlye it was ordeined for a remedye agaynste synne, and to avoide fornicacion, that suche persons as have not the gyfte of continencie myght marye, and kepe themselves undefiled members of Christes body. Thirdly, for the mutuall societie, helpe and coumforte, that the one ought to have of the other, both in prosperitie and adversitie.

At the most tenderly serious moment of their lives the young couple were to be solemnly informed before the public that their marriage was licensed copulation! This reduced sexuality to the farmyard level and the bed to a breeding pen. By the time this came up for revision in 1927 the climate had changed. At least the statement was put positively instead of negatively. The second reason for marriage then became: 'That the natural instincts implanted by God should be hallowed and directed aright; that those who are called of God to this holy estate should continue therein in pureness of living'.

In law, the wife was virtually the slave of her husband. The fact that he might be an enlightened, kindly and indulgent master did not alter that fact. The laws of the Hebrews and, indeed, of the later Roman Empire, had given more freedom and protection to a slave than the laws of England until recently gave to a wife. Throughout Europe, under the Mediaeval system, Canon Law had permitted a husband to whip his wife. In England wife-beating remained lawful until 1817 and did not become a ground for divorce until 1937. If a Roman patrician maltreated his slaves he could be compelled to part with them.

Both the money and the children of the wife belonged to her husband, who could deprive her of them at will. Even if a husband deserted his wife to live with another woman he could still claim the money his wife had earned for her own support. This occurred in the case of Caroline Norton, whose husband claimed her literary earnings while he was actually in a state of desertion and living with another woman. In the case of inheritance the law could be circumvented by the terms of the settlement but earnings did not come into that category. This position was rectified by the Married Woman's Property Act of 1882. Legislation passed in 1839 and 1886 sorted out the situation as regards the custody of children. Until 1857 divorce was virtually impossible, except by special Act of Parliament, but in that year the civil courts were empowered to grant a divorce to a husband on the ground of his wife's adultery. In 1923 the positions were equalised and the wife could then divorce her husband on similar grounds. It is only in 1970 that the obnoxious doctrine of the matrimonial offence and the guilty party have given way to the doctrine of irretrievable breakdown as the sole ground for divorce. Not until well into the twentieth century was the age of consent raised for girls from twelve to sixteen.

From all this it is clear that, to all intents and purposes, a woman was chained to her husband without hope of escape. She might be refined and gentle while he was brutish and perverted; but that made no difference. At the wedding service the bride was asked whether she freely consented to the marriage but she might be so young, and her parents so ill-conditioned, that the formula was meaningless. It is true that in any partnership the stronger and more intelligent character will take the lead; but it is also true that the weakest and most stupid person with a gun can always dominate the unarmed. Anybody can pull a trigger. The law put a gun into the hands of the husband while stripping the wife of all protection. It would usually be the weak, the brutish and the sadistic who would use this power given to them. There are far too many men who are psychologically disqualified from holding absolute power over another human being. Under the smooth externals there seethed an ocean of suffering and outrage. The Victorian home was in almost every respect a deplorable institution. It was an offence against the dignity of womanhood that the possibility of outrage should be legalised.

It was made the more galling by the wide prevalence of the double standard of morality. The husband could let his affections rove but the wife must remain like Cato's. The classic instance was that of Edward VII, who enjoyed a succession of love affairs while still maintaining an affectionate relation with his consort. His paramours were accepted in society without a murmur, which was natural when the King was the lover. But Alexandra, tolerant woman though she must have been, would never have dared to carry her relation with the man she loved to its consummation. There was one ethic for men and another for women.

These standards rested on two props, one material and the other mythical. In any society where the inheritance of property through the male line is an important element the chastity of women is likely to be safeguarded. There must be no doubt as to who is the father of a woman's child; but male escapades can be tolerated because they have no significance for inheritance. Also, there is the myth, convenient for the male, that the sexual desires of the female are less urgent and less easily aroused than those of the male and that, while the male displays masculinity by the multiplicity of his seductions, the female shows either wilfulness or frailty by permitting herself to be seduced. The notion that the woman might be the seducer was not contemplated. This is a curious reversal of the older belief that women are the source of all sensuality.

So far as it is possible to ascertain, the truth coincides with neither of these strange beliefs. On the evidence, just as men's natures range all the way from the Don Juan, through the natural celibate, to the effeminate homosexual, so women's natures range all the way from the nymphomaniac, through the natural spinster, to the active lesbian. The distribution appears to be fairly even.

Biology supports this view. In cellular structure nobody is either 100 per cent male or 100 per cent female. In recent years we have had athletes disqualified from entering competitions because, while anatomically they appeared to be female, on medical examination they turned out to be predominantly male. The statement that physical differences must have psychological consequences turns out to have relatively little significance. Since we cannot easily identify the physical differences, which vary from person to person, we cannot know what psychological consequences to expect. Generalisation becomes impossible. The fact that medical science and social custom are now diminishing the importance of the biological rhythms associated with childbearing reinforces this impossibility.

Although the differences between the sexes are often noticeable from the first hours after birth, psychological characteristics and behaviour are culturally elaborated. Sometimes the genetic drops are lost in the cultural flood. People tend to become what society expects them to be, conforming to the mores of their group. In Victorian times women were expected to be submissive, passive, meek, unintellectual and sexless. Except for the strong and high-spirited they tended to become so. As expectations change we are seeing a change in attitudes and behaviour patterns. These myths, then, that all women want to be dominated and all men to dominate, and that men are naturally polygamous while women are naturally monogamous, should be recognised for the nonsense they are. There is no foundation here for a double standard of morality. If men want sexual freedom for themselves, and claim the right to exploit the freedom of other women, they cannot reasonably refuse the same freedom to their wives.

These reflections are relevant to the question of women's vocational and political rights. The rise of women's liberation movements are a reminder how recently it is that careers have been open to women. Despite the succession of writers and scholars who, against serious discouragement, had demonstrated the intellectual abilities of women, and despite the ability they had displayed as monarchs of European countries, their sex was until about a century ago banned from all occupations except those such as teaching, nursing and domestic service or unskilled factory work, and was refused even the minimal political power conveyed by a vote in general and muncipal elections.

If women obtained an education it was because they were exceptional and seized it for themselves. For the most part, the girls' schools were derisory, concerned more with preparing their pupils for the social round than with serious academic work or training. Education for girls of the lower social orders was non-existent. Then, in 1849, Bedford College was founded and, in 1870, the Education Act made the minimal primary education of the Board Schools compulsory for both boys and girls. In 1878 London University admitted women to degrees and, subsequently, women's colleges were built at Oxford and Cambridge. In 1876 an enabling Act empowered universities to confer on women degrees in Medicine. In 1919 women were admitted to the legal and accountancy professions. Since then, women have made their way in nearly all phases of national life and, despite the tendency to abandon their careers after marriage, a few have reached the highest eminence. We would hardly expect to find them in the ranks of heavyweight boxers or weightlifters. They are still excluded from the ministeries of the Roman and Anglican Communions. It is acknowledged that there is no theological objection to their ordination and the ban is due solely to discreditable prejudice.

The movement that brought these successes culminated in the campaign for the vote. The Suffragettes, led by Mrs Millicent Fawcett, argued with pen and speech. The contempt shown for them by the reigning politicians taught the evil lesson that, if an unpopular cause wishes to make itself effective, it must resort to more forceful weapons than those of reason. Under the Pankhursts, mother and daughter, the Suffragists, a splinter movement, acted on this lesson with consequences that are well-known. Even the wisest and kindliest of statesmen showed that they could, when their prejudices were aroused, behave with stupidity and brutality. The lesser sort greeted the activities of the Suffragists with facetious obscenities. But the Suffragists won their case in spite of it. Following the vigorous participation of women in war work, in 1918 the Representation of the People Act gave the vote to women over thirty years of age. In 1928 it was extended to women over twenty-one and political equality was officially complete.

MARY WOLLSTONECRAFT

First of the feminist pioneers to demand full equality with men and parity of education was Mary Wollstonecraft (1759–97). A woman of exceptional, if inadequately trained, intellect her convictions were the flower of close observation and harsh experience. Her father was a drunkard who squandered his substance and terrified his family. As a girl, Mary had often to protect her mother from him. When she grew up she became a governess in private households, in those days the last resort of impecunious gentlewomen. In that capacity she could see the realities of married life at close quarters in the middle and upper classes. At one time she had a school of her own.

After suffering unrequited love for the painter, Fuseli, she went to Paris and there fell in love again, this time with an American, Gilbert Imlay. She lived with him unmarried and they had a child, Fanny, but after two and a half years he left her for another paramour. Twice Mary tried to commit suicide but eventually found happiness with the Radical writer, William Godwin. For the sake of the child with which she was pregnant the two married but she survived the birth of her second child by only a fortnight. The child became the Mary Godwin who married the poet, Shelley.

Mary Wollstonecraft's major work, *A Vindication of the Rights of Women*, is a torrent of impassioned argument, unsystematic and repetitive, which carries the reader along by the sheer force of its contempt and its invective. But her case is unanswerable. She derides the contemporary education of girls that turns them into servile dolls, fit only to be the playthings of lecherous men who, while outwardly setting them on a pedestal, inwardly scorn them.

Their conduct and their manners prove women to be in an unhealthy state for, like hothouse flowers, they are brought up only to please, and not to inspire respect. Their educators consider them:

> more as women than human creatures, have been more anxious to make them alluring mistresses than affectionate wives and rational mothers; and the understanding of the sex has been so bubbled by this specious homage, that the civilised women of the present century, with few exceptions, are only anxious to inspire love, when they ought to cherish a nobler ambition, and by their abilities and virtues exact respect.

This evil begins with the rich. Raised above ordinary wants, weak and artificial, their way of life undermines the foundations of virtue and spreads corruption through the whole of society. Their women are trained to be vain and helpless, living only to amuse themselves. Their education has tended to turn them into insignificant objects of desire. Always they have to accept the principles of living from others. But truth must be common to all, otherwise it will be inefficacious in general practice. The prevalence of chastity is necessary for the improvement of body and mind; but men will never be chaste while women are admired only for meretricious qualities. Who made men the exclusive judges of what women should be? The duties and morals of women must be comprehended by their reason, as with men, if they are properly to fulfil them.

Every profession in which there is great subordination of rank is injurious to morality, for the will and understanding of the individual are eradicated and the will of another is substituted for them. The author writes with searing derision of the military officers of her time, pursuing the trivialities of the social round, to show how servility and uselessness combine to enervate the character and to debase the virtues.

Mankind's pre-eminence in nature consists in the possession and the use of reason. But, among the human species, it is virtue that exalts one being over another. Now nobody is truly virtuous whose virtue does not arise out of his own understanding. The virtue that arises out of a facile conformity with convention is ethically worthless. Still more is it worthless when it is the consequence of the suppression by others of independent thought.

Women's understanding is subordinated to the acquisition of socially pleasing accomplishments. Yet the gifts of women must be the same in quality, even if not in degree, as those of men. Therefore, unless there are to be two types of virtue, the same treatment is required for each. The basic issue here is that of education. The most perfect education is that which is, 'best calculated to strengthen the body and form the heart. Or, in other words, to enable the individual to attain such habits of virtue as will render it independent'.

While it is true that, in physical constitution, men are stronger than women, and it is foolish for women to compete with them in physical prowess, that is no reason why it should be considered unwomanly to exercise and strengthen the body, and feminine to be weakly and always subject to the vapours. The education of women should be directed to healthy physical development as well as to the training of the understanding. Boys and girls should be educated together, without segregation. Mary Wollstonecraft would, in fact, have fully approved of the kind of education that is given in good mixed schools at the present time.

Contemporary women's education, she writes, is destructive of marriage. Brought up solely to please, a wife soon discovers that her meretricious charms cease to impress her husband, who begins to look elsewhere for novelty and excitement. Finding herself neglected, she has no inclination to cultivate her inner resources, but she begins soon to look elsewhere for new objects on which she can exercise her charm. By a strange injustice, while the husband's womanising is considered to be a sign of masculinity, the woman's sexual irregularities have to be clandestine. The seducer continues to enjoy the respect of society; the woman who carries in her arms the evidence of her seduction is condemned and an outcast. Hence the abhorrent evil of prostitution.

Yet women exercise a certain power over men. They are taught to command by servility and to secure themselves by cunning. In that they enjoy privilege without having earned it they resemble the rich and therefore do not develop the virtues. They are brought up as are tyrants, to have everything done for them and to expect as a right the outward show of respect from others. How, then, shall they use the power conferred upon them except in a tyrannical fashion?

Women's education is just as destructive of motherhood. Trifling employments render them triflers. They cannot govern children because they have never learned how to govern themselves. Parentage confers obligations without rights; but women expect rights without obligations. Parents should not be honoured unless they are worthy of honour.

But the fact of their subjugation does not by any means imply the inferiority of women. Men have not only endured subjugation but have often willingly submitted to it for the sake of some advantage to themselves. They have submitted with servility to kings and tyrants. That is the way of royal courts everywhere. In that respect there is no difference between men and women.

All the circumstances of womanhood render women incapable of satisfactory personal relations. Mary Wollstonecraft draws a curious distinction between love and friendship, the one excluding the possibility of the other:

Friendship is a serious affection; the most sublime of all affections. In a great degree, love and friendship cannot subsist in the same bosom; even when inspired by different objects they weaken or destroy each other, and for the same object can only be felt in succession. The vain fears and fond jealousies, the winds which fan the flame of love, when judiciously or artfully tempered, are both incompatible with the tender confidence and sincere respect of friendship.

It is plain that the author is here referring to the most senti-mental type of romantic love. The ideal love depicted by literary genius, she writes, if it exists at all does so only in the most exalted personalities. In reality, the pretence of the ideal is no more than a veil for sensuality.

Marriage should be founded upon friendship and esteem. Love in a man seeks pleasure in the wife and, in doing so, reduces her to licentiousness. The man is virtually seducing his own wife. This ministers to her own vanity and pleasure. Yet there is no real respect on either side because in all the other concerns of marriage the man expects obedience and servility from his wife. This is no basis for a permanently satisfying relation. True fulfil-ment comes of the mutuality, the commonalty of interests and of understanding, that is the basis of friendship.

When Mary Wollstonecraft wrote this she had not yet experi-enced her own unions with men. Perhaps she would have modi-fied her views had she been able to write from the standpoint of the serene happiness she seems to have enjoyed with Godwin. Through all this work there runs a thread of contempt for men that, in a measure, distorts her otherwise remarkable realism and independence of mind. Yet both men and women are what they are, on her own showing, because the condition of one half of the human race frustrates the potentialities of the other half. No generation could be better qualified than our own to appreciate the futility of a love that is identified with sexuality and to accept friendship, as she conceives it, as a more substantial basis for marriage. Love that depends upon the chemistry of the body, a merely glandular love, quickly evaporates, often leaving coldness or hatred behind. It is one of the dirtier tricks of nature that feeling such as this often deceives people into imagining them-selves to be possessed by the grand passion. Yet we cannot for that reason dismiss the ideal as a worthless fiction.

JOHN STUART MILL

Brought up from early babyhood by his father, James Mill, philosopher and economist, to be a scholar, John Stuart Mill (1806–73) became one of his century's most creative and most forward-looking students of human society. He had his own personal tragedy since, on the death of her husband, he married Helen Taylor, with whom he had been in love for twenty years. But his supremely happy married life with her ended at her death only seven years afterwards.

Mill was much less the impassioned crusader, much more the intellectual, than Mary Wollstonecraft, although he firmly supported the cause of women's emancipation throughout his life. In 1859 he published *On the Subjection of Women*, which was a reasoned attack on the condition of women in his time, which had improved a little, but only a little, since Mary Wollstonecraft's day. He attacks along the whole front and wrings the last drop of value from every argument.

Mill's thought pivots on a paragraph that comes near the end of his book:

> What marriage may be in the case of two persons of cultivated faculties, identical in opinions and purpose, between whom there exists that best kind of equality, similarity of powers and capacities with reciprocal superiority in them – so that each can enjoy the luxury of looking up to the other, and can have alternately the pleasure of leading and being led in the path of development – I will not attempt to describe. To those who can conceive it there is no need; to those who cannot, it would appear the dream of an enthusiast. But, I maintain with the proudest conviction, that this, and this only, is the ideal of marriage; and that all opinions, customs and institutions which favour any other notion of it, or turn the conceptions and aspirations connected with it into any other direction, by whatever pretences they may be coloured, are relics of primitive barbarism. The moral regeneration of mankind will only really commence, when the most fundamental of the social relations is placed under the rule of equal justice, and when human beings learn to cultivate their strongest sympathy with an equal in rights and in cultivation.

Apart from the phrase relating to the moral regeneration of mankind, of which as yet we see little sign, the rest of this statement
is so unexceptionable that nowadays only barbarians and reac-
tionaries would dispute it. Yet the arguments leading up to it will
still bear recapitulation. Mill starts from the position that the
subordination of women to men is not only wrong in itself but
also is one of the chief hindrances to human improvement. It
should be replaced with perfect equality, allowing neither
privileges on the one side nor disabilities on the other.

It is difficult to cope with the objection to this, says Mill,
because it arises out of feeling and out of ancient prejudice and is
therefore not amenable to reason. The only way round is to show
that the ancient traditions came into existence for reasons other
than their soundness. In fact, the old customs rested upon theory
only, because throughout history there has never been any
experience of any other system. From the origins of human society
muscular strength has given men the predominance. The subordination of women rested on the law of the stronger, which has
now been abandoned in civilised states; but the subordination of
women has persisted into a period that would never have permitted its establishment in the first instance.

To loosen the grip of this custom is particularly difficult because personal interest in the tyranny over women is not, like
other tyrannies, confined to a few rulers, but extends to all
males. By reason of the constitution of home and family these
have far better facilities for preventing uprisings than any other
holders of arbitrary power. They claim that this dominance is
natural; but does not unjust power always seem natural to those
who hold it?

Men want not only the obedience of women but their sentiment as well. They want willing obedience; and so they turn all
the influence of education into conditioning women to believe
themselves exactly the opposite of men. Since they are to be
entirely dependent, to be attractive is the main object of their
lives.

Vocation is no longer decided by birth or by law but by
individual preference and natural bent. Why should this principle

be abandoned where women are concerned? All careers and positions, except that of Royalty, are open to all males: why should the accident of birth exclude women? It is useless to say that women are unfitted for vocations that are now exclusively male. Nobody knows whether they are unfitted or not. They have never had a chance of displaying their qualities. Character is at least as much culturally as genetically determined and, if women were brought up differently in a society differently constituted, they would be different in themselves. If they did turn out to be unsuitable for certain professions they would soon drop out, just as incompetent men do, and no harm would be done. Let women find their own level by experiment.

It is odd that the one vocation from which they are the most rigorously excluded, namely politics, is the one in which they have shown the highest capacity. England has had two ruling queens, one of whom displayed a statesmanship far surpassing that of most of the male monarchs of her age. In other countries, notably Russia under Catherine the Great, women have shown fine capacity for government. In India, which Mill knew well from having served under the old East India Company, women who have never spoken to any men except for their husbands and close relatives, unless from behind a curtain, often act as regents for princely sons who are too enervated by vice to exercise their authority. They do so with wisdom and justice.

Men claim that women's nature is to live domestically; but they behave toward them as if they will do so only under compulsion. They fear that if women are free and equal they will demand better conditions of marriage. Any savage can acquire power over a wife; but the well-known maxims regarding men's unfitness to hold power apply just as much in marriage as elsewhere. A refined woman may find herself at the mercy of a brutal man without escape or redress. Her only protection is that of the scold or the shrew; but this avails her only against the gentler and least tyrannical of men. It is said that one of the partners in marriage must be dominant: but why? In a business partnership it is not considered necessary that one partner should dominate and between friends there is often complete equality. There is no reason why marriage should be different. Men and women should be equal before the law and equal as regards the ownership of property.

That mothers with children should wish to devote their lives to caring for them, and to household affairs, is natural and desirable; but that is no reason why, when circumstances are propitious, they should not pursue a vocation if they wish to. It is certainly no reason why unmarried women, or even married women at a later stage, should not make careers for themselves.

All occupations should be open to women. To argue the opposite it is necessary to maintain that all women are inferior to all men; that the ablest women are inferior to the most mediocre of men, which is a manifest absurdity. The only circles in which women do enjoy freedom and equality of education are those of reigning families and it is precisely there that the natural equality of men and women is most clearly evident. There are, in fact, few vocations in which women could not reach high rank, even if not the highest of all.

It may be true that women have not, over the whole field of human achievement, produced works of the highest genius. So few of them have the requisite background that this is hardly surprising. Where women have had the opportunity, as in literature from Sappho onward, their genius has been beyond question. The great Socrates himself had not disdained to learn philosophy from Aspasia.

As it is, women have to accept the principles of living, their beliefs, their way of life, their everything, from men. Their only reward is the approval of the conventional, which means that they have an entrenched interest in convention. In every family this means that the wife and mother is a built-in influence for mediocrity. Distinction is repugnant because different; and so men of promise fall back into mediocrity as soon as they are married. The way of progress is that of equality.

Chapter Eight

The Modern Period

PHILOSOPHICAL BACKGROUND

To dismiss three of the most influential philosophers of all time, Kant, Hegel and Marx, cursorily and in a few pages seems an impertinence; but the risk must be taken. Despite the huge volume of their writings, none of them treats of the present theme except incidentally or by implication. Their importance for us lies in the negative influence they exerted on some of the men whose thought we shall be studying in this chapter. It is unnecessary to trace the involved and difficult arguments with which they establish their conclusions.

Immanuel Kant (1724–1804) is important to us for the two categorical imperatives that he states in his *Fundamental Principles of the Metaphysic of Ethics*. These are purely formal principles, not intended to provide a code of behaviour, but to offer criteria against which we can test moral maxims. They are:

> Act as if the maxim of your action were to become through your will a Universal Law of Nature.

> So act as to treat humanity, whether in your own person or in that of any other, always at the same time as an end, and never merely as a means.

The first of these is a sophisticated version of the child's clinching argument: 'Suppose everybody did it; how would you like that?' As to the second, it is worth noting that Kant does not say, as he is often quoted as saying, that we should always treat everybody as an end in himself and never as a means. This would be absurd. An employer, for example, is under the necessity of using his employees as means. Kant is careful to introduce the qualifications, 'always at the same time' and, 'never merely'. An employer must consider his employees personally as well as functionally; which rules out slavery and rules out exploitation. It embodies the Christian principle of respect for personality.

Ethics here ceases to be individual and becomes social. Kant is not discussing how we should live our lives, whether we should live for pleasure or for virtue, nor what is the content of virtue. This is a relational ethic. We are not isolated selves wondering what to do. We are members of a human community and the nature of a community is to be a 'kingdom of ends'. Apart from this, in his *Practical Reason* Kant points out that love can never be forced or deliberate, but is always spontaneous, and therefore cannot be an ethical obligation.

In his early manhood, Georg Wilhelm Friederich Hegel (1770–1831), in reaction against dry Protestant dogmatism, and the rationalism of the Enlightenment, writes interestingly on the Christian religion. In an attempt to distil the essence from the Gospels he writes that the divine love is in every man and that it is by means of this love that human persons relate to each other and to God. If for the divine love we substitute the Absolute we shall be well on the way to understanding Hegel's matured philosophy. The Absolute does not transcend the real world but is the totality of the real. The Absolute objectifies itself in the multiplicity of the real. But this is a logical and not a temporal sequence: we are not to think of a pre-existing Absolute from which reality emanated or which created the real.

Now the Absolute is rational, which means that, since it is rationality that is objectified in the real, we can say that what is real is rational. Human affairs and the events of history follow rational courses. History therefore becomes the supreme judge of men and events. If the United States and Russia are the world's leading powers that is because of the rational development of history; and, if they blot each other out with nuclear weapons, that, too, is the progress of rationality. The Absolute comes to self-consciousness through human reason. The progress of philosophy is the advance of the Absolute in self-knowledge. The individual, and particularly the philosopher, is therefore of great importance for Hegel and it is quite wrong to represent him as submerging the individual in the totality – or in the State – as he is sometimes accused of doing. The individual is, in a sense, the Absolute's plenipotentiary in the accomplishment of its purposes. History is made by the great men, the Julius Caesars, the Lenins and the Lincolns, but their own private motives are overruled. Napoleon may have been moved solely by personal ambition, but history used him to make the new Europe.

A simple analogy may help to clarify this. A number of men meet, by chance, on a level field. Immediately the sporting spirit objectifies itself in them by forming them into two teams and setting them to play football. Before they met there was no sporting spirit already inhabiting the field and such a thing is inconceivable without men to embody it. But the men did not create it and nobody worked it up artificially. The spirit and the objectification occurred simultaneously and of their own accord. The sporting spirit then achieves self-consciousness in the decisions of the referee. Bertrand Russell comments: 'The Absolute Idea is pure thought thinking about pure thought. This is all that God does throughout the ages – truly a professor's God.'

Individuals become conscious of themselves only in relation. They become conscious of themselves when they see their own consciousness reflected in that of another person and when they can stand aside from themselves and think about the nature of the relation. Hegel's passage on the master-slave relation has become famous. Slavery arises out of war and terror. Fearing the threat to his own identity posed by the Other man, the master thinks to free himself of it, and to enlarge and confirm his own self-consciousness, by depriving the slave of his and turning him into a chattel or an instrument. But the truly free spirit rises above the situation and learns to disdain it. The master may then find the tables turned on him because, while he has been living parasitically in luxury and idleness, the slave has been learning to manipulate and use his master's property and his material environment. In the end, the slave enlarges his consciousness more than does the owner himself.

Hegel lays heavy stress on the triadic pattern, which is the characteristic movement of the Absolute, that he discerns running through all thought and through all historical events. This pattern consists of a statement (the thesis) and its contradiction (the antithesis), both of which are ultimately caught up in a synthesis. He applies this pattern to the family, with its immediacy of personal experience in the relations within it (thesis). As the members of the family reach maturity this tightly knit unit dissolves and the members separate from it to become independent individuals in their own right (antithesis). The next movement is for these individuals to become citizens of the civil society, organised as the State, which respects their individuality but at the same time has within it the values of the family (synthesis).

Hegel's treatment of the family probably reflects his own, happy experience for he writes movingly of the intimacies of family relations, especially that between brother and sister. In the family, mind appears as feeling. The physical difference of sex is a difference of intellectual and moral types. Husband and wife are actually welded together as a unity: 'With their exclusive individualities these personalities combine to form a *single person*: the subjective unity of hearts, becoming a "substantial unity", makes this union an ethical tie – *marriage*. The "substantial" union of hearts makes marriage an indivisible personal bond – monogamic marriage: the bodily conjunction is a sequel to the moral attachment.'

Since only the totality is fully real the individual comes nearer to his potentiality the larger the social group in which he participates. Active citizenship is enjoined upon him because the State is the culmination of the movement of the Absolute, the march of God through history. Hegel encourages personal relations within the State and, while he recognises that the needs of the State have priority, he will not have them furthered at the expense of the individual. Between the family and the State is a middle term, Civil Society. In society relations based on the free agreement of individuals are indispensable and give rise to rights independently of positive law.

It is not clear why Hegel stopped with the State instead of

going forward to the idea of a world community in which the
individual-in-relation would have found still greater fullness of
life. But he seems to have found value in the power struggle. He
lived through the period of the French Revolution and the
Napoleonic Wars. He saw how France had established the revolution under the impact of war and how Germany found a new
sense of nationhood in the confrontation with Napoleon. He saw
the threat of defeat shake people out of their self-satisfaction and
their false sense of security. He believed war to be one of the
ways in which the Absolute breaks out of the grooves of tradition
and conservatism. Because of his deification of the State and his
praise of war, Hegel became the favourite philosopher of pre-
1918 German militarism.

Karl Marx (1818–83) claimed to have turned Hegel upside-
down, holding that the material, and not the ideal, is the real.
The ideal is, for him, no more than the reflection of reality. At
the same time, Marx takes over from Hegel his insistence on the
triadic pattern of historical development. The combination of
materialism with this triadic pattern is dialectic materialism.
This, and not the social ownership of the means of production, is
his central theme. Marxism is not in any sense a theory of social
justice: it is a theory of history. It is due to sheer misunderstanding that idealists, dedicated to social justice, take Marx as their
prophet, for his interest in justice was minimal. Justice, in his
philosophy, is whatever serves the purposes of the ruling class.

One sentence in a letter to Engels, dated 4 November 1864,
throws a beam of light across the turbid morass of the Marxian
corpus. Marx is telling his friend about the preparation by one of
his committees of a declaration of principles. This is what he says
when he is writing to an intimate: 'My proposals were all
accepted by the sub-committee. Only I was obliged to insert two
phrases about "duty" and "right" into the preamble to the
statutes, ditto "truth, morality and justice".' Justice was shoved
in as a sop to sentimental proletarians!

Hegel had recognised that his dialectical triad could be used as
a means of interpreting only the past. It could not usefully be
applied to great historical movements until they were over their

peaks. He thought that these movements worked through the activities of ordinary men and women using their freedom for their personal ends, much as the classical economists thought that national prosperity came as the result of the pursuit of individual self-interest, without overall planning or government direction. Less modest, Marx thought the dialectical triad could be used for prediction. Accordingly he discovered a thesis, the bourgeoisie, which called into existence its antithesis, the proletariat. The next move was to be toward the synthesis, which would be the classless society, one of the inevitabilities of history and its culmination. His concern was not with the justice, or otherwise, of this classless society, but with its inevitability. Yet he was too impatient to wait for the inevitabilities of history to unroll in their own time and in their own way. They have to be helped along. This means manipulating society to fit the mould and forcing it to stay in the mould when it is made to fit. Had Marx been alive to witness the horrors of Stalinism he would have heartily approved had he thought that Stalinism was a necessary stage.

Marx understood history to be comprised entirely in the clash of classes. Individuals and outstanding leaders reflect in their minds the causes actuating these clashes but the causes themselves are material, not spiritual. He states this clearly in his essay on the philosophy of Ludwig Feuerbach:

> When therefore it is a question of investigating the driving forces which – consciously or unconsciously, and indeed very often subconsciously – lie behind the motives of men in their historical actions and which constitute the real ultimate driving forces of history, then it is not so much a question of the motives of single individuals, however eminent, as of those motives which set in motion great masses, whole peoples, and again whole classes of people in each people.

The individual is valued only as a unit in the mass. The interests of the class must always override those of the individual. Millions of khulaks starved to death or sent to rot in Siberia, for the sake of some theoretical point or some hypothetical gain, are acceptable sacrifices to the proletariat.

One of the inevitabilities that Marx failed to see – and might not have cared about if he had seen it – is that such a situation means the enfeebling or the destruction of satisfactory inter-personal relations. The leadership dare not allow free associations of individuals who might become powerful enough to break out of the classless mould. Indeed, any large grouping would itself constitute a social class and so would have to be destroyed, which is the real reason for the perpetual harrassment of the Christian churches in Russia and for Soviet anti-Semitism. It follows that there can never, under Marxism, be anything resembling electoral democracy because this depends on voluntary association. Even private individuals and their families must not be allowed to trust each other too much: they might conspire together. Loyalty to the class has to take precedence over loyalty to brothers and sisters and parents. Therefore there has to remain permanently in existence the apparatus of secret police, informers, spies and terrorism. The individual has to relate to the leadership, or to the proletarian class in the abstract, rather than to other individuals.

This is a paranoid symptom. In any organisation with paranoiac leadership this is the pattern of affairs. The leader will have to relate everyone directly to him and not at all to each other. If he can keep the membership at loggerheads, so much the better; they will not then be able to gang up against him, which is what he dreads.

It is a pity that Marx puts the brake on his dialectical triad when it reaches the classless society because it has further to go. The pattern has been repeated again and again since 1789:

thesis – a crisis situation of discontent
antithesis – revolution
synthesis – tyranny, which maintains the revolution and at the same time perpetuates the salient features of the old system

The notion that there can ever be a communist society in which freedom, voluntary association and interpersonal relations flourish, without first dropping Marx and all his works down a very deep well, is a mirage.

SØREN KIERKEGAARD

The succession of thinkers we are about to study came into existence as a movement of protest, partly against the philosophical idealism of Hegel and his successors, partly against certain tendencies in modern, technological society. All these men were deeply aware of the forces making for depersonalisation, for the submergence of the individual in the mass and for the erosion of freedom and responsibility. Consequently, they all lay the heaviest possible emphasis on the freedom of the will and on the responsibility of the human person for what he is and for what he becomes. They are known as 'existentialists' because their point of departure is not the 'I', reflecting upon the world from the standpoint of a god-like detachment, but the human person involved in a concrete situation. Even if they do not all use the phrase, they all take the line that 'existence precedes essence', which means that the human person, in his freedom, makes himself what he is as he lives his life from moment to moment. We *will* what we shall be. Passionate self-commitment is the hallmark of the existentialist.

If we had to discard every genius who was eccentric, the world would soon be short of geniuses. The fact that Søren Kierkegaard (1813–55,) known variously as the 'gloomy' and the 'great' Dane, was emotionally maladjusted and suffered from melancholia neither diminishes his brilliance nor discredits his thinking. Indeed, the torment of his mind might have opened to him insights denied to the rest of us. It is questionable whether his reputation suffers more from the uncritical adoration of enthusiasts or from the self-revelation that emerges from much of his writing.

To describe him as the founder of existentialism would be misleading, for existentialist thinkers are too individualistic to like being thought of as belonging to a school and most of them came to their convictions independently. But Kierkegaard was the first of the succession if not the father of it. His short life was spent in a series of violent reactions against the spiritual condition of the society in which he lived. He distilled what was for him the meaning of these reactions in turgid prose of insufferable verbosity. But he is worth study as a corrective of the exaggerations of our own society as well as of those of his own. Partly because it was written in Danish, his work at first received relatively little attention; but, during the early part of this century, it was widely read in Germany and, during the forties and fifties, it was translated into English and enjoyed a vogue in the Anglo-Saxon countries, chiming as it did with a mood of disillusion and anger.

During his youth, we have Kierkegaard reacting against the austere Protestantism of his beloved father who caused him overwhelming shock by the double sin of cursing God and marrying his servant before the death of his wife. While at the university Kierkegaard takes to the life of a playboy but then he reacts against that and undergoes a religious conversion. He falls in love with a young woman, Regina Olsen, but reacts against that and, after a year, disengages himself. He treats Regina badly and ever afterwards tortures himself with a remorseful search for self-justification. Partly, he imagines himself to have a vocation that is incompatible with marriage; partly, he feels himself to be temperamentally unsuited to it, an opinion that nobody is likely to dispute, as Copleston remarks. He determines to live as a bachelor and, as a consequence, has – inevitably – been suspected of homosexuality.

He reacts against the dominant Hegelian school which, he believes, submerges the individual in the totality and fails to do justice to his particularity. He regards the attempt to comprehend all reality in one grand, coherent system of thought as beyond human capacity. Hegelianism, he says, fails to chart a way of life, which should be the main purpose of philosophy. He reacts against the Church, which he charges with dissipating the power of the Gospel in irrelevant social activism, and watering down its message to avoid giving offence to fashionable society. He consistently reacts against the meretricious values of the society within which he moves. He reacts against the current liberal democratic ideas. These are a surrender to the crowd, which he sees as essentially untruth, a living lie, because it deprives men of their separateness and, therefore, of their responsibility. We can imagine what he would have thought about modern opinion-poll government. It is to the credit of his insight that, although the peril could, in his day, have been no bigger than a man's hand, he reacts against the depersonalisation inherent in industrial society. Finally, he reacts against life itself.

But Kierkegaard would not have dissented from this analysis of his life. Working in the borderland between theology and philosophy, the basis of his message is that truth does not arise out of the attempt to conceptualise reality by the application of the speculative reason but out of the exercise of will in moments of decision in the concrete situation of the individual, human person. This is a variant on the saying that if we do the will we shall know the doctrine. Kierkegaard is pre-eminently the protagonist of the person, although this leads him to elitism. To be sure, we weary of professional contempt for the 'crowd', the 'masses', the 'bourgeoisie', or whatever else happens to be the fashionable object of scorn, but Kierkegaard's recoil from mindless social conformity is genuine. He stands for integrity and independence. He wants the individual to take his life into his own hands and launch himself without reserve into his chosen course. This enlarges the personality and gives new meaning to life.

Since his affair with Regina Olsen meant so much to him a sketch of Kierkegaard's views on marriage will clarify much of what follows. He had a rare understanding of marriage and would, obviously, have loved to have been married himself. His renunciation cannot have been undertaken lightly. He puts his views into the mouth of a happily married public servant.

Marriage, he says, is 'decidedly the most important journey of discovery a man can undertake, every other sort of acquaintance with life is superficial in comparison with that acquired by a married man, for he and he alone has thoroughly fathomed the depths of life'. The same order of passionate self-committal is required as in spiritual love and in spiritual religion. The married man must be a true believer in marriage. The bond is not then felt as a bondage but as a liberation. Marriage is, for the married man, a perpetuation of the happy first love at the side of the woman from whom his life gained its significance. It may be true that the first ebullient enthusiasm does not last, but marriage has a mystical quality that knows how to fashion the first love into a stronger and more enduring love.

Married love has its own, special god, Eros, who is incarnate in it. Yet, surely, the God of Spirits has something to do with marriage as well. Certainly the priest says so at the wedding; but the God of Spirits has to be introduced in such a way that the marriage is not so caught up in the eternal as to cease to be special. We might say that, whereas paganism has a god of love but no god of marriage, Christianity has a god of marriage but no god of love, because for Christians marriage is the higher expression of love. If we rely only upon Eros, marriage becomes a matter of caprice; yet, if marriage is to be a duty, rooted in the spiritual relation with God, it will itself become purely spiritual and the psycho-physical synthesis that is the strength of Eros will evaporate into the eternal. So marriage is threatened from two sides, that of pagan reminiscence and that of spirituality. Marriage is the highest end, or intention, of the individual human existence, without which a man cancels earthly interests and retains only eternal and spiritual interest, which is exhausting. Yet marriage is not a blind urge or a compulsion but a work of freedom, which can be realised only in a resolution of the will.

This resolution must be present from the first moment, from the original occurrence of the love; for, if it is not, before the resolution is reached a change of mind might occur. If the immediacy, or the compulsion, of love is not matched by resolution the alternative is either to seduce or to break off hastily. Marriage itself can be a form of seduction. Reflection, or comparison, is not permissible for the married man for, if he reflects, he entertains a doubt, which breaches the immediacy of love and weakens the resolution. For the same reason, a man does not 'choose' his lady love for marriage because there must be no alternative. The woman must come to him as a gift, a divine gift. If not, then errant reflection has its opportunity and, again, resolution is enfeebled.

It is not the external attractiveness of a woman that establishes married love but the consciousness that each partner exists for the other, regardless of outside business or social interests. The notion that a woman blossoms for a brief period of her life and is then finished is nonsense. In reality a woman grows more and more beautiful as she matures and, especially, as she finds fulfilment in motherhood. So, too, the love grows and matures. Should a husband find that he has reason for suspicion of his wife, then jealousy is the highest honour he can pay both to his wife and to the relation that has existed between them.

We have now to take up another strand of the plot. It is for his threefold scheme of stages on life's way, worked out from his own experience, that Kierkegaard is best known. The first, or aesthetic, stage represents his playboy period. Here the word 'aesthetic' is used in the special meaning of its Greek derivation – feeling, sensation, perception. The first of Kierkegaard's stages is therefore the life of feeling, in which we live for the satisfactions of the moment. What is implied is not vulgar over-indulgence in wine, women and song, or eating, living and being merry. The first stager might be most fastidious in choosing elevated pursuits, such as music, literature and the arts, but always on the level of feeling and impulse, without central direction or meaning. Typical is the aimless philanderer who, when he wants a change, is clever enough to leave the seduced with the belief that it was she who initiated the affair and who also broke it off.

This way of life, which at first appears to be exciting and adventurous ultimately brings a bad taste. It yields no permanent satisfactions and at the heart of it is emptiness. The 'aesthetic' man reaches a condition when life is useless and absurd. He feels degraded; black despair with life itself takes possession of him. At this point he may either refuse to confront his despair, and shy away, continuing on the path of degeneracy or he may pull himself together in the realisation that he must acquire standards and principles. He now enters the ethical stage when he attempts to live by his standards and principles. But these ethical norms soon reveal their own sterility and inadequacy. The aesthetic keeps on dragging him back. The fundamental question of the meaning of life is still unanswered. The final stage is the religious, when a man makes the leap of faith in passionate self-committal to God.

Two points need clarification. First, when Kierkegaard speaks of salvation through despair he is not thinking, as he is sometimes popularly represented to be, of the brokenness that accompanies a personal calamity such as the death of someone dearly beloved or the collapse of a man's fortunes. Dives is damned not merely because his worldly affairs have gone well with him but because he has never had the courage to break away from the vanities of life. Lazarus is saved, not by his destitution, but because he has experienced in the depths the meaningless of life lived on the material plane and has looked beyond that.

Second, because Kierkegaard talks of the 'leap of faith', this is not to be taken to be blind acceptance of a dogma. Otherwise, the desperate man might throw the dice and leap from the bridge instead. While Kierkegaard does not believe that reason can demonstrate the presence of the Christian God, neither does he deny that there are pointers in that direction. At the ethical stage a man is under certain pressures, and conscious of certain indications, that move him towards faith. His will has already so structured his experience that faith is its natural climax. But the last step is a recklessness of self-committal.

Faith, in this sense, not only fulfils the moral law but transcends it. The test case is that of Abraham, knife in hand, ready to sacrifice his beloved son, Isaac, at the call of God. The divine demand is unlimited. Kierkegaard dwells on Abraham's overwhelming desolation at the prospect of the act he is about to commit, and on the arbitrariness of the demand. There was no rational motive behind the demand that Abraham could see; but, in confrontation with the divine, he must not refuse. This desolation, awe and terror, Kierkegaard calls 'dread'. It occurs because, at the religious stage, a man has entered a spiritual realm where familiar norms and prudential calculations no longer avail him and, alone, he confronts ultimate demand.

Now this faith-relation with God is exclusive. The person is reconstituted in separateness and solitariness. He becomes, in Kierkegaard's phrase, the 'Single One', and this singleness is incompatible with involvement in the world. It admits of no comparable relation with any human person. From the account given of his ideas on marriage it is now evident why Kierkegaard had to break with Regina Olsen. Marriage means the deepest possible involvement with the world, even to the acceptance of Eros as a god. In effect, Kierkegaard is pointing to the monastery as the most excellent way of life. He virtually endorses the double standard usually associated with Roman Catholicism; one standard for the religious, another for the laity. After total immersion in Kierkegaard some people have, in fact, turned to Rome. Kierkegaard's is a far more penetrating and subtle advocacy of the monastic principle than that usually pleaded on its behalf.

In taking the personal, in its particularity, as his starting point, Kierkegaard's weakness is that his thought is autobiographical rather than universal. We may, by study of his experience, enrich our own understanding; but because we have not shared his experience we cannot follow his development in our own lives, except artificially. No doubt, many have reached religious faith through disillusion, but not necessarily Kierkegaard's disillusion. Many there are, like the Psalmist, who, going through the vale of misery, have used it as a well, and have found that the pools thereof are filled with water. But these are usually splendid souls, already living in faith, who have learned how to distil sweetness from brackish wells. There are, also, many deeply religious men and women, who exercise their freedom decisively to will the direction of their own lives, who never experience this fundamental despair. They may, rightly or wrongly, convince themselves that despair is the only alternative to faith; but that is not what Kierkegaard says. In any case, probably in most people's lives, Kierkegaard's ethical and aesthetic stages co-exist, to be used as refuges from each other, while in moments of crisis the highest demands are met. When Kierkegaard wrote, Kant had already taken the personal as his starting point. The fact of our consciousness of moral obligation, he says, carries with it the implications of God, freedom and immortality. Except in the insane, this consciousness is not only deeply personal but is also universal.

Kierkegaard protests bitterly against Hegel because he submerged the individual in the totality. What Hegel actually said was that the Absolute willed itself into existence through the particular and came to self-consciousness through the individual person, a doctrine that, surely, gives as much dignity and status to the individual as anyone could wish. We remember how he attributed so much importance to personal relations as to show how the individual gains identity only in relation with the Other. As in musical counterpoint, a life's melody is enhanced by association with those of Others. By cutting the individual off from his ground, and having him will his own essence, Kierkegaard actually diminishes the individual. In the end, he is so individualistic as to deprive the person of all relation except that with the Absolute.

Kierkegaard reminds me of the soldier in a military formation who objects to saluting his officers. He might, if pushed, condescend to salute the Field Marshal. He thinks it humiliating to show respect to his military superiors. He imagines he loses his individuality and is submerged in the organisation. As a consequence, his officers despise him and he fails to win the respect even of his own equals. He has opted out of the organisation and so belongs nowhere. He is on his own, a nobody. But if he is willing to play along with the ethos of his organisation, to show the usual courtesies, and to salute his officers, he has everybody's respect and is accepted, not only in his own right as an individual, but also as a member of a proud tradition, with all the added status that gives. Kierkegaard strikes me as being the soldier who wants to opt out.

While Kierkegaard has much of value to say about love, it is always the love of subject for object, never the love of mutuality and involvement, which he disdains as merely love by inclination or preference. We have, he writes, a need to love and to show the fruits of love. As with the leap of faith, love has to be a passionate self-committal. We ought not to be constantly looking for the fruits of our love because that would imply the absence of this self-committal, as if we loved only in the hope of enjoying the reward of seeing the fruits. We have to *believe* in love.

In the great commandments we are told, 'Thou *shalt* love thy neighbour as thyself'. Here we are presented with a command to love. This seems to be paradoxical because it is usually understood that love is involuntary. But this is precisely what distinguishes Christian love from erotic love or friendship, which are love from inclination. These are based on the wrong kind of self-love or selfishness; because for this love we expect a return. Really, it is ourselves we are loving. Love such as this is not free but is governed by its object, which arouses the original inclination. Also, it is capricious and unreliable. It may die away as inclination and preference alter and may, even, turn to hatred when offended. Precisely because Christian love is under command, it is free and independent. Instead of being under the control of its object it wills itself and goes where it lists. It fulfils our need. Considered as obligation, love is secure against change. Agape in its extreme!

The command is to love Others *as we love ourselves*. Whereas this is often taken to mean that, as we love ourselves, so we should love our neighbour just as much, Kierkegaard takes it to mean the stripping away of self-love and the loving of Others *instead of* ourselves, thus identifying ourselves with the Others.

We are to love our *neighbour*, which means that there is to be no favouritism or partiality, as there is in the love of inclination. Of course, such love as this underlies erotic love and friendship but it is not the same as them. Since love is not dependent on inclination, nor upon the attractiveness or amiability of the object and, since it is impartial, everybody is our neighbour and our love must go out to everybody indiscriminately and without distinction. There are to be no comparisons between one and another. Love is consciously grounded in the eternal and therefore cannot turn to jealousy or hatred.

Love of neighbour in this sense is spiritual and belongs to Christianity. Spontaneous love, which includes erotic love and friendship, is love by inclination and belongs to paganism. Spiritual love displaces spontaneous love. That is not to say that there is anything wrong about spontaneous love; but there is nothing specifically Christian about it either. Perhaps we shall understand this better if we compare it with what Kierkegaard says about music. Since music represents feeling, or the sensuous (as distinct from the sensual), it is non-moral. Its function is to lift the particular instance of feeling into the context of the universal and this is not a specifically Christian function. Similarly, spontaneous love has a valuable function to fulfil but it is irrelevant to Christian faith.

Spiritual love is not romantic and does not inspire the poets. That is because it is to be done, or acted upon, rather than to be sung about. But there is no conflict between body and spirit at the root of the distinction between the different loves. Based on the senses, spontaneous love is a form of self-love but it does not exclude spiritual love, which can be at the base of every kind of love.

We appear to be left with the most cold-blooded, inhuman sense of duty that ever froze its object into paralysis. To call it love is flattery. By the time Kierkegaard has stripped away spontaneous love, inclination, mutuality, involvement with the world, social activism, marriage, friendship, and the sensuous, the area of life left to the spiritual is so small as to be negligible. Surely the spiritual should qualify and direct all human thought and activity. After all, when Jesus showed his example of how faith and love transcended the moral law it was by way of healing the sick, or providing food for his disciples, on the Sabbath Day, not in ordering people to murder their own children, which even Kierkegaard's deity is unlikely to do more than very occasionally.

MARTIN BUBER

If Kierkegaard was the prophet of the personal, Martin Buber was the prophet of the relational. Born in Vienna in 1878, he studied at the universities of Vienna, Berlin, Leipzig and Zurich. He came under the influence of the Jewish sect of the Chasidim and learned from them their special brand of practical mysticism. An active Zionist, in 1933 he was exiled and, five years later, became Professor of Social Philosophy at the Hebrew University in Jerusalem. In 1923 he wrote his *I and Thou* and, between 1929 and 1939, wrote a series of essays developing his theme which were later published together under the title *Between Man and Man*.

There are two types of relation, says Buber, the first of which is that between the subject, the 'I', and whatever it encounters in the natural world, which is the 'It'. The world plays no active part in this experience, only allowing itself to be experienced. This relation does not engage the whole of the 'I'. The other relation is that with another person, the 'I–Thou', which engages the whole being on each side of the relation. These, then, are the two primary words:

$$I - Thou$$
$$I - It$$

Whereas if we name an object in the natural world, a mountain, for instance, it was there long before anybody paid any attention to it, these primary words actually bring the relation into existence in the act of being thought or spoken. An object in the natural world, a tree, for instance, may become a 'Thou' if it absorbs the whole attention and fills the entire horizon. Words are not necessary to true conversation; only that two people experience one another. The 'I–Thou' relation can be turned into an 'I–It' relation if the 'I' differentiates itself and looks at the other merely as an object.

Buber writes:

These are the two basic privileges of the world of It. They move man to look on the world of It as the world in which he has to live, as the world, indeed, which offers him all kinds of incitements and excitements, activity and knowledge. In this chronicle of solid benefits the moments of the Thou appear as strange, lyric and dramatic episodes, seductive and magical, but tearing us away to dangerous extravagancies, leaving the well-tried context, leaving more questions than satisfactions behind them, shattering security – in short, uncanny moments that we can well dispense with. . . . Without It man cannot live. But he who lives with It alone is not a man.

As modern conditions of administration and technology involve us more and more deeply in the world of things, so the flashes of 'I–Thou' relations become more and more rare. The less we have to do with persons, as persons, the more of ourselves we devote to things. Of course, there is plenty of meeting between people on a purely superficial, or technical, level, but this has to do with questions of work, or the social trivia, and never rises to genuine encounter. People may spend most of their time among others in that way and never in their lives experience an 'I–Thou'.

> The development of the function of experiencing comes about mostly through decrease of man's power to enter into relation.

Yet the possibility of returning from the world of 'It' to authentic relation still remains, and in this rests man's freedom. Fate is excluded from the relational world. When a man looks at another merely, or observes him, all that he sees is the sum of his characteristics, a description of an object. He is not in touch with him in his uniqueness. It is when, in the exchange of glances, he sees what he cannot objectify that true meeting, or dialogue, occurs. That is when the protective armour with which we shield ourselves from the multitudinous influences directed against us falls from us and we are available to the address, whether wordless or not, of another.

Besides technical dialogue, which establishes understanding but no relation in depth, and monologue, in which two people are trying to impress each other with their statements, is genuine dialogue, now becoming more and more rare, in which true mutuality is established. The life of dialogue 'is not one in which you have to do with men, but one in which you really have to do with those with whom you have to do'. Again, 'Where unreserve has ruled, even wordlessly, between two men, the word of dialogue has happened sacramentally'. And again, 'The life of dialogue is not limited to men's traffic with each other; it is, it has shown itself to be, a relation of men to one another that is only represented in their traffic'.

I labour the point because 'dialogue' has recently become one of the fashionable words whose meaning easily becomes obscured by too facile use. There is to be dialogue between coloured people and white, between Communists and Christians, between trade unionists and employers, which is all very well provided these good intentions pass into deep-calling-unto-deep and do not trickle away in a spate of committees and academic discussions.

Every experience of a particular 'Thou' provides a glimpse through to the eternal 'Thou'. This is true mysticism; which is neither psychedelic vision, nor absorption into the divine with loss of identity, nor a glance into the undifferentiated unity in the depths of the self, but duality transcended relationally – the united 'I' and the boundless 'Thou'. The human-divine dialogue does not occur in moments withdrawn from the affairs of every-day life. It is not the loss of identity in the ocean of divinity. It is authentically relational. We enter into this dialogue by means of the signs that come to us through everyday events. As we know a poet by means of the numerous indications we see in his poetry of the manner of man he is, so we know God through the multi-plicity of signs visible to us in nature and in events. Religion, then, is not abstracted from life; it is, 'just *everything*, simply all that is lived in its possibility of dialogue'. We are not swallowed up but *willed* for the life of communion. Responsibility consists in our response to these signs that come to us through events. Through these signs, also, comes revelation; which is why Buber objects to dogma, with its once-for-all formulations, 'the most exalted form of invulnerability against revelation'.

Dialogue is not to be confused with love. Not even Jesus succeeded in loving every man he met. Of sinners he preferred only the loose, lovable sinners against the Law, not those who were on the right side of the Law but sinned against *him*. Jesus did not love those who hated him. Nor, for the matter of that, is dialogue to be confused with universal unreserve, with the senti-mentality of carrying the heart on the sleeve, which means only that there is no substance to lose. Love is beyond the physical, beyond ideas and beyond feelings. Feelings are entertained: love comes to pass by act of grace. Love is the responsibility of an 'I' for a 'Thou'. Hate is the negation of all relation because it is unable to say the primary word, 'I–Thou'. Yet it is nearer to relation than a being without either love or hate. Even hostility is better than no kind of attitude at all.

While Buber writes of Kierkegaard with understanding and sympathy, he is also deeply critical of him. Kierkegaard's 'Single One', he says, cannot be understood without an appreciation of his own solitariness. Augustine had his mother, and Pascall his sister, to maintain an organic connection with the world. But the central event of Kierkegaard's life was renunciation. So he finds that everyone should speak with God as with himself. But, answers Buber, whereas speaking with God is totally different from speaking with oneself, speaking with God is not totally different from speaking with other people. God wants us to come to him by means of the Regina Olsens he has created and not by renunciation of them. If we remove the object of love we remove it altogether and the void is not filled by producing an object 'from the abundance of human spirit and calling it God'. Who could possibly believe that God wants 'Thou' to be truly said only to him and not to others except in an inessential and invalid way?

Two more clarifications need to be made before we leave Buber to argue the point with Kierkegaard in the leafy celestial groves where departed philosophers earnestly converse. The value of marriage, writes Buber, is that the way to the infinite lies through fulfilled finitude. I want the other to exist because I want the particular one to exist and, from this, I learn to value otherness. Marriage occurs in that private sphere in which a man can identify himself with others without differentiation. We cannot, in the same way, identify ourselves with the body politic because the multiplicity of *that* otherness causes a cleavage. It is too big and numerous. We can be bound up (not bundled up) with the body politic without yielding ourselves unthinkingly to it. A man may endeavour to make the crowd no longer a crowd by changing it into a community of Single Ones. 'The Single One is the man for whom the reality of the relation with God as an exclusive relation includes and encompasses the possibility of relation with all otherness, and for whom the whole body politic, the reservoir of otherness, offers just enough otherness for him to pass his life with it.'

Community is dialogue in multiplicity. Collectivity, by contrast, is the bundling together of a multitude of individuals. It is based on an organised atrophy of personal existence. The multitude cease to be personal and become units in the mass. Community does not consist of a number of people who happen to exist side by side, like grains of sand, but of people living *with* each other, dynamically facing each other.

Political decision nowadays means joining one of several groups, each claiming to be authentic and to have the final answer to all political problems, and each claiming unreserved complicity. If the man of faith joins such a group, and so surrenders his personal responsibility, he has already fallen from grace; for, if religion agrees to be one department of life among many, and one autonomous group alongside others, it has already perverted the faith. To remove any realm from the relation of faith is to remove it from God's defining power. Whoever fails to let his faith be fulfilled in every aspect of the life he lives is trying to curtail the fulfilment of God's rule in the world.

Which is all very well; but, if all men of faith withdrew from political decision-making, the body politic would soon fall into the hands of the ill-conditioned and self-interested.

GABRIEL MARCEL

Few authors have written so felicitously as Gabriel Marcel on such subjects as hope, the family, fatherhood, fidelity. His thought gains force from having been publicised under the adverse conditions of the Vichy regime which, indeed, disapproved of his vigorous assertion of the significance of the individual. The difficulty in presenting an analysis of his thought is that he never organised it systematically. His tendency is to meditate around his chosen topic rather than to take a clear point of departure and move to a considered conclusion. His work is scattered over numerous learned journals and published papers.

Fortunately, a number of his lectures and essays, prepared in 1942 and 1943, have been collected in a single volume with the title *Homo Viator* (*Man the Traveller*). From these it is possible to lift some of the more rare jewels even if not to find a concise statement of a philosophy. It is of some significance that, although not brought up in a religious *milieu*, Marcel was received into the Roman Catholic Church at the age of thirty-nine. His own independent thought brought him to that decision.

Marcel believes that the adult retains throughout life the psychological pattern of childhood. Always he maintains his identity, his ego or self, in relation to other people, continuously making clear the separateness between them. The ego wants the recognition of others and offers itself to them for that. This ego is not reducible; it cannot be identified with any particular part of the personality, such as mind or heart, but is global, comprising the whole. The Other is a foil for its own self-satisfaction. For convenience we assume that the ego came first and the personality afterwards, but this pre-existent ego is fictitious: in reality the ego comes into existence only through the fact of being incarnate in a physical body and of acting in the events of life. Our *presence* always involves experience, the consciousness of existing among others. The *ego* is that part of experience that we want to safeguard against attack. Although its boundaries are not precisely drawn it does think of itself as self-contained territory from which trespassers are warned off.

Modern conditions of competition increase and exasperate this consciousness of being a separate *ego*, perverting it to self-worship – or 'egolatry'. 'I claim to be a person', writes Marcel, 'in so far as I assume responsibility for what I do and what I say. I am conjointly responsible to myself and to everybody else.' Person, engagement, community, reality: these concepts belong together. An essential characteristic of a person is to be available, which means that he is ready to accept opportunity and to undertake new enterprises and adventures. A person is less a *being* than a desire to rise above all that he is and above all that he would like to be and knows he is not. In short, a person is an eager participant in events, not a mere echo of others or a rôle player, but one who is constantly trying to transcend himself and his circumstances.

There are two ways of thinking about our experience that are clearly to be distinguished. If, as it were, we stand aside from our experience and view it objectively we are solving problems. For instance, I might be deciding on a school for my son. I send for several prospectuses and interview headmasters and then decide, on the evidence, which is the most likely to suit. This kind of thinking about a problem is what Marcel terms 'first reflection'. But suppose that my wife has told me that I am spoiling my son, and that I give in to him too easily, and that I ought to change my attitude. That is a question I cannot think about objectively because I am too deeply involved myself. My own inmost feelings and reactions are vital elements in the question and I shall never be able to find a cut-and-dried answer. The only solution might be that I should change my nature and become an entirely different kind of person. That I shall never know and if someone told me I should not believe him. Hence we have not so much a problem as a mystery, and the way in which I think about it Marcel terms 'second reflection'. Realistic thinking must now comprehend the total situation, including the observer, who is myself. The deepest human questions are mostly of this kind. This spirit informs all Marcel's own thinking, which makes his writing more reminiscent of practical religion than of abstruse academic philosophy.

In this spirit he writes about hope, which he defines as a positive response to a superficially pessimistic situation, a breakthrough from a situation of captivity, when we feel hemmed in by circumstances and events. Hope is significant only when we are in danger of succumbing to despair. This is not hope for particular things, such as that a crippling strike will be cancelled at the last moment, or that the bank rate will fall. It has little to do with what I have or expect to have. The hope that has deep significance is hope in life itself, arising out of belief, or confidence, in life. It may be hope in particular persons, or in people in general, going hand in hand with belief in them and love for them. It has nothing to do with calculation and argument about what the future is likely to bring forth but is a response from the depths. Hope such as this points to a transcendent reality because my hoping involves belief in the value of life and in the value of people and their universe. We cannot pin our hope on what has no value. If we put our hope and confidence in people, by implication we also put our hope and confidence in God.

Turning to the family, Marcel raises again his concepts of mystery and second reflection. The family is not a problem: we are involved in it too deeply and personally to consider it scientifically. It contains an element of the mysterious. To think of it objectively would result in a superficial and mechanistic interpretation that would bear little resemblance to the reality.

In early years a child feels himself to be the centre of the family, the focus of all attention, but later he finds that he is one of several, each of whom has his own system of relations within it. He begins also to develop a hidden, secret, life of his own from which others are excluded. By reason of the kind of person he becomes as he grows up he is a judgment upon those who called him into existence and brought him up. This fact establishes an infinity of new relations between them. He begins to realise that through his family tree, the tangle of great grandparents, great-great grandparents, great aunts and cousins scores of times removed, he is linked to the entire human race. Mankind is individualised in the singular creature he is. All human relations culminate in him. He is not the final term in a succession of causes and effects; the relations that constitute him are much more intimate than that and less mechanistic. He shares the inner meaning of life with those among whom he is coming to maturity.

But the family has entered into a period of crisis and dissolution due to a weakening, in the western world, of reverence for life. A process of devitalisation has corroded the familial institution. One effect of the Industrial Revolution has been to crumble the cohesion of personal relations, all the way through. There is current a detestable line of egalitarian thinking that leads to a resentment of any authority and a refusal to accept any hierarchy. A bitter jealousy arises at any suggestion of superior merit. To belong to a good family is supposed to imply unjust privilege and unfair advantage. Yet pride in family can be a creative influence. 'It is a response from the depths to an investiture to which it behoves a man to prove worthy.' He is involved in it and his roots are there.

But the traditional family rituals that gave cohesion and order and a sense of belonging are now cracking. Since the Industrial Revolution the family has been torn from its roots in the great rhythms of nature, which have been so speeded up as to have lost their meaning. To the city dweller the seasons of the year are irrelevant. Technology has obliterated them. To the townsman, living in an air-conditioned envelope, there is no difference between summer and winter. The individual has become trivialised by standardisation and by the impoverishment of personal relations. Always in search of distractions, and wishing to escape from the cosmic rhythms, people want only the meretricious glitter of their technological society. They think more of the external trappings of social life than of its substance.

On the subject of sexuality, Marcel writes that to think only in terms of its procreative function is to degrade it and to miss its depths. The dignity of the person is outraged when the joining of two persons is envisaged merely as a means of procreation. Both the union and the procreation are complementary to a creative process in which the destinies of parents and children are fashioned and in which all find fulfilment. The flesh will take a terrible revenge if it is treated merely as a means to the production of an heir. Yet the fact of procreation should give pause to the present multiplication of divorces because parents have brought into existence someone who has rights over them and to whom they have responsibilities. 'Everything seems to happen as though on the human level the operation of the flesh ought to be the hallowing of a certain inward fulfilment, an outgoing not to be forced since it springs from an experience of plenitude. . . . What a deep difference we must establish between husbands and wives who prudently secure for themselves an heir to succeed them, an heir who is nothing but a representative or substitute for them – and those who, in a sort of prodigality of their whole being, sow the seed of life without ulterior motive by radiating the life flame which has permeated them and set them aglow.'

Fatherhood is infinitely greater than any relation deriving from the physical nature. It is not to be summed up merely as causality nor even as finality. It is far more than a biological process for perpetuating the human race. Certainly it is not synonymous with procreation. Nor is it constituted by legal or social compulsion, or else it would be only an ephemeral and relative institution. The act of procreation is for a man merely a gesture. Except for the moment of physical union it matters little to him. He can accomplish it almost in absence of mind and forget it immediately afterwards. When compared with artistic creation it cannot even be regarded as creative. Looking at the matter in depth, the woman is by far the more active partner in procreation. Motherhood starts with a strong reaction to the circumstances of impregnation, which might have been against her will and bitterly humiliating, or might have been her own joyous act of self-giving in a partnership that is elevating and fulfilling. There follow the nine months of pregnancy with all that can mean. By contrast, fatherhood starts from nothingness.

Why should a man want children? That anybody can ask this question at all is symptomatic of the feebleness that has overtaken contemporary society. Contraception, another symptom of this debility, is altogether to be deplored as involving the destruction of the connection between man and life. There can really be no facile answer to the question why a man wants children. To outsiders, looking on as spectators, the wish seems to be gratuitous and irrational. But to the potential father it is vocational, an irresistible demand upon him, which is its own justification. We might as well ask why an artist wants to paint pictures or a musician to make music. All this seems incongruous only if we have an anaemic conception of what vocation can be.

Fatherhood is subject to a variety of perversions. Where conjugal love is nothing more than 'egoism in partnership' the original tenderness for the new-born child easily turns into jealousy and dislike or even, disproportionate though it may be, into active resentment. The proper authority of the father then ceases to be creative and dries out in a sterile and arbitrary coercion. In some families a debtor-creditor relation comes into existence. The parents blackmail their children by insisting on the good turn they have done them by bringing them into the world and by the sacrifices they have made on their account. On the other hand, there are parents who feel guilt for having brought children into the world at all and think themselves to be in some way indebted to them. There are fathers who want to fulfil their own failed ambitions through their sons or who plan their sons' lives with such pride that the boys grow up to find their future mortgaged and themselves in captivity to their fathers' hopes. At the opposite pole is an idolatry of the son that is nothing but a projection of the father's individuality and knows nothing of genuine love. None of these perversions has anything in common with that creative vocation that calls father and son to gain fulfilment in a developing relation. All of them end in spiritual dryness and sterility. A large family keeps them in check.

It would be absurd if a couple could not respond to the parental vocation merely because of some slight physical obstruction. The answer in such cases is adoption, which is not to be considered merely a pale and bloodless copy of real parenthood, but a means of grace destined to make up for the deficiencies of biological filiation.

PAUL TILLICH

Although not, strictly speaking, an existentialist, Paul Tillich can usefully be grouped with that tradition here because he learned much from it and respected it. In origin he was a German Jew who, in the early thirties, emigrated to America where ultimately he became theological professor at Harvard. His great, three volume *Systematic Theology* ranks him among the leaders of that upsurge of Protestant theology that began after the First World War in 1918 as a protest against the elements of disillusion and decadence in the western world, and that brought forward such men as Barth, Brunner, Bultmann, Niehbuhr and several others of the highest standing.

It is one of the causes of the ineffectiveness of the idealists of the present time that the words love, power and justice, three of the profoundest words in human language, are so much bandied about among them and so little thought about. Tillich fills in the gap in a series of lectures delivered in 1954 and later published under that title: *Love, Power and Justice.*

These three, he tells us, must be considered ontologically, which means that they must be considered in relation to being-itself, before we can usefully think about their operation in everyday life. We need to think of them in depth. In effect, this means that we abstract and abstract and abstract until we arrive at these concepts in their utmost universality and see them as arising out of the inmost nature of things. Tillich says that these concepts form a trinity of structures rooted in being itself. 'They precede everything that is and they cannot be derived from any-thing that is.' They are so closely related that to build any con-structive social ethic embodying the principles of justice is impossible so long as power is looked at with distrust and love is reduced to its emotional and ethical quality. Love is not an emotion although emotion is an element in it. Were it an emotion only, it would be nothing but a sentimental addition to power and justice without any significance. Love is not an addition to justice and does not transcend it but has its own proper function to fulfil in the administration of it. Justice is expressed in general principles and in legislation none of which can ever reach the particular situation of the individual. Love supplies this deficiency in justice.

This is a point of the utmost importance. To understand what Tillich means we have to realise that, for the achievement of perfect justice we should have to have a special law for each individual, because the circumstances of each differ from those of all others. But this is out of the question: legislation has to cover the whole multitude of people. We may instance the old marriage laws that admitted of virtually no exceptions to the life-long bond. This broke down because it allowed of no discretion in favour of the individual. Love plays its part when discretion can be exercised in relation to the circumstances of the case. We have a judge mitigating the severity of a sentence or calling for psychiatric advice. The same principle is applied when the Home Secretary remits a sentence. Wise legislation is always flexible enough to admit of this, which is why automatic sentences are always, everywhere and invariably wrong and to be condemned. Pure justice, says Tillich, is always unjust: it is love that adapts it to the concrete situation.

Ontologically, love is the moving power of life that drives everything that is towards everything else that is, the drive toward unity of that which is in separation. This presupposes a unity of essences, for things that are unlike cannot be brought into unity – as oil cannot be brought into unity with water. Love reunites radically separated individuals. Emotion is an element in it, an expression of the total participation of the being. Emotion is the anticipation of the fulfilment of the longing for reunion. Simple desire is the lowest form of love. The notion that love seeks primarily pleasure is false: it is the reunion it seeks and the pleasure is a side effect. The confusion between agape and eros arises out of this fallacy. These are not incompatible types of love but different qualities of the same love. The situation can best be summed up in the Greek word, *philia*. Tillich might with advantage have dwelt more on this word philia, which has the significance of mutuality. Some Greek authors as we have seen use its verb for the phrase, 'to kiss each other'.

How are love and justice related to power? The will-to-power does not necessarily mean the neurotic desire for power over other people. It is the dynamic self-affirmation of life, the drive of all things living to realise themselves with increasing intensity, the overcoming of internal and external negation, the possibility of overcoming non-being, which expresses itself in every encounter of everyday life. Power actualises itself through force or compulsion but is not to be identified with either of them. Force and compulsion are the tools of power. Power is *being* actualising itself against non-being. Compulsion and force are effective only when they are expressions of the actual power situation.

Tillich is saying here that we all want life more abundantly and that we are prepared to exert ourselves for it even if, in extreme cases, this involves the resort to physical force. If I see a hoodlum trying to enter my house I am hardly making an affirmation of life if I take no measures to stop him. On the contrary, I am feebly allowing non-being to creep in on me, and my friends might later find that the episode had ended in the negation of my being. Of course, we pass through every grade of experience before we reach that extreme. A businessman negotiating a deal, or a committee member arguing a point, are asserting themselves by the force of their own personalities. That is precisely what they are appointed to do and if they refrained they would be worthless either as negotiators or as committee members. Tillich is not thinking of power as an assertion of ourselves at the expense of others, which would be exploitation. He is explicit on the point that the more we carry others with us, or find ourselves at one with them, the greater our power. The committee member, for instance, is in a much stronger position if he can carry the whole committee with him instead of having to force an issue to the vote. The democratic statesman, who can rely upon the full support of his people, is in a much more powerful position than the tyrant, who has to terrorise them into obedience.

To state the matter in this way is to make clear that power is not incompatible with love. The more we conquer separation the more power we enjoy; but the process whereby separates are united is love. Therefore love is the foundation, not the denial, of power. But what of compulsion? Luther once remarked that, while sweetness and self-surrender were the proper works of love, violence was its 'strange' work. The right use of violence is to destroy what is against love; to clear the way for charity and forgiveness. Compulsion conflicts with love only when it frustrates the aim of love, which is the reunion of the separated, or when it destroys where it should be constructive. Tillich comments that compulsion is the tragic aspect of love, as Luther found when he had to support the princes of Germany in suppressing the peasant uprisings. Compulsion can be perverted to the interests of tyranny or for the maintenance in power of ruling groups who have forfeited the confidence of their people.

In a sophisticated way, Tillich is bringing us face to face with all the cliches and platitudes that bedevil the pacifist argument. How often have we been bored by the rhetorical question:'Would you stand idly by while a burglar assaulted your mother-in-law?' Answer, 'No. But I would not hurl a nuclear weapon at him either. I would pinion him while my mother-in-law telephoned the Police'. Thus, by means of violence, used with restraint, the interests both of love and justice would be served, and violence would be used creatively. By the injudicious use of violence I would have defeated the purposes both of justice, which is to render to each his due, and of love, which is to make a better man of the miscreant. To sum up, compulsion is indispensable but should be used proportionately to the requirements of love and justice, which, interestingly, has always been the principle of the British army when called to support the civil power.

It is on the basis of justice that the individual is united with the group. At the same time, as a principle, justice automatically passes judgment on all legislation. Were it not of eternal validity no criterion would be available for application to tyrannical laws. But love is the principle of justice while, at the same time, in the movement to reunion, it must be qualified by justice. The intrinsic claim of justice is that justice to one individual should be done within the structure of the whole organisation. A power structure in which compulsion works against justice to the individual is not strengthened by it but weakened. Justice is immanent in love which, without it, becomes disorderly and weak.

In other words, unless justice is done to me I can never be fully a member of any community, just as a slave, suffering from the injustice of being always used as an instrument, can never be a member of the community that so uses him. Accordingly, we must have an eternal principle against which we can measure the use of power. Otherwise, what appeal have we against the actions of tyranny? The tyrant can always plead 'reasons of State', and usually has, on the Machiavellian principle, and this has been held to justify any iniquity. Courageous churchmen have often stood against tyranny 'in the name of God', whereas the rationalist has often found himself bereft. The whole point of rationalism is that it is open to argument and it can easily find itself without any ultimate principle except that of logic. The tyrant easily confounds him with his reasons of State. But there is no argument against the man who claims to be in the counsels of God. Tillich would say that this coincides with his own appeal to justice as an ontological principle. Priests have been known to plead in defence of the secrecy of the confessional that, while they respected the terrestrial court before which they were expected to give evidence, their appeal was to a 'higher' court. It is a powerful plea because no advocate can shake it.

That being granted, justice is what an all-wise love would wish to achieve for each individual. It is prepared to use the instruments of power for the sake of achieving this. Such power may be that of persuasion or of personal charm; or it may be that of violence or the threat of violence. It may mean incarcerating a lunatic or a criminal both for his own protection and for that of the public. But the means used must in these, as in all, cases be appropriate to the end. The Anarchists are right in saying that the State organisation always involves power and that violence is implicit in it. They overlook that, without power, which may involve compulsion, there is neither justice nor love. The alternative to power is that there shall be no effective centre of decision in the community. That way lies, not the Anarchist's dream, but chaos for, if no decisions can be taken, what else is there except chaos?

Tillich makes an odd remark about self-love, which he denies on the ground that, since love is the reunion of the separated, and the self is a unity, to talk of self-love is a self-contradiction. But this implies that the self is a unity without internal differentiation, which is obviously untrue. Later, he states that in our relations with others we must observe justice to ourselves as well as to others if our love is not to deteriorate into chaotic self-surrender. He then realises that this appears to contradict what he had said previously and explains that it is not a question of the self doing justice to itself but to all the elements of which it is the centre. But is not that exactly what self-love means? The argument for self-love is, in fact, precisely the same as that of Tillich, that the love of a person who cares nothing for himself is worthless to anybody. Without self-love we deteriorate into non-being! This is an extraordinary lapse for Tillich but is little more than a question of terminology and does not invalidate his main point.

JOHN MACMURRAY

Professor John Macmurray, of Edinburgh University, pursues the existentialist argument to the extent of rejecting outright the traditional philosophy that takes as its starting point the thinking self, as with Descartes and his 'I think, therefore I am'. This philosophy, he believes, is precluded by its own methodology from answering the basic questions. It finds itself in the ridiculous position of having either to prove that the external world exists, which it cannot do, or to accept that it does not, which is absurd. In the recent period it has sunk into the sterilities of logical positivism.

In his Gifford Lectures of 1954, published as *Persons in Relation*, he claims that man should not be studied, except from the bio-logical point of view, as an isolated organism, but as a member of a community of persons in relation. The task of philosophy is to explore the structure of this personal world. Man is to be seen as actor, or agent, not as a multiplicity of centres of reflection. If the Self is conceived as Thinker, or Knowing Subject, the Other becomes mere image-in-the-mind and no verification is possible, which leads to the absurdity that I, alone, exist and that my experience corresponds to nothing outside me. We know we exist only when we meet a resistance. Therefore existence must be taken as the primary datum. Self, Mind and Will, considered as independent isolates, are metaphysical fictions arising out of a false conception of what knowledge is.

The idea of the isolated agent is self-contradictory. Any agent is necessarily in relation to the Other. I exist as an individual only in relation to other individuals; as one term in the relation, You and I. It is the relation that constitutes the person. Of course, it is possible to treat the Other person as an object, as a doctor does when he is examining a patient; but this is justifiable only when it is done in the interests of the Other person as a person. On the other hand, it is fallacious to think of society as an organism, for, in that case, the individual would be entirely subordinated to the totality. On the contrary, society consists of persons in relation, each for all and all for each. The relation is that of interdependence.

Likewise, the individual, from earliest babyhood, is not an organism but a real person. The baby's adaptation to its environment is not instinctive but intentional. There is a perpetual interaction between the intentions of the mother, as she attends to its needs, and those of the baby as it makes its needs known by crying or croons with pleasure at the satisfaction of those needs. From the beginning there is this communication which is the infant's sole means of adaptation to the world into which it is born. Human experience is always shared experience. The unit of personal existence is not the individual but two persons in relation; 'reciprocity' is the word that best expresses this. Organic development functions as a differentiating element as dependence upon the mother turns into interdependence, and as the child finds its own identity when it contrasts the family with itself as the 'other-than-I'.

This interrelation of agents is the ground of morality. A morally right action is one that intends community and makes for harmonious interrelations. Every individual agent is responsible for his actions to all the others. The modes of morality are three. The first is communal, because conduct is directed first toward the good of the others in the community. The second is the contemplative, which is egocentric and escapist. It implies that the real world is the spiritual and it involves withdrawal into the world of reflection. The third is the pragmatic, which is also egocentric. The conduct associated with this attitude is aggressive and is designed to achieve the agent's purpose at the cost of overriding others. It regards the material world as the real world.

Religion reflects and symbolises this social interrelation. Since the agent must act upon something, and since he cannot act upon what is different in kind from himself (as mind cannot act upon matter) the universe itself must be personal. So Macmurray closes his treatment of the subject with an assertion of belief in a personal God, transcendent and immanent.

JEAN-PAUL SARTRE

Up to the present, the existentialists we have studied have been theists in the sense that they believe the world to have been divinely constituted for a transcendent purpose. But there is another school, including such men as Heidegger and Camus, philosophers of despair, that denies this proposition. As a representative of this school I choose the most widely known and most popularly admired of them all, Jean-Paul Sartre, one of the heroes of the intellectuals of Saint-Germain and a man who has held in France a position of influence not unlike that held at one time by Bertrand Russell in this country. During the last war he was involved in the Resistance and since then has been active in left-wing politics. His major work, *Being and Nothingness*, was first published in France in 1943. A richly talented man, he has also expressed various aspects of his thought in a succession of best-selling novels and plays.

His outright denial of the existence of any kind of God is fundamental to his philosophy. Not only, he says, is the existence of God unproved, the idea itself is self-contradictory. There could not be any Being recognisable as a God. The system he worked out as an alternative so rattled the Establishment that he had to share the ordeal of more orthodox prophets, that of public vilification. His enemies wrote unrestrainedly and viciously. I have before me, for instance, a piece published by a Freudian psychologist to the effect that a study of Sartre's works shows him to be living in a state of exaggerated sexual excitement and that he has never passed out of the childish state of auto-eroticism; he has no real interest in other people except as a means of providing himself with improved auto-erotic pleasure.

That any professional man should write so offensively of a distinguished professor during his life-time is outrageous. In the first place, there can be no possibility of reply to that kind of vituperation, unless Sartre were to have engaged a panel of psychoanalysts to examine him in depth and publish a report. Second, how could anyone, however experienced, pass such a judgment without having first put Sartre through a prolonged course of psychoanalysis? If any practitioner who had done this subsequently published his findings the breach of confidence would have been such as to require his being struck off the professional roll. In any case, among psychoanalysts it is considered grossly unethical to use their specialist skills outside the consulting room. Had he wished to do so, Sartre could have replied in kind that this was the vindictive outburst of a man who had not yet emerged from the Oedipal situation and was still trying to establish his identity by fits of the tantrums against his parents. No progress is to be made by argument on these lines.

The importance of this is that the existentialists are often charged with thinking so autobiographically that their thought is valid only for people who share their personal experience. While this may have been true of Kierkegaard it is certainly not true of Sartre. He works out in intricate detail the consequences of the denial of the theistic proposition. Certainly he starts with experience, but it is experience that is common to everybody who is not sunk in deep coma: that consciousness is always consciousness of *something*. No scandalous autobiographical revelations in that! Sartre is not projecting his own neuroses: he is thinking universally. There is no need here, even if it were practicable, to accompany him on his labyrinthine researches into the structure of reality: but we can, I hope without distortion, abstract and paraphrase those elements that are germane to our subject.

We have to accept reality as it presents itself to the human consciousness as given. There is no substratum to support it; no reason for its existence and no cause. It is ubiquitous. Sartre uses the phrase *de trop*. It is differentiated into 'things' or 'phenomena', and this phenomenal world Sartre calls 'Being' or, more distinctly, the 'in itself', for it has no meaning outside itself.

Consciousness becomes what it is only as it meets the resistance of phenomena. It is emptiness, nothingness. Logically, it is prior even to the self. There is not an 'I' at the centre of awareness that uses the senses as instruments for filling the consciousness. On the contrary, before we can say, 'I think', consciousness has to be aware of the self. As to why these consciousnesses, these fissures in reality, these 'holes in Being', as Sartre somewhere describes them, come into existence we cannot say. They happen and that is that. Nor are we to think of consciousness and the body as separate entities somehow acting upon each other, as with the Christian idea of a soul and a body attached to each other like puppies tied by the tails. If they were different entities there would be no way in which they could act upon each other. Instead of thinking in terms of a material body and an insubstantial consciousness we should think of a single person of which body and consciousness are merely different functions.

All this is shattering to human conceit. We can no longer think of ourselves as being 'a little lower than the angels', the lords of creation, to whom the Almighty gave the earth with its wealth of flora and fauna for the service of our needs. For Sartre, we are no more than 3,000 million accidents disturbing the serenity of previously unbroken Being. But it is easy to make fun of Sartre, and easy to caricature him, but it is less easy to dispose of him.

Here we are then, consciousness, the 'for itself', interruptions in the continuity of the 'in itself'. We live also in time. The concept of the 'present' is a useful fiction. In fact there is no such thing. Like a missile flying through the air that is never anywhere because it is always in passage to the next place, so are our lives in time. Each moment we fling the present into the past and then pass on to the next moment. All our lives we are building up a past which is unalterable, dead, in-itself. Always on the edge of the unknown, we peer into the future seeking to reunite ourselves with the stability and serenity of the in-itself, dragging the next moment towards us. Since we cannot until death find the security and peace for which we crave there is always an element of unhappiness at the heart of the for-itself.

Looking back over the past, the determinist believes that he sees a causal chain of events, that our future is conditioned by our past history, our heredity and environment. But this is hindsight, wisdom after the event. Looking backward, any succession of events could be made to look like a causal series. In reality it is not so. Our freedom is unconditional and inalienable. We choose from the infinity of possibilities before us what line we shall take. Of course, the past influences us; but it is we ourselves who have made our own past in freedom and, in freedom, we select from the past which elements shall influence us. I might choose to make my schooling, my military service, my professional career, or my family background to be the governing influence at any particular moment: it is entirely up to me. The facts of my environment, that I live on the slope of a lovely valley, that I have a pleasant house, that my health is good, that it is a foggy morning, these are not determinants of my future choices but the raw material with which I work. Without factors such as these I would be in a vacuum without any possibilities whatever before me. As it is, I can, if I wish, choose to make a fortune. I may not succeed but the choice was mine and I am now free to make another. I may content myself with cultivating my garden or I may take to the streets and drink myself to death on methylated spirits: the choice is mine. What I am not able to do is to surrender my freedom. That is always with me.

Sartre points out that, even in the torture chamber, the object of the interrogator is to extract information of the victim's *own volition*. If he drives the victim to the point beyond which he is capable of choosing freely he ceases to be a for-itself and becomes instead a mere instrument. The skill of the interrogator is to drive the victim to the point where he thinks he can bear the agony no longer but where he could, in fact, bear it for a moment or two longer. He then freely makes the confession and carries the remorse of it with him for the rest of his life.

This sense of being interminably poised on a razor edge of decision, whether we like it or not, induces a feeling of despair or fear, that Sartre calls 'anguish'. We cannot see what frustrations we shall meet or how we shall let ourselves down. We might panic in the moment of action or display weakness in confrontation with opponents. We might be struck with a thrombosis or suffer violent indigestion during a vital negotiation. Anything may happen; anything may go wrong, and knowledge of this is destructive of our peace of mind.

People try to avert their eyes from this perpetual insecurity. They want to delude themselves that things are other than they are. This tendency Sartre calls being 'in bad faith' and this, too, is a condition from which we cannot escape. It is the permanent lie in the soul. Sartre instances an attractive woman who allows a man to make passes at her while pretending not to notice. She wants to be wanted but dare not let herself be seduced, yet she knows that if she snubs the man she will spoil their relation; so she acts as if the situation were normal. We might think of the more banal situation in which a man tells the woman he wants to seduce that his wife does not understand him. This excuses his own infidelity and at the same time persuades the woman that, in falling in with the man's wishes, she is not committing an immorality but is consoling the injured. Such is bad faith. Even in moments of sincerity with ourselves we are in bad faith because we are trying to make ourselves other than we are.

We have now reached the position where the human person, in his loneliness, and in the anguish of his freedom and his bad faith, projects his future and carves out his own destiny. This brings us to Sartre's famous formula, 'existence precedes essence', because, from the standpoint of simple existence we make ourselves what we are going to be. There are no transcendent principles or values to aim at; we generate these from within ourselves. But we do not exist by ourselves. There are those other 3,000 million. What are our relations with the rest of mankind? This brings us to the concept of the Other, in contact with whom we realise our individuality. Suddenly, when we least want it, we become conscious of someone looking at us. Sartre instances the man who is discovered spying through a keyhole. Caught in that posture by the look of the Other, he feels shamefully self-conscious. He realises that for the Other he is rather a contemptible Object and he is humiliated. It is as if the Other has taken possession of him. To recover himself he turns the tables on the Other and, by fixing him in his own stare, makes him the Object. Sartre appears to think that whenever we become pronouncedly conscious of ourselves this mechanism of being taken possession of is at work, with consequent resentment followed by reassertion of our own dignity. The natural relation with the Other is that of conflict. While this may seem sweeping, we can see what Sartre means if we look hard at the organisations to which we belong, when we shall realise that, by charm, fraud or force, nearly everybody is trying to assert the claims of his own personality against those of everybody else, until each finds his own level.

An episode from my own experience may illustrate the point. Some years ago I was charged with dangerous driving. This was desperately serious because, in the circumstances of the time, a conviction would have meant the loss of my appointment and my home as well as my pension rights and the destruction of such reputation as I had. Yet the charge was quite gratuitous. Here, indeed, was anguish! Through none of my doing this wretched affair came adventitiously to blast my own life and the lives of my family. The charge was, in fact, so ludicrous that my legal representative would not believe my story. I am sure he thought me a liar as well as a criminal. Yet these driving cases are so much a matter of chance, owing to prejudice against motorists, that innocence is no guarantee of acquittal. I had the choice of a hearing before the magistrates or before Quarter Sessions, but I was seriously advised that conviction was inevitable in any case because neither Court had ever been known to acquit anybody of this charge. I therefore saved my pocket by choosing the lower Court.

As we were waiting for the Court to open, my lawyer came rushing to me in high glee. 'The chairman of the Bench has crashed his car on the way here and is in hospital,' he said, 'you might stand a chance.' But as I caught the looks of the prosecution lawyers and witnesses, cocky and confident, while I was in a condition of sheer terror, I certainly experienced them as Sartrean Others, while I felt myself to be an objectionable Object.

But, as the prosecution witnesses went into the box, it became clear that their stories were derisory and that my own story was true. My lawyer and I were now looking at each other in a different way: we were *en rapport*. My own principal witness, my young daughter, gave her evidence with admirable poise and clarity. I was proud of her and began to feel quite a man again. When my own turn came I was able, under cross-examination, finally to turn the tables on my opponents and to make them look both criminals and fools. It was really they who were responsibe for the accident out of which the case arose and they had tried to get away with it by spinning a cock and bull yarn. By this time I was thoroughly enjoying the situation and my look at the prosecution witnesses, slumped on their benches in the depths of dejection, saw them as the most abject Objects. Even the Police looked sheepish. The adventitious misfortune of the Chairman had saved me from the adventitious threat the charge had created. My case was fairly heard and I was acquitted. This episode lived out within the space of a morning every phase of Sartre's philosophy of interpersonal relations.

For the Other, I am object; it seems to me that he possesses my freedom and constitutes me as what I am. But I am never able to stand in the Other's shoes and see myself as he sees me. His freedom and subjectivity are therefore a challenge to me. I should like to assimilate that freedom and that subjectivity but because the relation is one of pure externality I cannot. The relation is permanently unsatisfactory and I need a more secure and unifying one. What I need is love. Another parable may serve to elucidate Sartre's somewhat involved and paradoxical thought on this subject.

Imagine a gawky young fellow, safely emerged from the gang stage but not yet fitting in anywhere else, lonely in spite of his many 'mates', looking for a girlfriend and unable to find one. He daydreams of how they would enjoy each other; but somehow he is never able to relate. A failing statesman was once described as 'wandering around the House of Commons like an accident looking for somewhere to happen'. That is exactly how the youth feels – *de trop*.

> I a stranger and afraid
> In a world I never made
> (Housman)

sums up his predicament. He wants to stop feeling *de trop*. It is not only because he is bursting with frustrated sexuality that he wants a girlfriend. His deeper, unarticulated reasons are much more respectable than that. And, surely, it is not that he already wants to settle down as a married man or to gain prestige among his friends. In his heart of hearts he wants a secure niche in a frightening and lonely world and hopes to find it in the affections of someone else. He reaches out to the serenity and calmness of the in-itself and thinks he will find that kind of relaxation and quietness in the arms of his girl. Similarly, the young woman who behaves promiscuously because she is looking for a man who gives her the same cosiness and security that, as a child, she felt with her father is a familiar figure. Most of us have felt needs of that kind at some period of our lives: Sartre would say that we all feel the same all the time. So the gawky young fellow wants a girlfriend. It is not so much that he wants to love as that he wants to be loved, and therefore to belong. Almost anybody would do: which, again, is a familiar description of adolescent needs.

He wants to be loved for himself. It would not satisfy that a girl should want him only because he owns a motor-cycle and can take her pillion riding; although he would not be above using that as a bait. After all, when an impecunious duke marries an American millionairess it is the dollars and the title that are in love with each other, not the man and the woman. The duke will still want his mistresses and the millionairess her lovers. In the same way, a young woman feels humiliated if men want her only because she is good in bed. She wants to be wanted for what she is as a human person, not as an instrument for someone's pleasure.

Nor will it satisfy the young man to be one friend of the girl's among others, however intimate. It would mean that he was only one object among others. This is one aspect of affairs in which there is no safety in numbers. He wants to fill the girl's entire horizon. When he knows himself to be the supreme object of the girl's thought and attention, that she has no other longing except to be with him, that he is at the apex of the hierarchy of her priorities, then he imagines he will be safe, with his place in the world secure and an adequate reason for living. But he wants all this to be given freely, without compulsion or ulterior motive. If he lavishes expensive presents on her, or gives her money, at once her freedom evades him. He may dazzle her and he may appeal to her cupidity but, basically, he will be turning her into a prostitute. No! She will appreciate his gifts and he will enjoy giving them, but only if they come out of the depth of feeling, because he can hardly help himself giving them.

How can the young fellow win such love as this? If he were an experienced man of the world he would know how to present himself as desirable to the woman of his choice. But he is not; he is a shy and clumsy young fellow and so he has to continue feeling gawky and *de trop*, perhaps until some likeable girl in a similarly forlorn position, but with a little more *savoir faire*, sets her eyes on him. To win such love he must be prepared to offer a corresponding love. The girl must reach the point where she genuinely believes that it will be worth all the world for her to be loved by this young fellow and by nobody else. She must want his love in exactly the same way as he wants hers, freely given, without constraints or inducements. Then each will be to the other the privileged object and each will possess the other's freedom and subjectivity. That is why they want reassurance from each other that there is nothing they would not do for each other. They would sacrifice their best friends, break the law, go through fire and water. Often, a girl will put the young fellow through all kinds of secret tests before she dares to commit herself. This irritates the boy because he feels that she has no confidence in him for what he is and for his own sake.

Such is the ideal and, perhaps, it occurs more often than cynics suppose. But even that is not the end of the story. In the presence of a third party all three know each other as objects again, which is why the young fellow cannot bear to share his girlfriend with other young fellows. He loses his position of primacy and is jealous. That, also, is why lovers always prefer solitude and why having a parent to share their home is always a threat to a young married couple, however tactful and considerate the parent may be. The security each of the partner's gains is only relative. At any moment one may see the other as just one object among others against the background of the world, when the magic will vanish. There are instances when, on the wedding night, under conditions experienced for the first time, the bride suddenly realises her groom as a man totally different from the one she fell in love with not many months before. There are tragic occasions when the marriage does not outlast the honeymoon.

Sartre believes that at the highest moment of consummation the two lovers are still separate identities and their relation is still an external one. Hence its fragility. It is in the closest intimacy that the lovers become most aware of their separateness. Here, I am not sure whether the situation is as tragic as it looks. Without consciousness of their separateness, the desire for union and the satisfaction of bringing it about would both vanish together. Although lovers like to talk to each other about mutual absorption, and the obliteration of separateness, if it actually came about they would find undifferentiated unity rather boring. The fulfilment is in the perfection of the relation in spite of its precariousness. In complete unity the relation would vanish and there could be no love. I feel also that Sartre hardens his rigidities too much. Is there not, between lovers, a spiritual interpenetration, an emotional osmosis, as well as physical union? Beyond this question neither psychology nor philosophy can take us: we are left to interrogate our own experience.

In treating sadism and masochism as perversions of love, Sartre is on firm ground. Both are self-defeating. Sadism seeks to dominate and possess the freedom of the victim but in so doing destroys that freedom and finds itself confronting only a twisting agony. The masochist wants to surrender his own freedom to the Other but finds himself instead using the Other as his own instrument, as in the case of the man who pays a prostitute to flog him. On the subject of hate, Sartre is less sure-footed. Hate, he says, is the desire for the death of the person hated and this person stands surrogate for the whole of humanity. To hate one man is to hate your fellow men. But hate often derives from love, as I might hate a man who tries to entice the woman I am in love with. In this case I hate because I love. Usually we hate those who use for our injury the power they exercise over us or who cause us fear. What we fear we hate. We do not want the death of him we hate but to strip him of all dignity and self-respect so that he wishes he were dead.

It is questionable, too, whether Sartre is right in saying that to return the Look is to extinguish it. If we return the Look, he says, we see only a pair of eyes. Walking along the Strand, the people on the pavement are merely things in my way; animated, but still *things*. Suddenly I come across a group of workmen putting up barriers so that they can dig a hole in the road. A small man, hardly more than a midget, steps out of the group and takes a pick-axe, nearly as big as himself, and starts to bash the road surface with such venom as to make it seem as if he wants to cleave in twain the terrestrial orb entire. The scene strikes me as irresistibly comic. My eyes catch the eyes of one of the animated *things* and we both smile. In catching his eye I see him as a living person like myself, although I have never spoken to him, and I know him better than I know some people whom I have met frequently on committees for years. This look of mutual recognition is a form of egalitarian communication, a silent language, that is at least as significant as what has been called the 'Sartrean stare'.

Sartre's work contains much that is valuable and true. It can, indeed, exercise a powerful attraction. There is an exhilaration about the idea of unconditional freedom and of carving our own destiny. As for anguish, gamblers exploit it for their own amusement and find that the fear heightens the thrill of the game. Yet, if we look more deeply, unconditional freedom, with no reason why we should choose this way or that, would turn out to be unconditional stagnation. Freedom, as Hegel said, is grounded in necessity, while St Augustine rooted it in obedience to the divine will: 'In whose service is perfect freedom'. A world without values or standards, in which it was of no objective consequence whether mankind were annihilated by nuclear weapons or achieved Utopia, and where it mattered nothing whether I drank myself silly every day or led a nation in the ways of happiness and peace, would be a world of unconditional futility and boredom. We could hardly survive in such a world.

While it is right that we should not judge a philosophy by its consequences but by its truth, to find that a philosophy is quite unpragmatic is surely an indication that it is not an accurate analysis of reality. It may be that a better point of departure than the consciousness of something or other would be the historical fact that intelligent life has managed to survive on this planet for tens of thousands of years, and that the number of people who have been glad to be alive, and have known the deepest happiness, has not been few.

SIMONE DE BEAUVOIR

Known to be a close personal friend of Sartre, Simone de Beauvoir writes independently of him, although his influence upon her thought is discernible. Her most famous work, first published in French in 1949, and later published in English under the title, *The Second Sex*, might well be adopted as the Bible of the Women's Liberation Movement. Written in the spirit of Mary Wollstonecraft, it resumes the discussion of the status of womanhood and the relations between the sexes in the light of subsequent developments both social and scientific.

She makes no attempt to evade or diminish the fact of femininity. While there are no fixed entities, she says, determining given characteristics, the division of humanity into male and female nonetheless forces itself upon us. What she does emphatically repudiate is the notion that the difference between the sexes is to be defined in terms of biological functioning alone. Then what is woman? A man, she notes, would never write a book about the situation of the human male; but many authors, both men and women, have written books on the position of the female. Woman defines herself negatively in relation to man. The terms 'masculine' and 'feminine' are used symmetrically only as a matter of form. The masculine is the standard human type. Woman's biological function imprisons her in her subjectivity. St Thomas Aquinas defines woman as 'an imperfect man'. Man can think of himself without woman but woman cannot think of herself without man. She is the sex. Man is the subject – woman the Other. But why have women never insisted on reciprocity?

What they have gained, they have been given: they have never taken. The reason for this is that their situation deprives them of the means of achieving solidarity. It is the *couple* that is their social unit.'

There is a similarity between the position of women and that of Negroes. Both are in process of emancipation while a superior social class is trying to resist. A vicious circle has come into operation. Those who are treated as inferior become inferior in practice. But, in the case of men, their superior attitude to women is most often due to an inferiority complex or anxiety about their virility. To understand the situation we must throw aside current notions of superiority, inferiority and equality and start afresh. Feminist writings should no longer concern themselves with rights but with clarity. The word 'female' is itself derogatory: it imprisons woman in her animality.

Biologically, there is no truth in the supposition that the feminine plays the passive rôle. Asexual multiplication of living cells can continue indefinitely without degeneration. In any species, the male appears to be fundamentally unnecessary (i.e. from the standpoint of cellular multiplication). The differentiation of the gametes is accidental. Therefore the division into male and female is 'simply an irreducible fact of observation'. The chromosomes programmed XX give rise to the female and XY to the male. The two gametes together create a living thing. Biologically, the supposed passivity of the female in the union of sperm and the ovum is mythical.

The sexual adventure itself is immediately experienced by the woman as interior event and not as outward relation to the world and to others. After copulation, 'the male recovers his individuality intact at the moment when he transcends it . . . the female is at once herself and other than herself; and after birth she feeds the newborn upon the milk of her breasts.' In the higher forms of life: 'The male finds more and more varied ways in which to employ the forces he is master of; the female feels her enslavement more and more keenly, the more the conflict between her own interests and the reproductive forces is heightened.' Yet, continues Simone de Beauvoir, 'I deny that they (the biological facts) establish for her a fixed and inevitable destiny'. There is no living reality except as manifested by the conscious individual through activities in the bosom of society. Biology alone does not answer the question, why is woman the Other? Woman is to be defined as a human being in quest of values in a world of values, a world of which it is essential to know the economic and social structure.

While all of this is unexceptionable to plain reason, one qualification does need to be inserted. Simone de Beauvoir attributes the temperamental and attitudinal differences between the sexes to cultural influences, which are brought to bear from earliest childhood. By the kind of toys she is given and by the games she is expected to play, the girl child is guided into a socially acceptable feminine rôle. Against this statement must be placed the subjective impression of many parents that the differentiation is noticeable from the first days of life, long before any cultural influence has had a chance of being exercised, let alone of taking effect. It is precisely the male characteristics of aggressiveness and heedlessness observable at this stage which, in fact, give the girl-child the advantage in the learning process. While it may be true that culture is a more powerful influence than genetics in the formation of character, yet the genetic influence is not without importance. The statement that character is genetically determined but culturally elaborated would seem to be a more accurate formulation than that of Simone de Beauvoir.

To proceed: over against Soviet Communism, Simone de Beauvoir asserts that sex does not admit of integration with the social whole because there is in eroticism a revolt of the instant against time, of the individual against the universal. The erotic experience is one in which generality is always regained by an individuality.

As warrior, risking life, man proved that life is not for him the supreme value. It is not in giving life, but in risking life, that man is raised above the universal; that is why superiority has been accorded in humanity not to the sex that brings forth but to that which kills. Man's design is not to repeat himself in time: it is to take control of the instant and mould the future. In ancient agricultural communities maternity had prestige because of inheritance. Woman was assimilated to the earth because through both the permanence of life was assured. But this was ritualised in the religious worship of the Great Mother. It is always men who are politically and socially dominant. Man as transcendent, as tool user, could achieve his destiny only by dethroning womanhood as mystery and terror. The institution of slavery still further devalued womanhood by depriving her of usefulness.

During the Industrial Revolution womanhood entered into new opportunities because she was required in the factories. It is through labour that she has conquered her dignity as a human being. Yet, because she has still been tied to the family, she has still been subject to exploitation. Her earnings have been an extra to the family budget. Concurrently, womanhood has been freed from slavery to the reproductive process.

Man aspires both to life and to repose. Woman provides him with reciprocity without constituting a threat to him. 'Genuine love ought to be founded on the mutual recognition of two liberties.' But man demands that woman represent the flesh for its own sake. He does not see her body as the mediation of a subjective personality but as a *thing* sunk in its own immanence. Yet paradoxically, he dreads the suggestion of decay and mortality in nature and so devises artifices to conceal it. The Oriental, careless of his own fate, is content with a female who is for him a means of enjoyment. The Greek never found in the female, imprisoned in the women's apartments, the fellow being he required and so he turned to male companions. The more the male becomes individualised and lays claim to his individuality the more certainly he will recognise also in his companion an individual and free being.

JOHN COWBURN, S.J.

Father John Cowburn is a brilliant young Australian Jesuit who, after undergoing the training usual in his Order, studied at Innsbruck, Austria, under Karl Rahner and Emeric Coreth. Not only is he, as befits a Jesuit, steeped in the Scholastic tradition, he is also thoroughly acquainted with the existentialists; a good combination, especially in a man with a gift for synthesis. His erudition is, indeed, so considerable that, in setting out his conclusions, we round up many of the ideas we have already run across in this book and also gain the distilled essence of a number of contemporary authors for whom we have not had space. To all this, Cowburn adds cohesion and a sense of direction, besides his own original contribution. We appreciate him particularly for his clear definition and his organisation of his material. His work, *Love and the Human Person*, was first published in 1967.

First, he says, we must distinguish between the nature of a thing and its individuality; a distinction that can be illustrated by the contrast between a pen that we value merely because its nature is to be an instrument for writing, and a pen that is special for us because of some sentimental association. In the first instance, any pen would do: in the second, we would not part with this particular pen for a fortune. *Personality* is a higher order of individuality. A person is an individual whose nature it is to be rational. We see the difference by comparing the answers to the question, 'What is that?' (any one of a million pens) and, 'Who is that?' (one particular John Smith and one only). Personality perfects and includes individuality. A *person has* his nature as one of his possessions; rationality, a sense of humour, a phlegmatic temperament, a talent for music.

As we rise in the scale of being from the material to the highest products of nature we find increasing complexity and inwardness. Man's peculiarity is his consciousness and his liberty, which are what make the uniqueness of the individual human being. This is the person. But, as inwardness increases, so does association. Grains of sand do not associate, they merely happen to lie side by side. Association is stronger with the plants, which from their roots and their seed produce their own progeny. It is still stronger with bees and ants, stronger with the gregarious animals and strongest of all with man. A man is a knot of relations but he is still unique and his relations add nothing to his nature as a man.

Only persons have value in themselves and are not intended for the use of any other beings. A tool is valued for its usefulness as an instrument: a man is valued for what he is as a man. But we do not distinguish between a man and his nature as between two different things: always we consider the person as he is in his situation. The 'I' is soul, body, mind, spirit, thinking and all else that he is. He is subject as opposed to object. A man is a person by virtue of consciousness and self-commitment. We cannot avoid self-commitment.

A person can either accept or reject his own nature but he never entirely rejects it. Much is predetermined for him but, also, much is left undetermined and in this area he must choose for himself what he will be. The actions of a free man precede and determine his nature. We are part of the natural order and belong to it. Accepting that, we accept ourselves. What we do is done through us by the natural order and, in doing it, we bring the natural order to its full development.

Among the Scholastics, two theories of love were current, the physical and the ecstatic. Physical love arose out of the oneness of nature, as in parental love. Cowburn feels that the terms 'physical' or 'natural' love are open to misunderstanding and confusion owing to the popular usage of these words and suggests, instead, the contrast between 'cosmic' and 'ecstatic' love. Both imply self-love, which is the opposite of selfishness and, in reality, arises out of the hatred of the self. A proper self-love involves a desire to reproduce oneself. Fatherhood consists of (1) the objective communication of a nature (2) the will to do this. Physical presence is not necessary to paternal love. A son may develop his own interests and go to live abroad and may, ultimately, have little in common with his father, but this in no way diminishes the affection between father and son. Just as self-love is not selfish so paternal love is not self-interested. Nor is cosmic love of any other. As the father brings his child into the world without his consent so he assumes authority over him without his agreement. In the child, the father loves his own nature, which he has communicated to it. The child accepts the parents naturally and without deliberation, although he tests their authority. The father wants of the son that he reaches excellence

and that he recognises him as his father. The son has an obligation
to his father to pursue his own development. The filial relation
does not require the 'I – Thou' but may well lead to it. The tie of
nature is shown by the fact that, if a child is separated from his
parents at an early age he will move heaven and earth in later life
to find them and to renew his communication with them. It is as
if in finding them he found himself.

Here I must enter an objection. It is not to duplicate their own
nature that either mother or father want children, except in the
minimal sense of wanting children who are human and reason-
able! If a woman cannot bear children of her own she is often at
least as contented with adoption. This is no less true of a husband
whose wife is sterile. The satisfaction of parenthood is in bringing
up the child from earliest months and assisting it to develop its
own distinctiveness and independence. To ask why parents want
children is like asking why a sculptor wants to sculpt or a player
to play. It is their nature to do so and otherwise they would be
unfulfilled. After that there is no more to be said. It is a poor
filial relation that does not develop into the 'I – Thou'. This can
begin as soon as the child realises its own separateness. For this
reason the word 'authority' is unfortunate. What occurs is an
interaction between father and son in which the son will tacitly
acknowledge the superior experience of the father. But the son
may exercise his freedom by rebelling against even the best of
fathers. If a father takes his stand on his natural authority he is in
the right way to forfeit the respect of the boy as he grows up.

To continue: ecstatic love aims at the person himself in his
singularity, as in intersexual love or the love that binds friends. It
is the being in himself, taken as a totality, that is loved. Ecstatic
love is never for the beloved's qualities as such. Loneliness is the
fundamental problem of the self. In meeting and recognition is
the end of loneliness and of not being understood. To know a man
personally requires dialogue, which means intercommunication
on the deepest possible level. Love begins when the two consent
to each other as they are and as they exist. Love is not for the
potentiality of the other. If it were, it would not be for the person
at all but for the person as he might become. There is no decision

to love, but an occurrence of love. Nor is love desire: it is an act of the will, a self-commitment. Each is unique to the other. This is to love for the sake of the individual self, which is to love him as precisely the other. Loving in this way, a man is taken out of himself, which is why it is called 'ecstatic'. It means that a man wills the being of the other as he wills his own being. Self-sacrifice means precisely that. Cowburn recoils, understandably, from the idea that self-sacrifice springs from the love of virtue rather than from love of the other. Could that possibly coincide with the greater love that no man has than that he lay down his life for his friend?

Love is a unifying force: it is not union itself but union is consequent upon it. Love is a 'we' relation, without loss of identity on either side. It is not assimilation but unity. More precisely, it is union with a distinction not between opposites but between correlates. By paradox, each becomes more himself because of his identification with the other. For someone else to find fulfilment in me there has to be a me. This means synthesis rather than assimilation. Love is the gift of the self disinterestedly, but with the desire to be loved in return. It presupposes self-love. In the last resort, ecstatic love is unanalysable and inexplicable. It is neither rational nor irrational, but para-rational.

A gift is truly a gift only if it is willingly received with gratitude. Otherwise, it is not a gift but an unwanted imposition. Therefore there is always a return for a gift. In the same way, love is not fully love until it is reciprocated. Unconditional communication develops only when, in the depths of their being, self meets self on an equal footing. This relation is that of equality; but it is not equality in intelligence or virtue or talent but as persons. Thus the bride accepts in equality the authority of her husband.

Here again, the word 'authority' is inappropriate. It always implies coercion in the background and it totally misinterprets the marriage situation. Under modern conditions, any husband of a wife worth having who takes the authoritative stance is well on his way to finding himself back on the marriage market – rightly. Authority is for organisations that are too large to admit of the

'I–Thou' system of relations, which should be the norm for small communities. In a guerilla band, for instance, it is out of place: in a regular army it is indispensable. The statesman, Joseph Chamberlain, did himself no credit when, in soliciting the hand in marriage of Beatrice Potter, he insisted that she should in all things accept his authority. What he wanted of a woman, he said, was intelligent sympathy, not disagreement. Beatrice replied that, to her, this would mean intolerable servility and the affair came to an end. To expect this degradation of so superlative a woman as Beatrice Potter revealed an insensitive obtuseness surprising in such an intelligent man as Chamberlain. Later, Beatrice married Sidney Webb with whom she lived on terms of mutuality and equality and with whom she collaborated in numerous literary works and political activities. As John Stuart Mill remarked, in a business partnership there is not necessarily a dominant partner; why in marriage? It is nearly half-a-century since brides in the Anglican Communion had to vow love, honour and *obedience*. In the contrapuntal relation of marriage, in any situation, whichever partner has the skill or experience the circumstances require, spontaneously takes the lead and the other naturally accepts. Authority is irrelevant.

Cowburn continues that love is total. We give ourselves wholly just as we put all of ourselves into any free act. But the gift of self would be only a loan if made for a limited period (but is a gift never worn out or discarded?) therefore love is eternal. From this Cowburn believes that marriage can be deduced *a priori*.

Not egotism, but the readiness to love, is the primary relation. Friendship is strictly spiritual but conjugal love is, 'a single, combined operation of the will and the senses, the soul and the body, and, though it can be analysed into its two components, it has a real unity'. Friendship is not an impoverished version of sexual love but a relation in its own right which usually occurs when men are working together on some important enterprise. In conjugal, or romantic, love giving is physical and spiritual. The relation is objectified in the child, which is the image of the union. The sexual act is the expression of the two-in-oneness.

Father Cowburn would not thank me were I to omit mention

of his conviction that human love is a reflection of the divine love. To do so would be to overlook the main intention of his work. A principal aim of his thesis is to dispose of the theory that belief in the Divine love is a projection of the human longing for love; or that the attribution of love to God is an anthropomorphism. 'To say that only sexual love is the real thing and that "love of God" is a figure of speech,' he comments, 'is like saying that the painting in the gallery is nothing but a blown up version of the postcard on sale at the door.' But what Cowburn's more sophisticated opponents would say is that Freud and Jung burgled the picture from the gallery while the attendant's back was turned and left the postcard as a reminder. Cowburn concludes his volume with a section on the love-relation within the Holy Trinity.

THE DEPTH PSYCHOLOGISTS

In origin and intention, depth psychology was, and still is, therapeutic. To make of it a philosophy of life is to misconstrue what is essentially a methodology. It begins and continues in the consulting room with a sick mind that is to be restored to a wholesome condition. People seek the assistance of the analyst because they are hurting so badly inside, for no apparent reason, and are so at odds with themselves, that they may even be a danger to themselves and to others. With the help of the analyst they hope to regain the capacity for laughter, life and love. The analyst is a professional man, often with a high medical qualification and a long specialist training.

This being so, it would seem that there is no more a place in this book for a discussion of depth psychology than there is for a disquisition on cardiology or gynaecology. Until now we have been working on the level of freedom and responsibility, which is the level on which we have to live our everyday lives. There is no alternative to living on that level. We are not in the doctor-patient relation with the people we encounter as we go about our affairs. We have to behave as if all of us could make up our own minds and be held responsible for our decisions. I may have the best of reasons for believing the boss at my office to be a raving paranoiac, who is causing infinite suffering and damaging the business because of his derangement, but I have to take him as he is and act toward him as if he were free and responsible. Such smatterings of psychology as I have been able to acquire may help me to understand him and to exercise patience but I cannot put him on the couch and psychoanalyse him. Similarly, the boss who tries to dissect the motives and feelings of his subordinates in a quiet chat is a peril to be given a wide berth, if only because, being untrained, he will not know how to allow for his own subconscious reactions. He is too personally involved to be objective.

At the same time, it is also true that depth psychology has exercised a profound influence on interpersonal relations and on public attitudes to many social problems. The literature of the subject has had a great vogue; partly owing to healthy curiosity about the human make-up; partly because of its aura of the occult and esoteric (new analyst is old witch doctor writ large); partly because of the pleasurable shock it gives to conventional prejudices. Some of the leading ideas, and some of the terminology, often misunderstood, have become part of the normal furniture of the mind. The medical profession at first regarded the new methodology with proper caution but have since learned much from it; for example, the previously unsuspected importance of psychical influences in the aetiology of disease.

It is, perhaps, in the administration of the law that the new way of looking at human nature has had the most obvious influence. Here the change in attitudes has been revolutionary. Like all beneficial revolutions this has been brought to pass by the dynamic of ideas, without a drop of bloodshed and without a single demonstration. But the whole emphasis has shifted from retributive to remedial punishment. Judges and magistrates nowadays are, in many difficult cases, reluctant to pass judgment without first remitting the prisoner for medical reports, especially in the children's Courts. Group psychotherapy is now an accepted element in the prison system. Cruel legislation against homosexuals has been repealed.

Pundits used to pontificate, without contradiction, that nobody ever returned for a second birching, until some bright person thought of counting, when it was discovered that a large proportion (about 70 per cent) returned. Psychologists could explain that the treatment engendered such a black hatred of mankind that the victim went away a confirmed public enemy. When a judge so far forgot himself as to opine that a sound thrashing would benefit the youth before him, an enterprising journalist went to investigate. He found that the poor lad's father was an ex-sergeant major who had belted him every day of his life. Before the beginning of this century only a few exceptional humanitarians would have dreamed that there might be anything to investigate.

For the family, a multitude of popularly written books and pamphlets convey to parents the latest thoughts of the child psychologists on the upbringing of children. The vile phrase, 'spare the rod and spoil the child', is now seldom heard. It is known that the rod is more likely to create delinquency than to cure it. The work of the psychologists has, also, gone far to dispel the glutinous miasma of guilt that used to envelop the subject of sex. Here, the guilt does infinitely more damage than the deed. Even on the most superficial level this is evident. Having been unwise, or carried away by feeling, a girl becomes pregnant. In guilt-engendered fear of the guilt-engendered scorn of the neighbours, her parents fling her out to make her way, destitute, to the squalor of North Kensington, where she has no recourse but to drugs and prostitution. The parents then lament noisily over the vice statistics. At a deeper level it is now known how morbid guilt can bring on illness and can wreck the marital relation.

We have learned to look askance at moral indignation and we have learned the truth of Shakespeare:

> Thou rascal beadle, hold thy bloody hand:
> Why dost thou lash that whore? Strip thine own back;
> Thou hotly lust'st to use her in that kind
> For which thou whipp'st her. The usurer hangs the cozener.
> Through tatter'd clothes small vices do appear;

Robes and furr'd gowns hide all. Plate sins with gold,
And the strong lance of justice hurtless breaks;
Arm it in rags, a pigmy's straw doth pierce it.

King Lear

Moral condemnation is the obverse of morbid guilt. It is whole-some only when reserved for the evils that genuinely deserve it; for cruelty, hypocrisy and injustice, the weightier matters of the law.

Of course, there is another, less admirable side. Half-understood, ill-digested psychological concepts have distorted ethical attitudes. Emancipation from sexual guilt, and from inhibitions and taboos, is often taken to imply emancipation from all restraints and standards. No psychologist of any repute has ever said that! But this provides a convenient excuse for indiscriminate sexual promiscuity and the disregard of social obligations. It is imagined that *all* guilt is morbid: but, if we have behaved un-worthily, it is unhealthy not to feel guilty unless amends have been made. Morbid guilt is remorse for nameless deeds that have never been committed; guilt, perhaps, driven into the depths at an early age by foolishly strict or religious parents. The emanci-pated are often far more intolerant of the traditionalists than the despised traditionalists are of them. There is a tendency to dis-count all tradition as being of murky or superstitious provenance. Principles, standards, religious beliefs, are psychologisms to be discarded in favour of 'doing your own thing', which usually turns out to be the most blatant psychologism of them all. Slick, generalised, psychological explanations are found for all be-haviour. If a man is faithful to his wife, he is afraid of sex; if he likes the company of women, he is a mother-fixated Don Juan; if he prefers male company, he has not emerged from the Oedipal situation; if he has a taste for solitude, he is narcissistic. If two women are friends, they are lesbian; and so on, and so on. All this is degrading to interpersonal relations. Yet, if a balance could be struck, it would probably be found that the good that has flowed from the popularisation of the ideas associated with depth psychology far outweighs the evil. Enlightened Humanism has found in these ideas an instrument that it has used to good effect.

Until the early years of the century, psychologists had confined themselves either to studying the surface of consciousness or to counting the instincts in the bundle of them that was supposed to constitute human personality. In 1900 the Viennese neurologist, Sigmund Freud, started the new movement with his revolutionary *The Interpretation of Dreams*. Later, the other two of the great trinity, Adler and Jung, worked with him for a time but then broke away to form traditions of their own. But they never abandoned Freud's central insights and they continued to use his method.

Simply stated, this was based on the discovery that the springs of human behaviour rise far below the surface of consciousness and that, by penetrating to them through the free association of ideas and the study of dreams, the analyst could enable the patient to understand himself sufficiently to regain control over the unrecognised forces and long forgotten memories that were the causes of his disturbances and so rid him of his neuroses. The differences between the interpretations of the structure and development of the human personality offered by this trinity were strongly marked. There has been plenty of room for adjustment and redevelopment by those who learned their first lessons in depth psychology from them. Behaviourists and clinical psychologists add to the Babel. But, in practice, there is more consistency than at first appears; for the tendency among practitioners is to an eclecticism that selects from the masters and their successors the salient truths that apply in the particular cases before them. The almost religious dogmatism that characterised many of them in the early days is now less prominent.

In general, the weakness of the Freudian school, and of the traditions that spring from it, is to be narrowly individualistic. The human person is for them a test-tube in which a variety of chemical elements bubble and boil and froth together until they overflow. All human conduct is selfishness and hedonism and the natural relation between people is that of conflict. So I shall leave Freud and his school, with their Oedipal dubieties and their

incest phantasies and their infantile sexuality and their reduc-
tionism *ad absurdum* and turn, instead, to another who started in
this tradition, but who broke away in a direction more interesting
to us, and more promising for the understanding of society,
Ian D. Suttie, whose work, *The Origins of Love and Hate*, was first
published in 1935.

Gregarious animals, says Suttie, differ from the solitary mainly
in the length of time they nurture their young. This suggests to
him where to look for the secret of human society, which he
finds in the dominating need of the new-born child to retain
contact with the mother. Long after the sensory gratifications of
the breast have become superfluous, the need for comfort,
attention and support remains. As separateness and identity
develop, the child finds substitutes for this mother-baby relation
in social co-operation, competition and culture. 'By these substitutes we put the whole social environment in the place of the
mother.' We have a mental and cultural *rapport* instead of
maternal caresses. Friendship, also, develops out of the love
relation with the mother but comes about by a shared concern
for the same interests rather than by concentrating attention upon
each other.

Dread of loneliness is the conscious expression of the urge for
self-preservation, which is what originally attaches the child to
the mother. Out of this emerges not only the power to love, but
the need to love. The child's tantrums are aimed at inducing the
mother to accomplish the child's wishes. What the child cannot
tolerate is being ignored; it actually wants to be punished because that means it is receiving attention. Fear in a baby can find
expression only as an appeal to the mother. 'Earth hath no hate
but love to hatred turned and hell no fury but a baby scorned.'
Suttie is sure that all hatred derives ultimately from love.

At first, the baby does not distinguish between itself and the
mother. This 'binity', the undifferentiated two-in-one, comprises the baby's entire universe. Then there comes the gradual
discovery of the not-self as an external power making for pleasure
or displeasure, because the not-self is associated from the beginning with anxiety and resentment as well as loving feeling.

The child makes angry claims against it. As time passes the child learns to compensate for loneliness or rejection by phantasy memories of past gratifications.

In the initial stages the mother-child relation is one of complete equality. The mother gives the breast: the child gives the mouth. It is a paradisial state when all the baby's acts are acceptable. Then comes a period when the child's wishes are not uniformly acceptable; weaning, toilet training and the like, which involve frustrations, insecurity and irritability. Each refusal ranks for the child as a rejection and so there has to be repeated effort to restore the love relation. The baby's attitude becomes ambivalent: on the one hand is the longing and the love; on the other, anxiety, apprehension and anger. The cause of these negative feelings has to be removed by the reestablishment of harmony. So, all through life, we induce other people to do things for us for the sake of the reassurance this provides that we are loved. Thus we seek power as a means to the acquisition of love and not vice-versa. The refusal of the mother to give attention is as much a rejection of the child's proffered gifts as a withdrawal of her own. The reaction of the child is a feeling of badness or unlovableness, and, also, anxiety, hate and aggression.

As against Freud, Suttie writes: 'I consider that the germs of goodness and love are present from the very beginning and that our traditional method of upbringing frustrates this spontaneous benevolence and substitutes a "guilt-anxiety" morality for natural goodness.' By contrast with Freud's individualism, Suttie's psychology is relational. But, he continues, inhibitions on his giving tend to direct upon others the child's attitudes to his parents.

Various human emotions are different forms of the same social feeling. The greater the love, the greater the hate formed as a result of its frustration. Thus we have: love threatened = anxiety; love denied = hate; love refused = despair; unworthiness of love = guilt and shame; loss of love = grief; sympathy with the object of love = pity. Whether these equations of Suttie's fit all cases is open to question. For instance a man does not necessarily hate a woman who fails to reciprocate his love. He is more likely to feel a sense of bereavement. But there is deep insight into his later remark that the disposition of love is the centre of all the bitterness of human nature, which leads many people to the cynical denial of its reality. The need to give love and to have it accepted is as real as any of the bodily wants. Self-sacrifice is demanded of the other as the only guarantee that the love is both accepted and returned. The basis of asceticism is that love is not real if it is pleasurable: it must be sacrificial. The taboo on tenderness, so characteristic of the Anglo-Saxons, creates an artificial distance and a consequent emotional barrier between men and women.

The origin of society is to be found in the band of brothers and sisters formed under each mother. The parents imposed morality by the threat of the withdrawal of love.

Chapter Nine

Future Tense

Nothing is so frustrating either to the social dogmatist or to the legislator of morals as the transformations that occur within the human personality. No sooner do they imagine themselves to have human nature neatly docketed for all time than it slips away, leaving them looking foolish. Since these transformations are always accompanied by changes in the style of relations between persons, which are the subject matter of the dogmatists and legislators, the articles of faith and the commandments they have laboriously compiled lose their relevance and their work has to be done all over again. The ethical debate moves to new ground and argues from different premises. The interpersonal relation is perennially a subject of intense discussion precisely because it can never be trapped in a formula.

But the Establishment, at any time, is what it is precisely because it consists of people who have introjected the code into themselves. It has become the material of their consciences. As a consequence, when their assumptions are challenged they are horrified at what comes to them as a threat to the very ground of their personal security. Hence the resistance to change of the institutions in which the mores of the Establishment are embodied; the legal systems, the churches and education. With the sanctions of religion and tradition behind them, their first impulse is always to resist and often enough they are right to do so; but the results are rebelliousness, social upheaval, moral collapse and the generation gap.

However changeless the basic ingredients of human nature may be, the physical constitution, the appetites and the intelligence, the structure of the personality is never static. The earlier psychologists did a disservice by attributing rigidity and permanence to their several-tiered psyche. The psyche is not architectonic but fluid. A river with several currents, frequently altering its course, is a better simile for it than a building. We should think more in terms of process.

Yet Freud himself, in his *Interpretation of Dreams*, drew attention to one of the most far-reaching transformations of all. To illustrate, he contrasts the dramatic handling of the incest theme in the *Oedipus* of Sophocles (c.425 B.C.) with that in Shakespeare's *Hamlet*. Whereas in the *Oedipus*, he writes, the childish incest phantasy is overtly reproduced, in *Hamlet* the theme is so deeply concealed as to be unrecognised for what it is even by the author. Freud attributes the difference between the two to the progress, during the millennia separating them, of repression in the emotional life of humanity.

There is no need to go all the way with Freud, in treating the incest phantasy as a universal experience, to appreciate the truth in this and its importance. In all his plays Shakespeare, surely no less a dramatist that Sophocles, nowhere drags such preternatural horrors from the depths as Sophocles does in narrating the experience of Oedipus and Jocasta. Until Freud reminded him, modern man had most likely forgotten that such depths existed. Incest was for him no more than the unsavoury crime of undiscriminating lust. For Sophocles both the compulsion and the answering taboo were present to imagination as appalling realities. The stronger the taboo the more powerful the urge.

But the contrast between Shakespeare and the Greek tragic playwrights is displayed on a far larger canvas even than that. Not even in the *Tempest* or *Macbeth* does Shakespeare exhibit such a strong consciousness of the influence upon human affairs of suprahuman powers as they do. It is true that the later Greek playwrights made fun of the gods, while the philosophers politely ushered them off the stage; but the forces they represented, the ineluctability of destiny, the tenacity of retribution, harmony and strife, were constantly recurrent themes. In *The Tempest*, Prospero was fully in command: the spirits did his bidding. No character in Greek tragedy was ever in that happy position. Men were at the mercy of powers beyond their control.

C. G. Jung offered an explanation of this reversal and, in doing so, further developed Freud's analysis. This is the diminishing capacity for religious experience of people brought up under the conditions of western civilisation. It could, indeed, be said with truth that this incapacity and technological civilisation go hand in hand because, while the intellect of Europe was absorbed in celestial concerns, it was not interested enough in terrestrial affairs to create modern technology.

Religion, said Jung, grew out of the projection into the celestial regions of certain archetypal patterns originating in the depths of the unconscious. There they became objectified and enjoyed an autonomous life of their own. This accounted for the recurrence in the old mythologies the world over of certain tremendous themes: the Great Mother (the Virgin Mary, Isis, Astarte); the cosmic conflict between the powers of light and darkness (Christ *v.* Satan, Ahura Mazda *v.* Ahriman); the virility symbols (Apollo, the heroes of the Sagas).

Nowadays fewer and fewer people are capable of this projection and nobody has been able to provide a clear explanation why this should be. It can be suggested that the whole scientific and technological climate is against it. In opening up interstellar space astronomy has destroyed the dwelling place of the supernatural. A man working all his life with machines cannot find it easy to regard the stories of Christmas and Easter as anything more than charming fairy tales. When people had the myth of Persephone constantly reenacted before their eyes in the annual resurrection of nature they seemed less alien.

So, if the archetypes are not securely locked away in the cellars of the psyche, they have to be content with projection onto the local football team or a racing driver while, for many, the Afrikaaner Nationalists are always available to deputise for the myrmidons of Hell. But these are neither as mysterious nor as exciting, and certainly not as comforting, as the Heavenly Hosts. Jung warned that these forces in the depths of the psyche must have an outlet and that we could not expect to continue sitting on the volcano without scorching our backsides. In the event, when eruptions have occurred, a whole nation has turned paranoiac or multitudes of young people have gone after odd Dionysiac cults, aided, only too often, by marijuana or LSD. But the Hippies have to enjoy their frenzies without Dionysus: they make do with the current pop idol. Except for sporadic outbreaks the supernatural is excluded. Each generation is more terrestrially-minded than the last and millions are bored with life.

For a third example of a change in human nature, there is the obvious and rapid transformation of the feminine personality, which will assuredly bring about a change in the male. It is no mere freak of fashion that approximates the dress and hair-styles of men and women to each other. Men are less ashamed than they were of appearing womanish and women are less ashamed of appearing mannish. Why should there be shame when, freed from perennial fears and weaknesses and relieved by technology of their muscular disadvantage, women take their place side by side with men in the great world? A modern young woman not only has a different way of life from those described by Mary Wollstonecraft but is a different kind of creature. This does not mean that, in all respects except the biological, men and women need become identical. By all means, *vive la différence*, but let it be a different difference.

These developments in human nature have deeply affected interpersonal relations. The stiffening of the integument that contains the untamed forces of the psyche creates barriers between individuals at the deeper levels. With the decay of religious faith the universe has become a much lonelier place. The dayspring from on high has deserted us and we are no longer on speaking terms with the angels. Or is it we who have deserted them, as we have opted out of the Communion of Saints? The scientific explorers who described what has been happening in the psyche of western man, and whose prestige as a consequence swayed the multitudes with their unbelief, disclaimed the rôle of philosopher or theologian and excused themselves from asking whether the supernatural they discarded did not represent deeper realities than they had ever dreamed of. When we have recovered our balance we may learn to regard this as the great *trahison des clercs* of the twentieth century. The testimony of the mystics throughout the ages, with their claim to have transcended the supernatural of the archetypes and to have reached ultimate reality, that the universe is not a lonely place and that, in fact, love is of its essence deserves at least as much respect as the indemonstrable and much disputed theories of Freud and Jung.

In the meanwhile, our isolation is reflected in our behaviour patterns and is further deepened by our social conditions. The utilitarian principle has replaced absolute values without offering any satisfactory answer to the question, 'useful for what?' Each of us must 'do his own thing' (surely as vapid a phrase as any that could be spoken!) because we are left without a destination and without maps and because there is no guidance. We are not bound together by common observance of an objective norm and each has to find his own way. With the absolutes, the sense of sin has gone, too, or at least has transformed itself into anxiety, which is all the more painful because there is no answering promise of redemption. We no longer fear either God or the Devil; but fear of each other, of ourselves, of tomorrow and of the impersonal forces of international finance and world politics fills half our hospital beds.

Recovery from this collapse is bound to be slow and painful. New life does not come into existence by the resolution of a committee. At the close of *The Phenomenon of Man*, Teilhard de Chardin writes that, if we look at the world from the point of view of the suffering involved in change, 'We soon see under the veil of security and harmony which, viewed from on high, envelops the rise of man, a particular type of cosmos in which evil appears necessarily and as abundantly as you like in the course of evolution – not by accident (which would not much matter) but through the very structure of the system'. This is an element in the 'anguish' of which Sartre writes. The present crisis is not the first in the history of mankind and there has always been agony. Each generation has to take up its own burden and to advance in its own way.

There arises the question, if changes of this magnitude occur in human nature, how can we understand the thoughts and experiences of people who lived in the distant past? We can extend the question: how can we understand our own contemporaries, the Indians, the Japanese, or the Eskimos, whose cultural background and traditions are so different from our own – or our own parents? The short, but inadequate answer, is that some of the worst of tragedies result from the fact that we cannot understand groups different from ourselves, living on our own doorsteps! Modern means of communication, of which so much good was expected, seem only to make matters worse. We are so flooded with aimless chatter on the level of the lowest common denominator that the silence on the deeper levels becomes more painful.

Yet we are all products of similar natural processes and we all live out our lives under the same skies and this gives us at least enough in common to recognise each other's humanity and to communicate. Honey tasted as sweet to Achilles as it does to me and a smile expresses pleasure and a scowl expresses anger in every age and climate, although the occasions of our smiles and scowls may be different. Were we not able to communicate across the barriers between us, or over the centuries, all literature and all history would be bogus; but the historian knows that he faces an insoluble problem in trying to enter into the meaning of the past, knows that he cannot avoid interpreting it in the terms of the present, but does his best. When I read Plato and Aristotle I am well aware that I do not experience the full flavour of their writings in the way their contemporaries did but I also know that I learn from them and that what I learn is worth the effort.

This is one aspect of the question as to how we can communicate at all with anybody whatever; how we come to believe, even, that associated with all those bodies we see around us are minds similar to our own, capable of thoughts and the expression of them similar to our own? It raises profound issues of metaphysics and epistemology and various answers have been given. In the end, the most satisfactory answer is the pragmatic one; that we do communicate in fact and that it works! If we could not, survival itself would not be possible.

At the lowest, we communicate technically. For example, when doing business with a businessman we talk in terms of commercial transactions. Provided he is reliable, and knows what he is talking about, it is of no consequence who he is. Any businessman would do as well as any other. If we are discussing science with a scientist we talk in terms of his discipline and have no interest in him apart from that. In some instances a computer would provide just as satisfactory a conversation. This can become so lifeless and mechanical that in business nowadays people try artificially to drag in a measure of humanity by the use of Christian names. At a higher level, the man we meet for relaxation at golf or at bridge is a bundle of qualities. He plays well, has a sense of humour, is discreet and a lively conversationalist. But he is still interchangeable; if he leaves the neighbourhood or dies we send the appropriate messages and find another companion. In a small community, such as a family, or between people who deeply care for each other, we relate differently. We meet a person in his individuality and nobody else will do. Each is more than the sum of his qualities.

Speech, gesture and facial expression are in these instances means of conveying thought and feeling but are far from carrying the whole of the relation. In my experience with my contemplative friends in the monastery there was a deep sense of community despite the strict rule of silence – they would say because of it. In each person is an area of privacy, impenetrable to the observer, the centre of his freedom and an inner core of value. It is with this that love is established. Max Scheler offers a similar thought:

> Personality is that unity of substance, baffling observation and eluding analysis, which the individual experiences as inherent in all the acts he performs; no 'object' therefore, let alone a 'thing'.

Persons, he says, cannot be objectified, in love or any other genuine act, not even in cognition. We know people well only in community. The more authentic the love, the greater the knowledge.

In our encounters on this level we spontaneously exercise an intuitive insight, an empathy, beyond the interpretation of words and gestures, that illuminates the mind and the feelings of the Other. As to whether this can be accounted for by familiarity has been the subject of experiment. Stories we hear of communication through dreams between people in different continents are scientifically unreliable; but there does appear to be more authenticity in Professor J. B. Rhine's experiments in extra-sensory perception. First published in 1934, the results of these experiments showed that if a person sitting in a room picked a card at random from a full pack, another person in a different room with no means of communication could guess what card he was looking at with a regularity that excluded chance. Not all scientists are convinced and it may well be that the relaxed attitudes necessary for this type of communication would be impossible under laboratory conditions; but the accumulation of evidence for some kind of intuitive insight is impressive. It coincides with popular belief which, in a matter of this kind, is not to be despised.

Whether we can have similar insight into the personality of a historical figure who has been dead for centuries is another question. Yet it is possible to become so saturated in his thought, so familiar with his life and times, as to feel as if we were in his physical presence and to entertain a personal affection for him. In such an instance, the man's writings convey a richness of meaning that is denied to those who have read them merely as a text-book. Committed Christians, who have daily pored over their Scriptures and meditated upon them, and who have toured the Holy Land and practised the *imitatio Christi*, often have this experience.

This possibility of the fusion of personalities should be at the basis of any realistic theory of love. Especially in heterosexual love, which is the most intimate form of human community, the lovers are not two *egos* hygienically kissing each other through a muslin protecting their separate identities. While they still retain their independence as persons they are participating in each other. The most appropriate metaphor is that of musical counterpoint, in which two or more melodies, each a tune in its own right, are intertwined to create a harmony that enriches both and is greater than both. The sexual act is symbolic of this. Not intended primarily either for procreation or for pleasure, because this implies the partners using each other as means to an end, or to be unitive, because the unity exists already, it is simply a joyous expression of relatedness. That without it men and women alike feel frustrated is an indication that relation and community are among the deepest human needs. When these needs are unfulfilled, when there is no community, no mutuality, unsatisfactory substitutes make their appearance.

It is not due only to glandular stimulation that, when entering into a love relation, or, indeed, when participating in any good friendship or community activity, a person's vitality is enhanced and the whole environment assumes a psychedelic quality. It is because we become more truly ourselves and more conscious of our kinship with nature. Max Scheler writes of:

> that emotional identity of human beings in the unity of universal life whose natural aim and end in the biological order of development is their loving union in the sexual act; this being the only case of *mutual* fusion into universal life which we have so far been able to identify as normal to human beings. And here we stand, in fact, at the gateway to *every* kind of emotional fusion with and into the cosmos itself.

Looking at western society from this standpoint we can begin to appreciate how deep is its crisis. It is true that there is already a reaction against some of the forces threatening the integrity of the individual that have aroused the protests of existentialists. But much better understanding is required of the spiritual nature of the crisis. Political and social leaders, and the moralists who lecture at them, tend to deal only with the material problems such as housing, and then not always percipiently, or with symptoms, such as pornography. The deeper problems are ones that cannot be treated by legislation; while the social revolution that so many of the younger generation look for as a solution would not cure the sickness but only reflect it. Indeed, one of the effects of the welfare legislation of the past half-century has been to roll back the floods of physical misery and reveal the mire of spiritual unhappiness they concealed.

There are times when the sheer revulsion of the human spirit insists upon a reversal of present tendencies and there are times when technology solves the problems it creates. We have feared, for instance, the threat implicit in modern administration and in industrial processes which have seemed to standardise the individual and submerge him in the mass. But there are signs of a new dialectic coming into operation. The Huxleyan and Orwellian nightmares may still be imposed upon us but no longer as the ineluctable demand of the machine. As an example, we may take the division of labour which ultimately reduces the worker to the level of the robot, doing simple repetition work that could, actually, be done better by a mentally deficient, and is an insult to humanity. Yet, it is now slowly coming to be recognised in the more enlightened firms that this not only produces all the symptoms of poor morale but defeats its own purposes of cheapness and efficiency. Managements are compelled in their own interests to introduce schemes for job enrichment, group working and the delegation of responsibility.

So far as the customer is concerned, automation makes for less standardisation and more diversity. In administration, modern office systems and electronic machines relieve both staff and public from obsession with wearisome detail and monotonous chores for more creative activities. Of course, these techniques could be used in the service of Big Brother but there is enough awareness of the danger to forestall it if the will to do so is present. The bürolandschaft style of office lay-out is intended to give humanity a chance as well as to develop efficiency.

To be aware of a problem is to cope with it. For more than a generation leaders of the educational profession have been conscious of the threat to the person and, sometimes with more adventurousness than wisdom, have made the all-round development of the personality a high priority. Perhaps we do not like some of the products: the student activists, the Hippies and the Beats; but at least we must acknowledge that the more thoughtful of them are expressly refusing to accept submergence in their suburbs and their slums.

When we walk through a crowded shopping centre, we do not

see the 'faceless masses' that have been made so much of by the facile but the lineaments of experience and suffering. Looking deeper, we find the profoundest existential decisions, responsibly taken: a woman sacrificing her career to care for an invalid relative; another sacrificing marriage for a career; a man preferring social conformity to the greater excitements and rewards of a life of crime, for social conformity need not be 'mindless'. If clothes are an indication of individuality, each wears whatever pleases him or her, regardless of the fashion houses. Even in mass communications, there are still too many media and too many voices to admit of the public conditioning that has been foreseen.

But the threat to human relations is real. If it is true that the relation constitutes the person, when relations are impoverished there may not be individuals to crush. As Buber remarks, the more we concentrate on technology the less we have of real dialogue, of the 'I–Thou', and at present the greater emphasis is on technology. It is here that the danger of mass communications lies. They substitute public address for dialogue and conceal their destruction of the 'I–Thou' relation by supplanting it with attitude surveys and random interviews.

One of the worst influences is the excessive mobility of population. Credit is due to those stubborn people who, when their industry closes, resist the pressure to leave the homes that have been theirs for generations. They are standing for real values. But the system requires the mobility of the factors of production and so they have either to uproot themselves or to join the rejects of society. This is not even economic, for the social cost of bringing industry to the people is much less than that of taking the people to industry. A tree will not grow well if it is constantly being dug up and replanted.

Planning authorities often display a supreme insensitiveness to human need, as if hygiene were their only concern. It is not that the rashes of little boxes they scatter over the countryside all look just the same but that their regulations tend to compel the dispersion of families and to enforce loneliness. They will throw together thousands of houses without ever thinking of the little amenities that encourage the formation of community, the corner pub, the little shop, the working men's club, the discothèque, the public library and the swimming pool. Then they are painfully surprised when gangs of hooligans roam the streets and they call in the Police. The churches alone have been alive to the realities and have strained their resources in the search for answers. In many instances the slums are preferable to the housing estates. Each household has been the centre of a network of family relations and friends who have provided support and companionship for each other. Coronation Street is in many respects a happier place than Wythenshawe.

Especially among the aged, but desperate also in hundreds of thousands of bed-sitters in the big towns, loneliness has become a scandal. Women are harder hit than men because convention still ordains that it shall be more difficult for women to take the social initiative. If a middle-aged man of only moderate means advertises in the marriage-mart columns he is likely to have over fifty replies from women so bereft as to be ready for any chance. At a lunchtime discussion group of city workers I was taken aback to be told by them unanimously that they actually liked the rush-hour crowds because they provided their only human contact during the day.

Marriage and the family provide only an inadequate answer to this problem. Seldom in history has the family been so impoverished, partly because the outward forms of the post-Reformation system have been retained, while the conditions that favoured it have vanished and only vestiges of its substance remain. It would be absurd to suppose that a system appropriate to an agrarian and pastoral society could survive unscathed into the technological period. The nuclear family of the present day would have seemed to our forefathers a grotesque travesty of what a family should be.

In search of a solution, groups of young working women club together to rent a house in which they can live in free-and-easy community. There are groups of families in America living together in the same way, recapturing something of the intimacy of village life. There is much to be said for this. The colonies of artists in Cornwall have found their own answer. Anglers, musicians, sportsmen and others find community based on like-mindedness rather than on location. It is easier to diagnose the sickness than to prescribe remedies but with this sickness the diagnosis may be the biggest contribution to the treatment.

What the pattern of intersexual relations will be in the future is a matter for surmise. It is not a matter for hysteria: sexuality has a built-in, self-regulating mechanism that prevents it from running completely wild. People who fear that relaxation of the rules will lead to a permanent orgy of national promiscuity really are overestimating the sexual capacity and desire of average people. In any society there will always be pools of decadence but, generally speaking, the practice of free love turns out to be a squalid business that soon sickens the practitioners. If, for a trial period, all restraints could be removed and the moral question left open I surmise that, after a brief interlude of anarchy, most people would be found living much as they are now, with young folk pairing off and forming permanent unions. But there would be a much wider fringe of normal people whose lives followed different patterns of their own making.

For some years an unplanned experiment on these lines has been working itself out in certain circles. More than ever before, young people, particularly of the intellectual type, have been insisting upon the freedom to find their own way and they appear to be finding it along these lines. There are a number who cannot afford, or who do not wish, to observe the conventional require-ments of entering into matrimony but whose unions often turn out to be just as stable and at least as valuable as those of any who can and do. If they value the relation they have to respect each other because they can freely come and go without worrying about social or legal sanctions.

Yet, even in these circles, unwritten conventions do come into existence, if only because people need guidance in the conduct of their lives and know they need it. They also need to know how they stand with each other and what relations exist between their acquaintances. Otherwise there are embarrassments and quarrels. What is objected to is the clumsiness of the law in dealing with the intimacies of life. Legislators and magistrates have to make and apply the law with a view to the masses of people and not even the most understanding of judges can quite make it suit the special needs of the individuals in front of them. It shows an advance in sensitiveness that the law has recently in large measure withdrawn from the sphere of private morality, between people who are capable of looking after their own affairs, and confines itself more to protecting those who need protection. Severity and interference can be much more damaging than licence.

With the embodiment in law of the doctrine of irretrievable breakdown, divorce has been rationalised; but there is still strong resistance to divorce by consent. Surely there could be no better grounds for divorce than that both partners want it. For couples to be compelled to remain together against their will is abrasive and traumatic and there is no point in trying to do it. In future, couples who have come to the parting of the ways will not have to undergo the humiliation and public scandal they have had to endure in the past.

But the fate of the children remains an unsolved problem. Radical solutions, such as that of abolishing the institution of the family altogether and substituting the kind of community life of the *kibbutzim* fail to attract. Social arrangements have to be made for people as they are and not as we might think we would like them to be; and the plain fact is that, even in Israel, most people do not want to live in *kibbutzim* and would be miserably unhappy were they compelled to do so. Perhaps the only satisfactory solution to the problem of the children of broken marriages is that the prospective parents should be totally sure of each other before they undertake the responsibility of bringing children into the world.

The lifelong marriage of one man to one woman, they still say, is the ideal. Certainly it is the ideal – for those for whom it is ideal. On the evidence it is not ideal for everybody. The holy noises in the Anglican marriage service, 'love, honour, obey, till death us do part' are sentimentally appealing but nobody has any moral right to exact that vow. In some instances it would be wrong to continue the marriage. I think of a woman friend, a literary person, whose husband turned out to be a homicidal maniac who chased her around the house with a carving knife. The cherishing part of her vow she had to pass over to the male nurses in the asylum where he was sent for life; but was she really expected to continue loving and honouring him? That is the extreme case: but there is nothing in human experience to suggest that when the life force brings two people together it necessarily binds them permanently. Often it is capricious. A couple in the United States, who were of deeply religious convictions, amicably decided after fifteen years of happy marriage that they were no longer contributing to each other and would be well-advised to separate. Having been married in church in the presence of their friends, they invited their friends to a second service, this time to mark their divorce; thanksgiving for their years together, prayer for their own and each other's future.

Several factors likely to have profound social consequences can usefully be listed together in summary form:

The first casualty of the population explosion may well be society's esteem for parenthood. Women will feel dispensed from the obligation of bearing children and many, who feel no vocation to motherhood, will prefer careers.

The second casualty of the population explosion is likely to be the sanctity of life. There will be increasing demands for the euthanasia of the chronically ill, the aged, children with deformities and hereditary diseases and for the sterilisation of criminals and the mentally deficient. These demands will always be made under the cloak of humanitarianism.

Since more and more married women will be pursuing independent careers they will often be expected to live in different localities from their husbands, whom they will meet only at weekends and during holidays. This will mean that both partners will want to form liaisons outside marriage and this may well be accepted by both partners as a condition of marriage.

The progress of medical science increasingly releases women from domination by the rhythms of life and so enlarges their freedom and independence while diminishing their specifically feminine characteristics. While reliable contraception releases women from the fear of pregnancy it still further cuts them off from nature.

Antibiotics take the terror out of the sexually communicated diseases.

The progress of technology furthers the artificiality of civilised life and deepens man's alienation from the cosmos.

The demands of the economic system increasingly atomise the individual.

Had these changes come upon us one by one we might have been able to cope with them adequately. Having more or less taken us by surprise, all at once, as a totality they provide a formidable challenge. While they have a strongly positive as well as a negative aspect, it is noticeable that they affect women far more immediately and profoundly than men and give women a much more difficult problem of adjustment.

It is to the credit of the Women's Liberation Movement that it has recognised this tendency and is trying to come to grips with it. Some of the movement's less balanced supporters spoil their case. For example, the proposal in the United States that women should relieve themselves of dependence upon men by living as lesbians is creditable neither to heart nor head. Deeper understanding of the condition will probably remove the stigma from homosexuality in both sexes, but to recommend this as a basis for the reorganisation of society is too trivial even to be worthy of arguing. The more serious intellects of the movement exaggerate the present serfdom of women and often misconceive the true nature of their case.

I take as my first example, the American writer Kate Millett who is herself married. In her book, *Sexual Politics*, she writes that when the movement for the emancipation of women secured its immediate political aims, a counter-revolution set in that robbed the victory of its substance. Male dominance reasserted itself. She instances the writings of D. H. Lawrence, Henry Miller, Norman Mailer and Jean Genet. On this evidence, she has had to scrape the western world pretty thoroughly to find her dirt. All these are authors who gain their audience by causing shock, which is enough in itself to indicate that they

are not typical. We have noted before the fallacy of general-
ising from a few authors, imagined to be representative, to the
condition of a whole civilisation. We are in a vicious circle: do
we take the authors to be representative because we see that
civilisation is like that, or do we take it that civilisation is in a
certain condition because we take these authors to be representative?

To regard the over-compensatory sexual phantasies of a handful
of men such as these as indicative of western attitudes, and as
evidence of a general hostility to women, is nonsensical. Their
writing is not even realistic, although it is supposed to be
detailed observation. Try lying in a bath, divesting a woman of her
saturated dressing gown, and then having intercourse with her,
in the manner described in Mrs Millett's long opening quotation
from Henry Miller, and see for yourself! Mrs Millett interprets
the behaviour of Miller's hero as an example of masculine
exploitation of women's animality and of the desire to humiliate,
and of women's concurrence in this. But she has it wrong! The
incident described was, in fact, an example of feminine animality
exploiting masculine vanity! More probably still, man and
woman were both exploiting each other: it often happens so.
Mrs Millett really cannot build a case on this kind of adolescent
prurience.

She has a good bash at Freud, whose theories of feminine
psychology, based on envy of the male genitals, she rightly believes to be degrading to womanhood. But this was far from being
the aspect of Freud's thinking that had the most influence. In any
case, Freud was not the only psychologist of influence during the
early part of this century. Adler and Jung were always there,
confusing the issues. In fact, what probably influenced the public
most of all was a serious misunderstanding to the effect that Freud
recommended unrestrained sexual indulgence as a means of dealing with the inhibitions. Actually, Freud recommended nothing
of the kind but the notion that he did provided a convenient
rationalisation for those who wanted one.

In my own, necessarily limited, observation, I have not seen
this counter-revolution or this devaluation of womanhood. I can

think of no serious author who would countenance them. What I have seen is women gradually rising above the disabilities and prejudices of the past and carefully picking their way in the new world, and among the new opportunities that have been so dramatically and suddenly laid open to them during the past couple of generations. For, if Mrs Millett is disappointed by women's response to emancipation, she would do well to reflect that the adjustments required may take much more time than she allows.

Germaine Greer (*The Female Eunuch*), brought up in Australia and now a don in an English university, makes a much more serious contribution. Yet, while recognising many injustices, I cannot see womanhood at the present time being in quite the depressed state she describes. It may be that she has been influenced by her own home during childhood, which does not seem to have been of the happiest, and by her Australian background. In matters of this kind we are all in some measure limited by our own experience, so I shall without diffidence refer to mine.

I was born the youngest of seven children (two daughters and five sons) and my father was an Evangelical clergyman of the Church of England, vicar of a northern industrial parish. In the better sense of the term ours was rather a 'Puritan' home. For instance we had to attend Church four times on Sundays and family prayers every evening were a crashing bore. First, we had to listen to my father reading a long screed from the Bible and then had to kneel at our chairs, backsides toward the centre of the room, and listen to his rambling prayers. I suppose it must have left an influence because we all in later life, according to our lights, which may sometimes have been dim, worked for the better ordering of human affairs.

In spite of her large brood, and we were too poor to afford a maid to help her, I do not remember my mother having felt oppressed or downtrodden. I would gladly have challenged anybody to downtread her. The ensuing devastation would have been hilarious. My mother did not regard her family as a burden, but more as a vocation from on high in which she gloried. The

sacrifices she expected would be required of her in the service of
this vocation she made in the spirit of glad obedience, without
self-pity and without repining. She still found time to share my
father's pastoral work, and was much loved by the women of his
parish. This does not mean that she was never deeply fatigued and
never longed for relief because it would not be true. Our home
was sometimes a battleground: I clearly remember hurling the
furniture at my dearly beloved brethren. But I do not recall there
having ever been intersexual conflict. My parents were anxious
that my sisters should have satisfactory professional training and
qualifications, not only as a safeguard against the uncertainties of
life, but also for the sake of the better contribution they would
make to human society. Any remarks made derogatory to women
would meet with instant reprimand.

When I look around at the serried ranks of nephews and nieces
and in-laws I call to mind some twenty women, none of whom
strike me as feeling oppressed or downtrodden, although I have
not quizzed them all on the subject. All of them have followed
creative careers and most of those old enough to have brought up
children beyond the toddling stage have resumed their careers, in
some instances at a much higher level than before. Yet I would
not say that we are in any sense an exceptional family. We may
have a fair share of northern gumption and guts. I hope so.

But there is much of positive value in Dr Greer's writing. It is
true that legal emancipation and the career open to talent are not
yet fully reflected in social conventions and manners. Women are
still not expected to take the initiative in social encounters with
men, still have to be 'taken' everywhere, still have to be paid for
as if they had no money of their own, are still treated with an
artificial deference that in reality is patronising, still supposed to
be fragile. They have not yet fully succeeded in throwing off the
conditioning that makes them not only expect all this as a right
but actually regard it as a privilege. They still allow themselves to
be influenced by the myths that women want to be dominated
and that their rôle in sexual relations is passive. If there are few
men who can carry authority gracefully, there are still fewer
women, and as business executives, ill-at-ease in a situation that is

not customary for women, they react temperamentally and with misplaced conscientiousness. I am told that they are more at home in the Civil Service, where there is an accepted etiquette and where status and relations are more clearly defined. Women are more than ever subject to exploitation as the principal consumers, particularly by the torrents of inane and offensive advertising that are poured over them, the appeal of the cynical to the gullible.

Dr Greer is surely right in maintaining that the way to break out of this vicious circle is not by hysterical gestures, nor by aping masculinity, nor by trying to form exclusive female communities which, like women's convents, could do no more than watch the stream of development pass them by. Her own answer is that women should exact a true respect by developing their self-respect and their distinctiveness, that they should take their affairs more into their own hands and that they should insist on genuine equality in personal relations.

One baneful influence against which Dr Greer might well have directed her fire is male jealousy, which has had a profoundly formative influence on our mores, and which militates against the easy mingling in society that is a precondition of feminine dignity and independence. The obverse of possessiveness, jealousy is not entirely ignoble, since it arises out of a high valuation of the object of rivalry. If I do not care whether my wife comes or goes I feel no bitterness against the man who filches her from me. I may actually be pleased with him. But if I think she is a queen among women and love her passionately I turn upon him with hatred. Jealousy arises, too, out of the fear of losing emotional security and, sometimes, out of the fear of losing material security. There is a fear of personal failure, which is a blow to our vanity if, having loved, we have lost to someone else.

Unjustified jealousy, arising out of baseless suspicion, indicates a lack of confidence. The love I profess is a self-deception. It is myself that I love. The lowest form of jealousy is that which is worked up because it is expected of us and because we are afraid of becoming a laughing stock as cuckolds. One of the lingering myths is that the sexual act has a deeper significance for women than for men. But –

> When lovely woman stoops to folly and
> Paces about her room again alone,
> She smooths her hair with automatic hand,
> And puts a record on the gramophone
> T. S. Eliot

In a period such as the present, when so many new developments are upsetting the accepted ideas, we ought to expect confusion. Institutions, such as some of the Churches, which content themselves with taking their stand stubbornly on the traditional codes, will merely be ignored and left behind because they are no longer realistic. They forfeit their credibility. The ethical debate has to be conducted on different ground. The old sanctions have lost their power. We can no longer, for example, base sexual discipline on the fear of illegitimacy. We can argue only on the ground of integrity and respect for personality, our own and that of others. To argue effectively we need a high doctrine of the human person and his relation with the cosmos, such as we have found in our references to the work of Max Scheler.

I have no intention here of trying to pontificate on all the issues that arise or of trying to set out ethical rules for them: abortion, family planning, artificial insemination H or D, the contemporary home, the position of children in the nuclear family, trial marriage, extramarital sexual relations, homosexuality . . . and so on. These are not the subject matter of this book. But I hope that we have by now established the criteria whereby such rules as are necessary can be elaborated: whether they are compatible with respect for personality, whether they enhance or diminish interpersonal relations, whether they make for enriched community.

Most of the authors we have studied have linked the questions of the nature and ideal of interpersonal relations with the religious and metaphysical questions. In authors such as Plato, Kierkegaard and Sartre, we see how deeply this influences their conceptions. Nowadays it is more usual to think in ethical terms, which are intended to be regulative of those relations, and it is often assumed that ethics cannot be derived from religious or metaphysical principles. It may be, and probably is, true that by examining the requirements of satisfactory living in human society, we could reach an ethical code as exalted as any that prophets or saints have proclaimed. Convincing a man of the reasons why he should not steal a march on his fellows and enrich or fulfil himself at their expense by disregarding this natural law is quite a different matter. There have always been plausible reasons for exploitation. But religion, of whatever provenance, makes two contributions of which a rationalist ethic can know nothing. One is an analysis of the human predicament in the context of its insight into the meaning of existence; the other is a personal motive of overwhelming power. Ethics offers maxims of behaviour: religion, whether Bhuddism, Christianity or Voodoo, offers a way of life and a conception of man's destiny. It is from these that the ideal of interpersonal relations ought to be derived and by these that the conduct of them should be qualified at every moment.

But to what religion or metaphysic ought we to commit ourselves? History has brought us to a point at which traditional orthodoxies have lost their authority and we are presented with a host of alternatives without there being any compelling reason why we should opt for one rather than another. This is an unhealthy state of affairs. Parents and teachers who are reluctant to 'indoctrinate' their children fail to realise what an intolerable dilemma they are preparing for them. Hegel used to advise his students to start their philosophical education by mastering one system thoroughly; for this would at least provide them with a standard of comparison and a point of departure, even if it were only to be rejected later. That is one reason why it is regrettable that religion is not taught more seriously in schools.

Christianity is the most obvious candidate for our self-committal but if we are in that condition of uncertainty we shall be unlikely to make progress by the study of Christian dogmatics. We may ponder the Creed clause by clause, asking whether Jesus was born of a virgin, whether he rose from the dead and whether he ascended into heaven, but unless we begin with a prejudice we shall reach no conclusion. The theologians of the past were mistaken in resting their case as heavily as they did on the historicity of these dogmas. A corpus of doctrine that can be overthrown by pinpoint linguistic research, or by the unexpected discovery of an ancient document, has very shaky foundations indeed. Nowadays it seems too easy to explain away or otherwise dispose of the events described in the Gospels. At some point in our thinking we shall feel constrained to ask whether their historicity is of any importance for, sooner or later, we shall be brought up against the fact that the Creeds do not so much provide an outlook on life as presuppose one. We can accept them only if we have already taken up a certain attitude. But if we can take their statements to be prototypes of human spiritual experience, they will come alive and will illuminate that experience. It will not matter very much then whether they are mythical or historical.

The centre of the argument now shifts. Taken separately, the validity of these dogmas is of little consequence. The question hinges on whether, as a totality, they represent symbolically the fundamental truth of the constitution of the universe and of human destiny within it.

At this point, reason leaves us stranded. We have to fall back upon experience. Unfortunately, experience is difficult to communicate. I have already referred to the evidence of the mystics; but their experience is not ours and we know it only at second hand, which for most people is not good enough. In the end we shall have to take the leap of faith, like Kierkegaard, towards a religious interpretation of life or against it. But I think we have experience of our own which at least points the way. I have drawn attention to the fact that, in the movement of love, we are not projecting a feeling from within ourselves but are entering into an experience which enhances our sense of unity with the cosmos. It is an easy transition from this to objectify love and to conclude that it is of the very being of the cosmos. Plato thought similarly about beauty.

We have similar experience of goodness as objective reality.

Ordinary people who, as Iris Murdoch puts it (*The Sovereignty of Good*), have not been corrupted by philosophy, experience the good as a series of demands upon them from outside, revealing themselves in particular situations. They do not imagine it to be a value that they create in their own minds. They feel the demands of the good as absolute, which is why they always try to persuade themselves that even their naughtiest deeds are done in a good cause. The good is to be striven after and is available to the pure in heart. The movement of love is always toward the good for the beloved.

Here, then, is a holy trinity – love, beauty, goodness. We need only attribute intelligence to them (and they are hardly conceivable without it) and we have the personal Deity of the Christian faith.

Let us not be deceived: this really is a matter of faith, built on experience. The primary question is whether we believe in persons and in people, in life itself. Is our belly reaction to the cosmos that of cynicism and despair or that of aspiration and endeavour? It is often in moments of personal crisis that we ask this question most searchingly. If we take the line of cynicism we find that ethics crumbles for we shall be on the defensive in an alien world. No truly 'I–Thou' relation will be possible for we shall have no confidence. Sartre ruthlessly follows his argument where it leads when, starting with the meaninglessness of existence, he finds that conflict is of the essence of the interpersonal relation. In defining love as the pursuit of the serenity of the in-itself he virtually equates love with the longing for death.

Take the line of hope and confidence and we find, with Buber and Marcel, that the essence of the interpersonal relation is the affirmation of individuality and that the long altercation between agape and eros is transcended in a higher mutuality. Love is the fullness of life.

These are the alternatives.

Bibliography

AESCHYLUS, *The Suppliant Women*, tr. Gilbert Murray, Allen and Unwin, 1930.
— *The Eumenides*, tr. Gilbert Murray, Allen and Unwin, 1905.
ALIGHIERI, DANTE, Vol. 1, *The Inferno*, Vol. 2, *The Purgatorio*, Vol. 3, *The Paradiso*, the Italian text with translation in terza-rima verse by Melville B. Anderson, World's Classics, Oxford University Press, 1932.
— *The Divine Comedy*, tr. Rev. H. F. Carey, Everyman, Dent, 1908.
AQUINAS, ST THOMAS, *The Summa Theologia*, tr. the Fathers of the English Dominican Province, Burns and Oates, 1920.
ARISTOTLE, *Nichomachean Ethics*, tr. D. P. Chase, Everyman, Dent.
ASCH, SHOLEM, *The Nazarene*, Putnam.
AUGUSTINE, ST, *The City of God* (2 vols.), tr. John Healey, Everyman, Dent, 1945.
— *Confessions*, tr. E. B. Pusey, Everyman, Dent, 1907.
— *Homilies on 1 John*, Library of Christian Classics, VIII.
— *Augustine's Later Works*, SCM Press.
— *The Good of Marriage, Adulterous Marriages, Holy Virginity*, The Fathers of the Church, a New Translation, Vol. 27, St Augustine, Treatises on Marriage and Other Subjects, edited by Roy Deferrari, Fathers of the Church Inc., 1955.
DE BEAUVOIR, SIMONE, *The Second Sex*, tr. H. M. Parsley, Jonathan Cape, 1953.
BUBER, MARTIN, *I and Thou*, tr. Ronald Gregor Smith, T. and T. Clark, 1937.
— *Between Man and Man*, tr. Ronald Gregor Smith, Routledge and Kegan Paul, 1947.

BURCKHARDT, JACOB, *The Civilisation of the Renaissance in Italy*, various English translations, first published in German, 1860.

BURLEIGH, JOHN H. S., *The City of God, A Study of St Augustine's Philosophy*, Nisbet, 1949.

BURNS, C. DELISLE, *The First Europe, A Study in the Establishment of Mediaeval Christendom*, A.D. *400–800*, Allen and Unwin, 1947.

BURY, J. B., *A History of Greece*, Macmillan, 1945.

CALVIN, JOHN, *Institutes of the Christian Religion* (2 vols.), tr. Henry Beveridge, James Clarke and Co. Ltd, 1949.

CAMERON, T., *The Kindly Laws of the Old Testament*, Lutterworth, 1945.

CHAUCER, GEOFFREY, *Troilus and Criseyde*, edited by John Warrington, Everyman, Dent, 1953.

CHAYTOR, H. J., *The Troubadours*, Cambridge, 1912.

— *The Troubadours of Dante*, Oxford University Press, 1902.

COLE, WILLIAM GRAHAM, *Sex in Christianity and Psychoanalysis*, Allen and Unwin, 1956.

COPLESTON, FREDERICK, S. J., *History of Philosophy* (8 vols.), Burns and Oates, 1946–56.

— *Contemporary Philosophy*, Burns and Oates, 1956.

COULTON, G. C., *Mediaeval Panorama*, Cambridge, 1943.

COWBURN, JOHN, S. J., *Love and the Person*, Chapman, 1967.

CROXALL, T. H., *Kierkegaard Studies*, Lutterworth, 1948.

D'ARCY, MARTIN, S. J., *The Mind and Heart of Love*, Fontana Library, Collins, 1962, first published by Faber and Faber, 1945.

ERIKSON, ERIK K., *Childhood and Society*, Imago Publishing Co.

EURIPIDES, *The Iphigenia in Tauris*, tr. Gilbert Murray, Allen and Unwin, 1910.

— *The Trojan Women*, tr. Gilbert Murray, Allen and Unwin, 1905.

EYRE, EDWARD, editor, *European Civilisation, Its Origin and Development*, III, *The Middle Ages*, Oxford University Press, 1936.

FINDLAY, J. N., *Hegel, a Re-examination*, Allen and Unwin, 1958.

FIRKEL, EVA, *Woman in the Modern World*, tr. Hilda C. Graef, Burns and Oates, 1956.

FREUD, SIGMUND, *The Interpretation of Dreams*, tr. A. A. Brill, Allen and Unwin, 1913.

GEORGE, W. L., *The Story of Woman*, Chapman and Hall, 1925.

GILSON, ETIENNE, *History of Christian Philosophy in the Middle Ages*, Sheed and Ward, 1955.

— *The Spirit of Mediaeval Philosophy*, Sheed and Ward, 1955.

GINSBERG, MORRIS, *On the Diversity of Morals*, Heinemann, 1956.

GORE, GUILLAUME and GOUDGE, *A New Commentary on Holy Scripture*, S.P.C.K., 1928.

GREER, GERMAINE, *The Female Eunuch*, MacGibbon and Kee, 1970.

GRIFFITH, EDWARD P., *Marriage and the Unconscious*, Secker and Warburg, 1957.

HAMILTON, ELIZABETH, *Heloise*, Hodder and Stoughton, 1956.

HAZO, ROBERT G., *The Idea of Love*, Concepts in Western Thought Series, Frederick A. Praeger, 1967.

HECKER, EUGENE A., *A Short History of Women's Rights*, Putnam, 1910.

HEGEL, GEORG WILHELM FRIEDRICH, *Phenomenology of Mind*.

HOARE, F. R., *Eight Decisive Books of Antiquity*, Sheed and Ward, 1952.

HOBMAN, D. L., *Go Spin you Jade, Studies in the Emancipation of Women*, Watts, 1957.

HOOKER, RICHARD, *Of the Laws of Ecclesiastical Polity*, Everyman, Dent, 1907.

INGE, W. R., *The Philosophy of Plotinus*, Longman, 1928.

JASPERS, KARL, *Man in the Modern Age*, tr. Eden and Cedar Paul, Routledge and Kegan Paul, 1933.

JUNG, C. G., *Psychology and Religion*, tr. R. F. C. Hull, Routledge and Kegan Paul, 1958.

— *Psychology and Alchemy*, tr. R. F. C. Hull, Routledge and Kegan Paul, 1953.

JUNG, C. G., *Psychology of the Unconscious*, tr. Beatrice M. Hinkle, Routledge and Kegan Paul, 1919.

KANT, IMMANUEL, *Principles of the Metaphysics of Ethics*, tr. Thomas Kingsmill Abbott, Longmans, Green and Co., 1929.

KIERKEGAARD, SØREN, *Either/Or*, tr. David F. Swenson and Lilian Swenson, Oxford University Press, 1946.

— *Fear and Trembling*, tr. Walter Lowrie, Princeton University Press, 1946.

— *Stages on Life's Way*, tr. Walter Lowrie, Oxford University Press, 1945.

— *Works of Love*, tr. Howard and Edna Kong, Collins, 1962.

KORNER, S., *Kant*, Pelican, 1955.

LECKY, W. E. H., *History of European Morals, From Augustus to Charlemagne*, Longmans, 1911.

LEWIS, C. S., *The Allegory of Love*, Oxford University Press, 1936.

LODGE, R. C., *Plato's Theory of Ethics*, Kegan Paul, Trench and Trubner, 1928.

LUCAS, F. L., *Greek Poetry for Everyman*, Dent, 1951.

LUCRETIUS, *De Rerum Natura*, with an English translation by W. H. D. Rouse, Loeb Classical Library, Heinemann, 1924.

MACKINNON, D., *Borderlands of Theology*, Lutterworth, 1968.

MACMURRAY, JOHN, *Persons in Relation*, Gifford Lectures, 1954, Faber and Faber 1956.

MARCEL, G., *Homo Viator*, tr. Emma Crauford, Gollancz, 1951.

MARITAIN, JACQUES, *Moral Philosophy*, Geoffrey Bles, 1951.

MARX, KARL, *Capital*, tr. Samuel Moore and Edward Aveling, edited by Frederick Engels, Allen and Unwin, 1938.

MARX-ENGELS-LENIN INSTITUTE, Moscow, *Karl Marx: Selected Works*, Lawrence and Wishart, 1942.

MESSENGER, E. C., *Two in One Flesh*, Sands and Co., 1950.

MILL, JOHN STUART, *On the Subjection of Women*, Everyman, Dent, 1929.

MILLETT, KATE, *Sexual Politics*, Rupert Hart Davis, 1971.

MOORE, GEORGE, *Peter and Heloise*.

MUGGERIDGE, KITTY and ADAM, RUTH, *Beatrice Webb: A Life*, Secker and Warburg, 1967.

MURDOCH, IRIS, *Sartre*, Fontana, 1967, first published by Bowes and Bowes, 1953.

— *The Sovereignty of Good*, Routledge and Kegan Paul, 1970.

NEDONCELLE, MAURICE, *Vers Une Philosophie de L'amour et de la Personne*, Aubier, 1957.

NIEBUHR, REINHOLD, *The Nature and Destiny of Man* (2 vols.), Nisbet, 1941–43.

NUTTALL, GEOFFREY, *The Faith of Dante Alighieri*, S.P.C.K., 1969.

NYGREN, ANDERS, *Agape and Eros*, S.P.C.K., 1932.

OVID, *The Art of Love*, tr. J. Lewis May, Bestseller Library, Paul Elek, 1959.

PLATO, *Lysis*, tr. J. Wright, Socratic Discourses, Everyman, Dent, 1910.

— *Republic*, tr. Davies and Vaughan, Macmillan, 1921.

— *Phaedrus*, tr. J. Wright, Five Dialogues of Plato, Everyman, Dent, 1942.

— *Symposium*, tr. Michael Joyce, Five Dialogues of Plato, Everyman, Dent, 1942.

PLOTINUS, *The Enneads*, tr. Stephen McKenna, Faber and Faber, 1917–30.

PLUTARCH, *Moralia*, tr. F. C. Babit, Loeb Classical Library, Vol. 2, 1962.

RASHDALL, HASTING, *The Idea of the Atonement in Christian Theology*, Bampton Lectures, 1915, London, 1919.

REICH, EMIL, *Woman Through the Ages* (2 vols.), Methuen, 1908.

RUSSELL, BERTRAND, *History of Western Philosophy*, Allen and Unwin, 1946.

SARTRE, JEAN-PAUL, *Being and Nothingness*, tr. Hazel E. Barnes, Methuen, 1956.

SCHAER, *Religion and the Cure of Souls in Jung's Psychology*, Routledge and Kegan Paul, 1951.

SCHELER, MAX, *The Nature of Sympathy*, tr. Peter Heath, Routledge and Kegan Paul, 1954.

SCHUSTER, ERNEST J., *The Wife in Ancient and Modern Times*, Williams and Norgate, 1911.

SCOTT, MELVILLE, *The Message of Hosea*, S.P.C.K., 1921.

SCOTT-MONCRIEFF, C. K., *The Letters of Abelard and Heloise*, Chapman, 1925.

SELTMAN, CHARLES, *Women in Antiquity*, Thames and Hudson, 1956.

SIKES, J. G., *Peter Abailard*, Cambridge, 1932.

SMITH, G. A., *The Book of the Twelve Prophets*, Vol. 1, Hodder and Stoughton, 1899.

SPENSER, EDMUND, *The Faerie Queen*, Everyman, Dent, 1929.

STERN, KARL, *The Flight From Woman*, Allen and Unwin, 1966.

SUTTIE, IAN D., *The Origins of Love and Hate*, Kegan Paul, Trench and Trubner, 1935.

TAYLOR, G. RATTRAY, *Sex in History*, Thames and Hudson, 1953.

TEILHARD DE CHARDIN, PIERRE, S. J., *The Phenomenon of Man*, tr. Bernard Wall, Collins, 1959.

THODY, PHILIP, *Sartre*, Studio Vista, 1971.

THOMSON, J. A. K., *The Ethics of Aristotle*, Allen and Unwin, 1953.

TILLICH, PAUL, *Love, Power and Justice*, Oxford University Press, 1954.

— *Systematic Theology* (3 vols.), Nisbet, 1953–64.

TORRANCE, T. F., *Calvin's Doctrine of Man*, Lutterworth, 1949.

TREVELYAN, G. M., *English Social History*, Longmans, 1942.

TROISFONTAINE, ROGER, S. J., *Existentialism and Christian Thought*, tr. Martin Jarrett-Kerr, C. R., Dacre Press, 1949.

WADDELL, HELEN, *Peter Abelard*, London, 1933.

WOLLSTONECRAFT, MARY, *The Rights of Women*, Everyman, Dent, 1929.

XENOPHON, *Banquet*, tr. James Welwood, Socratic Discourses, Everyman, Dent, 1942.

— *Memorabilia and Oeconomicus*, tr. E. C. Marchant, Loeb Classical Library, Heinemann, 1959.